The Early Care and Education of Deaf Children in Ghana

PERSPECTIVES ON DEAFNESS

Series Editors
Stephanie Cawthon
Harry Knoors

Innovations in Deaf Studies: The Role of Deaf Scholars
Annelies Kusters, Maartje De Meulder, Dai O'Brien

Educating Deaf Learners: Creating a Global Evidence Base
Edited by Harry Knoors and Marc Marschark

Evidence-Based Practices in Deaf Education
Edited by Harry Knoors and Marc Marschark

Teaching Deaf Learners: Psychological and Developmental Foundations
Harry Knoors and Marc Marschark

The People of the Eye: Deaf Ethnicity and Ancestry
Harlan Lane, Richard C. Pillard, and Ulf Hedberg

Deaf Cognition: Foundations and Outcomes
Edited by Marc Marschark and Peter C. Hauser

How Deaf Children Learn: What Parents and Teachers Need to Know
Marc Marschark and Peter C. Hauser

Research in Deaf Education: Contexts, Challenges, and Considerations
Edited by Stephanie Cawthon and Carrie Lou Garberoglio

Diversity in Deaf Education
Edited by Marc Marschark, Venetta Lampropoulou, and Emmanouil K. Skordilis

Bilingualism and Bilingual Deaf Education
Edited by Marc Marschark, Gladys Tang, and Harry Knoors

Early Literacy Development in Deaf Children
Connie Mayer and Beverly J. Trezek

The World of Deaf Infants: A Longitudinal Study
Kathryn P. Meadow-Orlans, Patricia Elizabeth Spencer, and Lynn Sanford Koester

Approaches to Social Research: The Case of Deaf Studies
Alys Young and Bogusia Temple

Deaf Education Beyond the Western World
Edited by Harry Knoors, Maria Brons, and Marc Marschark

Co-Enrollment in Deaf Education
Edited by Marc Marschark, Shirin Antia, and Harry Knoors

The Handbook of Language Assessment Across Modalities
Tobias Haug, Wolfgang Mann, Ute Knoch

The Early Care and Education of Deaf Children in Ghana

Developing Local and global understandings of early support

Ruth Swanwick, Daniel Fobi, Yaw Offei, and Alexander Oppong

Great Clarendon Street, Oxford, OX2 6DP,
United Kingdom

Oxford University Press is a department of the University of Oxford.
It furthers the University's objective of excellence in research, scholarship,
and education by publishing worldwide. Oxford is a registered trade mark of
Oxford University Press in the UK and in certain other countries

© The several contributors 2024

The moral rights of the authors have been asserted

All rights reserved. No part of this publication may be reproduced, stored in
a retrieval system, or transmitted, in any form or by any means, without the
prior permission in writing of Oxford University Press, or as expressly permitted
by law, by licence or under terms agreed with the appropriate reprographics
rights organization. Enquiries concerning reproduction outside the scope of the
above should be sent to the Rights Department, Oxford University Press, at the
address above

You must not circulate this work in any other form
and you must impose this same condition on any acquirer

Published in the United States of America by Oxford University Press
198 Madison Avenue, New York, NY 10016, United States of America

British Library Cataloguing in Publication Data

Data available

Library of Congress Control Number is on file at the Library of Congress

ISBN 978–0–19–287227–2

DOI: 10.1093/oso/9780192872272.001.0001

Printed and bound by
CPI Group (UK) Ltd, Croydon, CR0 4YY

Oxford University Press makes no representation, express or implied, that the
drug dosages in this book are correct. Readers must therefore always check
the product information and clinical procedures with the most up-to-date
published product information and data sheets provided by the manufacturers
and the most recent codes of conduct and safety regulations. The authors and
the publishers do not accept responsibility or legal liability for any errors in the
text or for the misuse or misapplication of material in this work. Except where
otherwise stated, drug dosages and recommendations are for the non-pregnant
adult who is not breast-feeding

Foreword

As I write this foreword, my colleagues and I are in the process of planning the 6th International Conference on Family-Centered Early Intervention for Children who are Deaf and Hard of Hearing (FCEI 2024) themed 'Connect, Communicate, Collaborate'. This crucial FCEI 2024 theme highlights the power and necessity for deaf, hard of hearing, and hearing individuals—parents, professionals, and community members alike—to connect, communicate, and collaborate.

The book you are about to read, *The Early Care and Education of Deaf Children in Ghana: Local and Global Understandings of Early Support*, serves as an excellent representation of this theme. A collaborative effort that bridges deaf (all levels and ways of being deaf) and hearing perspectives across continents, cultures, and professional fields, this book stands as a testament to the potential that lies within connection, communication, and collaboration.

Early childhood care and education (ECCE), often termed the bedrock of a child's well-being and development from birth to age 8, serves as the focal point of this book. Despite the global emphasis on ECCE and children's rights, as underlined by Ghana's historic ratification of the United Nations Convention on the Rights of the Child (UNCRC), the reality for deaf children in Ghana continues to be a work-in-progress. Typically, children are not identified as deaf until the age of 6 years or older, due to an infrastructure that lacks resources for newborn hearing screenings.

Yet, the story does not end with identification. Once identified, the needs of deaf children often go unmet due to various factors, from the stigma that surrounds being deaf to a lack of proper training for professionals tasked with supporting deaf children and their families.

Utilizing a bioecological approach, the team of co-authors and contributors of this book, from diverse backgrounds and experiences, collaborated to explore ECCE practices in Ghana. Ultimately, they propose inclusive paradigms and practical interventions that build upon local knowledge and practices.

The first section of the book sets the stage by discussing the local and global challenges surrounding ECCE, with a specific focus on deaf children. The subsequent chapters provide context related to Sub-Saharan Africa, including perspectives on being deaf as a child, values of child rearing that influence parenting styles, and the legislative and historical context of ECCE.

The second section of the book features research carried out by the authors and contributors on ECCE for deaf children and their caregivers. Chapter 5 outlines the framework for their research, discusses factors that influenced their methodological approach, and reflects on ethical dilemmas faced by their team. Subsequent chapters present project findings from experiences of caregivers, multilingual context of ECCE, role of professionals, and participation and leadership of deaf adults. The final chapter reflects on the insights gained from the research and their broader implications for understanding ECCE in Sub-Saharan countries.

While reading through this book, I was reminded of the complex and nuanced nature of early childhood education, particularly within diverse cultural settings. It underscores the need to consider diverse infrastructures, policies, cultural attitudes, and ideologies to shape early childhood education programmes. I hope that this book will not only spark further research and dialogue but also lead to more inclusive and culturally sensitive early childhood education programming for young deaf children and their caregivers in Ghana and beyond.

For example, as chair of the Deaf Leadership International Alliance (DLIA), an organization dedicated to advocating for deaf leadership within early intervention systems, I view this book as a valuable resource aligning with DLIA's objectives. For instance, the chapter addressing deaf adult participation and leadership in ECCE examines deaf leadership history and research outcomes. It highlights the necessity of involving deaf adults and recognizing the substantial impact of our life experiences within early childhood education systems. The collaborations illustrated in this book serve as excellent examples of integrating deaf adult perspectives, emphasizing the crucial role of deaf leaders in ECCE.

I invite you to learn from the experiences of the authors and contributors, whose work spans geographical and professional boundaries, illustrating the 'Connect, Communicate, Collaborate' theme of the FCEI 2024 International conference. Together, we can positively impact young deaf children on a global scale through connection, communication, and collaboration.

Elaine Gale
Associate Professor, Department of Special Education
Hunter College, City University of New York (CUNY)

Acknowledgements

We wish to acknowledge the people and organizations in the UK and in Ghana that made this work possible.

We were supported in the first instance by the British Academy who funded the original research project thus facilitating this longer-term and productive UK–Ghana collaboration.

The University of Leeds and colleagues, especially in the Research Support Services and the School of Education, supported the undertaking of the project work, helped us during Covid with work-arounds, and encouraged all aspects of the research, writing, and impact activities.

We would also like to thank Deaf Child Worldwide for giving us a platform to disseminate our work and helping us to connect with other deaf education projects in the global South.

In Ghana we are especially grateful to the caregivers, education practitioners, and clinicians who so generously gave of their time to talk to us about their experiences and to the caregivers who welcomed us into their homes.

The University of Education in Winneba, Ghana, supported the project activities in Ghana and have continued to facilitate an ongoing research collaboration with University of Leeds.

The work could not have developed without the support of the Ghana National Association of the Deaf who played a central role in advising and collaborating with us from the start and who have been instrumental in the development and dissemination of video-based materials for caregivers and practitioners.

Many individuals have helpfully guided and advised us through the project work and the writing process. We would especially like to thank Dr Elaine Gale from the City University of New York for her enthusiasm and interest throughout and for helping us to develop and connect our work to the wider community of deaf leaders in the early support of deaf children.

As a writing team we have all in different ways been supported by our colleagues, friends, and families who have been patient and understanding during times of frustration and who have celebrated along with us at every success.

Contents

Co-authors Affiliations	xi
Contributor Affiliations	xiii

1. **Introduction: The Writing Context, Vision, and Objectives** — 1
   Ruth Swanwick, Daniel Fobi, Yaw Nyadu Offei, Alexander Mills Oppong, Joyce Fobi, Obed Appau, Derrick Asomaning, Richard Doku, and Linda Amanvida Gibbah

2. **Childhood Deafness in Sub-Saharan Africa** — 21
   Daniel Fobi and Derrick Asomaning

3. **African Childhoods** — 41
   Alexander Mills Oppong and Obed Appau

4. **The Early Care and Education of Deaf Children in Ghana** — 58
   Yaw Nyadu Offei and Linda Amanvida Gibbah

5. **Researching Childhood Deafness and Early Support: Ethical and Methodological Implications** — 77
   Ruth Swanwick and Joyce Fobi

6. **The Experiences of Caregivers of Deaf Children** — 91
   Ruth Swanwick and Obed Appau

7. **The Multilingual Context of ECCE for Deaf Children and their Families in Ghana** — 109
   Ruth Swanwick and Joyce Fobi

8. **The Role of Professionals** — 133
   Yaw Nyadu Offei and Linda Amanvida Gibbah

9. **Deaf Adult Participation and Leadership in ECCE** — 149
   Daniel Fobi, Derrick Asomaning, and Richard Doku

10. **Early Childhood Care and Education of Deaf Children: The Development of Knowledge, Theory, and Practice** — 169
    Ruth Swanwick and Daniel Fobi

Index — 187

Co-authors Affiliations

Ruth Swanwick, School of Education, University of Leeds, UK

Daniel Fobi, Department of Special Education, University of Education, Winneba, Ghana

Yaw Nyadu Offei, Department of Special Education, University of Education, Winneba, Ghana

Alexander Mills Oppong, Department of Special Education, University of Education, Winneba, Ghana

Contributor Affiliations

Obed Appau, Department of Special Education, University of Education, Winneba, Ghana

Derrick Asomaning, Department of Special Education, University of Education, Winneba, Ghana

Richard Doku, Ghana National Association of the Deaf, Accra, Ghana

Joyce Fobi, Department of Special Education, University of Education, Winneba, Ghana

Linda Amanvida Gibbah, Ghana National Association of the Deaf, Accra, Ghana

1

Introduction

The Writing Context, Vision, and Objectives

Ruth Swanwick, Daniel Fobi, Yaw Nyadu Offei, Alexander Mills Oppong, Joyce Fobi, Obed Appau, Derrick Asomaning, Richard Doku, and Linda Amanvida Gibbah

Introduction

This book examines how an understanding of social-cultural and resource dynamics can support early education programming that helps young deaf children progress through early childhood development and remain on-track in terms of language, communication, learning, and psychosocial well-being. The organization and content of the text centres on the knowledge and understanding developed through a collaborative UK–Ghana research initiative that examined the early childhood care and education (ECCE) of young deaf children in Ghana[1]. We frame this empirical work within current discussions of ECCE in the context of deaf children focusing specifically on the experience of caregiving, childhood deafness, and early support in sub-Saharan Africa (SSA).

The research and development work that we describe in Ghana provides a specific case study that we draw on to discuss the issues of deaf ECCE in the wider African context. Our focus is specifically SSA, and our use of this term encompasses Central, Southern, East, and West Africa where there are geo-political and cultural commonalities and shared deaf education histories. We also use this term in the context of reporting statistics and demographics and referencing other's work. We suggest that the theoretical and practical

---

[1] The research project described in this book was funded by the British Academy (ECE 190031).

Ruth Swanwick, Daniel Fobi, Yaw Nyadu Offei, Alexander Mills Oppong, Joyce Fobi, Obed Appau, Derrick Asomaning, Richard Doku, and Linda Amanvida Gibbah, *Introduction* In: *The Early Care and Education of Deaf Children in Ghana*. Edited by: Ruth Swanwick, Daniel Fobi, Yaw Offei, and Alexander Oppong, Oxford University Press. © Ruth Swanwick, Daniel Fobi, Yaw Nyadu Offei, Alexander Mills Oppong, Joyce Fobi, Obed Appau, Derrick Asomaning, Richard Doku, and Linda Amanvida Gibbah 2024. DOI: 10.1093/oso/9780192872272.003.0001

2   Care and Education of Deaf Children in Ghana

implications of this project are pertinent to other multilingual agrarian and collective socio-cultural contexts where there are similar resource issues around ECCE support and infrastructure. We use the terms 'low- and middle-income countries' (LMICs) to highlight these resource commonalities. We also use the term 'global South' in our writing making a distinction between nation states and countries of the South and those of the Western world in the regions of Europe, Australasia, and the Americas. This distinction underlines gaps in wealth and power but also conveys a sense of the spaces and people implied, recognizing that these terms conflate diverse economic, social, and political experiences.

Our ambition to bring a new and context-sensitive contribution to the examination of early education programming for young deaf children goes beyond the translation or modelling of Western concepts. We do not seek to make comparisons between contexts but rather to juxtapose little known, indigenous knowledge on early childhood care practices and conceptions of deafness, with established knowledge in the field. This endeavour involves a review and critical discussion of the existing knowledge base surrounding early childhood deaf education that is inclusive of the contribution of scholars and practitioners in the global South. We will thus explore traditional and contemporary perspectives on childhood deafness and caregiving that are meaningful to the African early childhood deaf education landscape to project and advance voices from this context. Our approach involves the use of a bio-ecological lens that examines local cultural, knowledge, and infrastructure resources to identify the challenges and opportunities for the early childhood care and education of young deaf children and their caregivers in the development context. This approach emphasizes the complex interactions between multiple systems of influence on individuals' development, including their immediate environment, their larger social context, and the interactions among these contexts (Bronfenbrenner & Morris, 2006). These influences include biological, individual, family, peer, and media factors, as well as cultural and historical forces that impact how humans change over time.

This is a co-authored text that brings together the experiences, understanding, and knowledge gained by our UK–Ghana research project team as we conceptualized, developed, and completed our research into deaf ECCE in Ghana. An important part of this process has been the way in which our thinking has developed individually and as a team and our ongoing reflections on the positionality of this work in the wider global context. As we set out the plan for the book and began to collectively write materials for different chapters, we realized that our different positionalities, perspectives, and the way in which we worked together needed to be made explicit as essential context for the way in which we have approached the writing and as part of our ultimate knowledge and capacity-building objectives.

As a writing team we feel an urgent need to address gaps in the global research and—in even a small way—shift the traditional flow of knowledge to open the potential of South–North illumination and learning. To do this effectively requires an openness about our individual backgrounds and expectations, as well as our collective and individual perspectives on deafness and early childhood, and a description of the writing process itself. Taken together this essential background contextualizes the book's structure, content and voice, and situates the text within the available and established scholarship in this field.

This chapter provides information about each of the book contributors. We each say a little bit about ourselves, who we are and what we do, our cultural context, our experience in deaf education and/or in the social context, and our role in the project and the book. These personal stories have been written by hearing team members. Deaf team members preferred to video-record signed narratives in the first instance that they then translated into written English. Following these individual stories we outline the book objectives, and collectively what we bring to the writing process and these aims. We describe our approach to writing the book and ways in which the academic confidence and capacity of the writing team were developed through this process. Finally, we provide an overview of the structure of the book.

Contributor Stories

Alexander Mills Oppong (co-author)

I am a teacher of deaf and hard-of-hearing (DHH) students and my specialism is the documentation and the teaching of Ghanaian Sign Language (GhSL). I have over 30 years professional experience as a teacher of DHH students. I have taught from the pre-school (kindergarten) through to secondary and tertiary levels. I initiated the teaching of GhSL as a programme in the Department of Special Education at the University of Education of Winneba in 1996 and have since taught GhSL to undergraduate and post-graduate students and documented GhSL text books.

I joined the international UK–Ghana (University of Leeds–University of Education of Winneba) project as one of two co-investigators (Co-Is) with the objective of listening to the views and preferences of caregivers regarding the resources they will need to care for their deaf children. In the SSA context where poverty, stigmatization, and language deprivation persist, we hope to replicate this project in other contexts to build an objective understanding of the resources available to caregivers. My contribution to the book centres on the African socio-cultural context of childhood deafness, contextual theories of childhood and beliefs, and values about childhood and parenting in SSA.

Being inclined to the 'positivist' and quantitative paradigm, this is my first experience of working with qualitative methods. Thanks to the mentorship of the principle investigator (PI) I have found myself acceptingly and willingly immersed in the qualitative paradigm of research. I am grateful for the research training and time given to this as part of the project structure that encompasses new knowledge, skills, and research repertoire. This collaboration and academic preparation helped shape me personally for this project and will enable us to build more research capacity in this field in the global South.

Daniel Fobi (co-author)

I have over 15 years' experience working as a sign language interpreter for deaf people. I grew up in a multilingual environment and can speak four different languages. My journey as an interpreter began with my involvement in the church and my university studies. As an undergraduate student, I had a colleague who was deaf so anytime his interpreters were absent, I stepped in to support him and this helped me understand deaf people since we shared the same residence and attended the same church. My interpreting skills also improved since at the university we did about 16 different courses in an academic year, which required a lot of interpreting skills to switch between courses. At the same time, I supported interpreting at church, which gave me religious exposure to interpreting. I have worked as an interpreter in other contexts including health, law court, basic school, and political platforms. Through this, I have developed my knowledge of deaf people mainly through the interpreting lens and at the higher education level.

My journey as a teacher of deaf children began at the basic school level where I taught deaf students mathematics and then moved into tertiary classrooms where I taught sign language and other deaf education courses to student teachers of the deaf. This experience of the linguistic abilities, language development, and academic performance of young deaf people informed my subsequent research studies. My early research was based on the educational inclusion of deaf students at the tertiary level and the mental health of deaf adolescents. Through the UK–Ghana ECCE project I have developed a deeper interest in early years deaf education research in the SSA context.

Introduction: Context, Vision, and Objectives   5

I am committed to building networks within this region that support the development of scholarship and research among hearing and deaf academics and practitioners. This project collaboration and mentorship from the PI has helped me begin to expose and project Southern theories of deaf education. In my role as project coordinator, working with the UK PI and Ghana Co-Is and research assistants, I have learned different ways of constructing deaf identities in different contexts. I have also been inspired to take a positive approach to my writing and build networks between deaf and hearing people to support inclusion for all.

In my approach to this shared text, I believe that in developing the deaf ECCE knowledge base in the SSA context we as researchers need to be truthful about the realities of the context and project them accordingly. This in no way suggests that I project a deficit view of deafness and deaf people in the SSA context. However, I think that if we hope to promote multimodal communication, collaborative research, and developing sustainable research capacity every aspect that we intend to improve must be thoroughly examined. We must highlight the infrastructure and logistical challenges surrounding the early support of deaf children and develop strategies for mitigating these challenges. At the same time, we need to be able to recognize the resources that are available to us. As a co-author I aim to dissect the existing issues and project the working strategies that stakeholders in early education for young children and their caregivers are experiencing to others who find themselves in similar contexts.

Derrick Asomaning (contributor Chapters 2 and 9)

I am the only child of my biological father and the first of my mother. My mother remarried, and we live at Kasoa. I have two stepsiblings and a younger brother. I am the only deaf person in my paternal and maternal extended families. My father is an Akyem[2] and my mother is an Assin. My maternal family speaks Fante. During my adolescent years, we located to Accra where we lived among Ga families who spoke Ga. During this time, I learned the Ga language as a subject at school and from friends in the community. Thus, I speak three languages: Twi, English, and Ga. I learned GhSL at the university during my first degree in Special Education.

---

[2] Ghana consists of different tribes or ethnic groups, such as the Akan, Assin, Ga, Fante, Ewe, Dagbani, and Gonja, with over 73 languages, such as Twi, Fantse/Fante, Ga, and Ewe., but English is the official language of the country.

6   Care and Education of Deaf Children in Ghana

My wife is hard-of-hearing and I have a hearing daughter of two and half years old. At home, I communicate with my wife through simultaneous communication—we sign and speak at the same time. I always communicate with my daughter through speech although I sometimes teach her simple GhSL vocabulary. I also communicate with my parents and in-laws through speech. When I visit my uncles and aunts, we use speech and writing to communicate. I use speech as expressive communication, and writing and speechreading as receptive communication. I use the same method when I visit offices such as the bank.

As a teacher of deaf children and a research assistant with interest in deaf and inclusive education, I am currently teaching at a regular school. I use speech during lessons and speechread responses from my students. Where I am unable to get what they say, I ask them to write their responses or questions. I communicate with teaching colleagues through speech and writing. I use the same method of communication at church. In the larger community, I use speech and speechreading.

At the university where sign language interpreters are readily available, I use them when going to offices or talking to lecturers who do not know sign language. I always use sign language when I am in the company of deaf people, such as when I meet deaf friends, visit the Ghana National Association of the Deaf (GNAD) office, or a school for the deaf. I personally prefer speech to sign language especially when it comes to expressive communication. There are two main reasons for this. Firstly, I do not want to lose my ability to speak. Continuing to use speech helps me to maintain this ability. Secondly, almost all the people around me, whether family, colleagues, students, friends, and community members, are hearing individuals, who do not know sign language. Thus, the preferable mode of communication is speech. Although I accept my deafness, I am more inclined to hearing perspectives than Deaf cultural views. This is probably because I became deaf later in my life (aged 26 years) and have always lived in a hearing culture.

Together with two other deaf adults, I have been involved in developing the project resources and materials for young deaf children and their families. These included parent–child interactions and GhSL vocabulary videos as well as deaf adults' documentaries in which some deaf adults shared their experiences of deafness. In addition, we developed a handbook that serves as a manual to the video resources so that deaf children and their families can watch the videos and use the manual as a guide. These resources are interactive, informative, and educative. They were designed to assist families of deaf children in providing support, care, and education in the early years. I also assisted in writing for publications and conferences.

Having been deaf for 10 years, I have experienced the difficulties that families especially hearing families with no prior experience of deafness encounter. These difficulties which are mainly about communication are very serious in the early years where young deaf children need love, care, and support from family members. Due to my background as a deaf individual and a teacher of the deaf, I was able to offer practical views on some of the issues that the book addresses such as early identification and intervention, social exclusion and marginalization, and inclusion of deaf children in education, health, religion, and community participation.

Joyce Fobi (contributor Chapters 5 and 7)

I have worked as a teacher of the deaf and a sign language interpreter in academic and social contexts in Ghana. I worked as a research assistant on the UK-Ghana ECCE project that underpins the production of this book. My role in the project team centred on the development of the interviews, the recruitment of participants, and data collection and analysis. I transcribed and analysed interview data and provided contextual information to the project. As a contributor to some of the chapters in the book, my goal is to enrich the text by providing contextual information based on my experience in the field, and of the caregiving context.

Throughout my years of experience I have come to understand that working with deaf individuals and coming to a proper understanding of their identity, culture, language, and communication requires a lot of knowledge, skills, and training. I realize that most deaf individuals are born and raised in hearing families. Most of these families have little knowledge and experience in relation to early identification, intervention, educational placement, and the communication options available for their deaf children, and how this provision can enhance children's developmental progress. I firmly believe that with the correct infrastructural support available for early identification and intervention, the severe impact of deafness could be lessened. In education, I have also come to believe that deaf children are just like any other 'normal' hearing individual and can be educated in any educational setting when they are identified early and given the right intervention and support. Many deaf individuals have realized the importance of being educated at the highest level despite the challenges some encounter because there are a few deaf adults who serve as role models for them as they occupy dignified and top positions in various sectors in the country. They do not allow their disability to overshadow them from achieving highest level of education.

8 Care and Education of Deaf Children in Ghana

Linda Amanvida Gibbah (contributor Chapters 4 and 8)

I am a deaf graduate with a Bachelor of Education, Special Education from the University of Education, Winneba. I specialized in the education of deaf children and sign language. I am currently working as a project lead with GNAD, Accra. Having lost my hearing at eight years of age, I went through a lot of difficulties both in school and the community where I live. Being called names, mocked, and ignored were all forms of discrimination I faced daily. Until now, I usually encouraged myself to ignore such happenings and to focus on making society a better place to thrive. Actually, I have encountered two persons in my family who are deaf, one a young lad (now 10 years old) and the other an elderly woman. Though, I am not aware whether deafness runs in the family, from what I heard, the young lad was misdiagnosed with a certain illness when he was a toddler so the medications prescribed to him at the hospital severely damaged his right ear and rendered him profoundly deaf. As for the latter, I only got to know her at a family gathering.

Being taken through hands-on learning and practical experiences in the education of deaf children during my four-year programme at the University of Education, Winneba, from 2013 to 2017, I have realized that deaf children are just like any other hearing children. However, deaf people often acquire language late. Currently, the education system for deaf children is progressing considerably better than previously. This is because, in the past, society doubted the abilities of deaf children and did not feel the need to enrol them in school because the majority assumed it to be a waste of time and resources or they believed it was not beneficial to educate deaf people. This negative old-fashioned perception is what is preventing many parents and families from providing the deaf children in their care with the needed educational support.

Having been engaged in a four-month internship as well as a one-year national service[3]in one of the schools for the deaf in Accra, Ghana, I have observed that, deaf children tend to perform better in all areas of academic and outdoor learning when they receive the necessary motivation and support throughout their education. For instance, a child with a family that supports and provides them with the necessary attention performs better academically and socially than one who does not receive any support or attention. The

---

[3] Ghanaian students who graduate from accredited tertiary institutions are required under law to do a one-year mandatory national service to the country. This service provides graduates with practical exposure on the job, both in public and private sectors, as part of their civic responsibilities. They are usually paid a non-taxable allowance at the end of every month. The amount is usually based on what will be approved by the Ministry of Finance. Currently, they receive 709.04 Ghana Cedis or £50.61 (at £1 = Ghc14.01) per month.

communication flow may be easier if families, caregivers, and teachers know how to interact with them in sign language.

My role within the project was as a research assistant alongside two other deaf colleagues. We teamed up with the support of the Co-Iss to gather information on deaf leadership targeting deaf adults and their roles in the education and upbringing of deaf children. Among them too were some documentary videos depicting deaf professionals as they engaged in their day-to-day activities at work.

These professionals also shared their experiences of difficult social encounters and gave encouragement for parents. The documentary videos were intended to demonstrate to parents, caregivers, and others that being deaf does not make one incapable so they should be inspired to encourage and support any relative who was born with deafness or acquired it later in their lives.

Working alongside the project team, I have contributed to some of the journal publications including one on deaf leadership in ECCE. Through this project, I have learned that deaf adults play a very important role around children who are deaf by being exemplary figures in their lives or acting as a support system to parents. We need to continue to involve parents and other community leaders in the education of deaf children, and to encourage the government to support ECCE programmes with funding. With the publication of this text we hope to raise deaf awareness and increase the visibility of young deaf children and their caregivers in Ghana so that policymakers are empowered to transform ECCE for deaf children in Ghana and develop sustainable research capacity.

Obed Appau (contributor Chapters 3 and 6)

I am a hearing person and I live in a multilingual community where people speak different languages, including Twi, Fantse, Ewe, Ga, and use GhSL. Living in a multilingual community makes life interesting and at the same time challenging where learning, speaking, and communicating in different languages is essential.

I am a sign language interpreter and lecturer in deaf education in the Department of Special Education at the University of Education, Winneba. I have interpreted for deaf students since 2008. Currently, I teach and supervise undergraduate students and I provide support services for deaf students across all the educational levels in Ghana. I am an activist for deaf students in education in that I advocate for deaf students on issues concerning their language and communication, their access to education through interpreting, and for assessment modes and teaching pedagogies that meet their learning needs. I am motivated in the work by my long experience in deaf education of meeting deaf individuals who cannot communicate with their hearing parents due to language barriers.

I worked as a research assistant on the UK-Ghana ECCE project that underpins the production of this book. I was one of the research assistants s involved in the project fieldwork and my main responsibilities were data gathering and analysis. This involved interviewing deaf and hearing caregivers, teachers, and health practitioners via telephone calls and WhatsApp. My contribution to this text involves bringing contextual information, gained from my experience of interacting with caregivers, teachers, and health practitioners, to the writing. I hope that this contribution will enhance readers' understanding of the dynamics surrounding the experiences of caregivers and their young deaf children in SSA.

Richard Doku (contributor Chapter 9)

I'm the first child in a family of six children. I lost my hearing at 17 years of age of. Among my siblings, I am the only one with a disability (deafness). I had my basic education with hearing children. I was in my junior high school first year when I lost my hearing. I then gained admission to the Senior High Technical School for the Deaf (Sectedeaf) at Mampong Akuapem in the Eastern Region of Ghana. This was where I learned sign language, and I began my life journey as a deaf person and learned about the deaf culture.

After senior high school, I was lucky to gain admission to the Presbyterian College of Education in 2005 and graduated as a professional teacher in 2008 with a Diploma in Basic Education Certificate. I taught for about five years before going to the university to study Special Education and Mathematics at the University of Education, Winneba, where I had a familiar environment. There were quite a good number of deaf students. The university also had a lot of sign language interpreters. I graduated in 2017 with a bachelor's degree in special education and mathematics. I am currently a master of philosophy (second year) student at the same university.

I work with GNAD as a sign language officer for the organization's current project on the 'Recognition and Promotion of Ghanaian Sign Language'. Among some of my roles are teaching GhSL at the University of Cape Coast and developing GhSL curriculum for public and deaf schools. I also assist in developing learning materials to support the curriculum being developed.

Our draft work on the curriculum for deaf schools is awaiting a forum where it would be presented to Special Education Division, as a starting point for a general GhSL curriculum for deaf schools.

After losing my hearing and spending a few years in deaf school and within the deaf communities, I began to feel different. For instance, I no longer feel that the Ewe language is my mother tongue. I sign and write English, so that seems to matter the most. When I am with my deaf colleagues, there seems to be nothing in which I am different from them, neither do I see any of them differently in terms of religion. In fact, I have been to various churches and even to Friday prayer meetings (Al'Jumah) with my Muslim deaf friends. I no longer define my culture in terms of a specific religion; I do not have a specific tribal language, no specific food, no specific dress code or tribal events to attend; neither do I identify with a particular geographical location. Culturally, I want to be defined in terms of my sign language; where I use my hands and body to talk, and where my emotion is shown by my facial expressions. I want to be defined by people with similar identities: deaf identity—we talk and make background noise, we can sign all day long, we meet together irrespective of language, religious denomination, wealth, class, age, what have you.

My engagement in this project commenced in October 2021 as a research assistant along with two other deaf colleagues. My roles included data collecting, analysing under supervisors and developing ECCE materials to support the project activities. In the production of the ECCE materials, we interacted with parents of deaf children, and other deaf adults who had stories to share. The parents and deaf adults were filmed. We produced two documentary videos featuring deaf children and parents communicating and interacting at home. We also produced three videos featuring deaf adults where they shared their life and work experience. Additionally, we developed five video materials to assist parents/ caregivers and all other persons who come into contact with deaf children, to learn basic sign language to be able to communicate and interact with them.

This project has given me insights into what deaf education is all about and the roles I could play as a deaf adult in support of improving deaf education. I am utilizing my experience from the ECCE project to conduct a study on the 'Coaching roles of deaf adults in the education of deaf and hard of hearing children'. In the future, my hope is to conduct further studies to address the effects of educational environment such as large class sizes and overcrowding in students' dormitories on deaf students' academic performance.

Ruth Swanwick (co-author)

As a language teacher and teacher of the deaf in the UK, I came to this project with quite a few years of experience of working in deaf education as a hearing teacher and then as a teacher trainer. I came into deaf education when the sign bilingual approach was taking off in some UK schools and services and I was excited by this, given my keen interest in bi/multilingual language use and learning, and have championed for bilingual practice for all my professional life in this field.

With this professional background, I came to this project with an understanding of the importance of early exposure and access to language and of the need to provide prompt and objective support to caregivers. Of course, my experience had been in the UK where universal newborn hearing screening came into place in 1997 and where now a confirmation of childhood deafness can be made as early as early as the first 4–5 weeks. This confirmation importantly triggers support and intervention from qualified education and health practitioners (Avard et al., 2007; Carling et al., 2022). I had very limited experience of working in a low-income context where this infrastructure cannot be taken for granted. One of the challenges for me with this background has been to work with the early support context as I see it and not to approach the project work or the writing with expectations and assumptions that are borne of my own professional and cultural experience. A very important aspect of this project for me has thus been the avoidance of imposing knowledge and expectations from a northern to a southern context and seeking instead to bring southern knowledge, experience, and theory to the fore.

My work in bilingual education had fostered in me a focus on the language and learning resources of deaf children as the starting point and an expectation of respect for the linguistic and cultural experience of being deaf. I have worked, and trained teachers to work, from an asset-based perspective and to frame practice decisions based on resource rather than on a deficit view of deafness. Again, this philosophy needs to be understood with the Western context of my experience where constructs of deaf identity (Chapman & Dammeyer, 2017; McIlroy & Storbeck, 2011), deaf gain (Bauman & Murray, 2014; Skutnabb-Kangas, 2014), and an individual rightsbased agenda are a part of the educational and academic discourse. In the context of the work in Ghana I have had to personally re-examine these constructs that do not embrace global deaf childhoods and the intersection of childhood deafness with other aspects of disadvantage including poverty, ill-health, stigma, and social and economic marginalization.

The funding structure for the project described in this book required a UK PI but at the same time provided an opportunity for equitable distribution of resources across both research contexts. Nonetheless the leadership and onus of responsibility for the overall project work rested with the UK PI. There was a continual tension in this set up. Whilst being the PI for the project work, I was aware at all stages of the work that the local expertise was with the Ghana project team and wanted to ensure that this was at the forefront of the processes. However, the experience and know-how needed to deploy the rich local knowledge and expertise within the expectations of a UK funding structure was uncomfortably within my remit. This has demanded hard work across the team in coming to understand one another's perspectives. We have spent as much time discussing how to work cross-culturally as we have been discussing the work. It is for these reasons that everything about this project and the writing process has been a collective process where the development of capacity and confidence through mentoring and support has been a central component of team activities.

Yaw Nyadu Offei (co-author)

As a teacher of the deaf and an audiologist, I teach both undergraduate and postgraduate students in the Department of Special Education at the University of Education, Winneba. As a practicing audiologist I screen and diagnose hearing loss, and provide clinical, educational, and counselling support in terms of education, communication, and amplification options available for deaf children and their caregivers. My research interest is in early identification and intervention for deaf children. In this context, I have developed an infant hearing screening tool called the LittlEARS (MED-EL) Auditory Questionnaire (LEAQ), and the Adaptive Auditory Screening Test (AAST) that is available in the Asante, Akuapem, and Fanti languages of Ghana.

As a hearing teacher, and a trained deaf educator with an audiology background, I believe in maximizing the use of residual hearing through amplification and exploring all forms of communication options for the deaf. From my experience in deaf education and the social context of Ghana, I have learned that a significant number of children in schools for the deaf in Ghana have substantial residual hearing and could, with proper amplification and appropriate classroom support, learn alongside their hearing peers. Unfortunately, few mainstream schools in Ghana have trained teachers of the deaf who can provide appropriate support to deaf children in regular classes. Parents are therefore often advised to send their children to a school for the deaf, even though this would not be their preferred choice.

I trained as a teacher for the deaf in the early 1990s when sign language was discouraged and oral approaches to communication for deaf people predominated. I have seen this change over time with the increasing provision of sign language as an option. I personally advocate for all forms of communication by whatever means possible. This view has sometimes exposed me to criticism from deaf people assuming that because I advocate for the use of cochlear implants and hearing aids that I am against deaf people and their culture.

I am one of two co-investigators on the UK- Ghana project and a co-author for the book. In this role I have led the writing of two of the chapters and co-ordinated the Ghana writing team with the support of the project officer. I have been able to bring my rich experience in deaf education and clinical practice and have been able to engage with allied professionals (speech and language therapists, paediatricians, physiotherapists, teachers of the deaf) as well as deaf adults and caregivers as part of this process.

Collective Vision for the Book

As these individual stories illustrate, we bring diverse backgrounds and experiences to the writing of this book. As a writing team made up of largely Ghanaian members of different cultural and linguistic backgrounds, we reached a consensus on our approach, objectives, and priorities. Our priority was to ensure that everyone involved in the project had a voice in the book and that our writing reflected the cultural context of the work and the different experiences of being deaf in this context. We do not conceptualize our approach as belonging to either a social or a medical paradigm but seek to understand deafness and caregiving in the cultural, historical, and social context of Ghana, recognizing the intersecting issues of health, poverty, disadvantage, and stigma that are characteristic of such a context.

Our objectives centre on the need to bring Southern experience and perspectives on the early care and education of deaf children into the wider ECCE literature. This involved a precarious balance of situating the work in the wider research field without leading with Western theory and perspectives. Linked to this was the need to build capacity for academic writing and engagement beyond Western work. These principles were a driver for the way in which we organized and managed the writing process.

We established a core writing team that comprised the PI, Co-Is, and project officer from the original research project. The core writing team developed the overall intellectual direction of the book that was also shaped by the findings from the project research activities. We used relevant literature on the language and communication of young deaf children and their caregivers, and the child rearing practices within SSA to provide a context for the writing. In our approach to the writing, we sought to draw on and bring to the surface individual professional expertise and research interests as well as personal experience, knowledge, and understanding of different cultural contexts. According to individual strengths and thematic interests, each of the core team members led on the writing of different chapters and worked in mentoring pairs with early career project members who had less experience of academic writing. The early career scholars chose to contribute in different ways to the drafting and redrafting of the English text. Specifically, the research assistants on the team were able to bring their in-depth experience of the field work visits, interviews, and observations to identify appropriate data sources and provide contextual examples to support the text. Our deaf project colleagues offered more personal narratives on different themes in the text in GhSL video format that they then translated into written English. We have woven aspects from these stories and reflections into the text to enrich the descriptions, broaden the discussion, and sometimes challenge perspectives.

The Structure of the Book

Chapters 2 to 5 of the book introduce local and global issues about early childhood care and education. These sections provide a critical discussion of the academic context of this work and set the scene and methodological approach for the Ghana project work. The following four chapters describe the main areas of focus and impact of the Ghana project work. These centre on the experience of caregivers, the multilingual context for development, multi-professional working, deaf participation, and leadership in ECCE. The two final chapters discuss the impact and capacity building implications of the work and offer a final discussion of the North–South learning brought about through this work.

In Chapter 2, we examine the medical and social implications of early childhood deafness in the SSA context. The chapter provides an overview of the available data on childhood deafness within this context and outlines the

ECCE challenges resulting from limited resources and the identification and intervention infrastructure needed to support children and caregivers. The chapter describes the consequential social and educational exclusion experienced by deaf children and their caregivers in this context in various aspects of life including education, health, and religion. Despite our individual and collective stance on the linguistic and cultural perspectives on deafness and social models of disability we felt it important to highlight from the start the realities of being and caring for a deaf child in a low-resource context.

The aim of Chapter 3 is to introduce the socio-cultural context of SSA and discuss traditional or pre-colonial African conceptions of childhood, disability, and deafness. We will focus on African child-rearing practices and what it means to be a child in Africa and set out important contextual issues. This includes the exploration of African worldviews, philosophies, and conceptions of being and knowing on childhood. Many of these constructs were disrupted and nearly destroyed by the colonial project. Traditional values that can be brought to bear on understandings of child-rearing practices in Africa include the Ubuntu model of disability (Chataika et al., 2015) and the communitarian sense of solidarity, family care, and social cohesion, as well as the general primacy of community. The chapter examines the depths of traditional African social life for positive contributions to child-rearing that lay a firm foundation for developing ecologically valid, contemporary early years' resource and capacity-building later in the book that will draw on solutions and indigenous models inspired by African theory and ethics.

The Ghana context of early years support for deaf children is introduced in Chapter 4. The chapter provides a discussion of what early support of childhood deafness means for a country like Ghana that is undergoing rapid development and change in terms of urbanization, cultural values, understandings, and behaviours, and what questions we need to ask about early years support to inform policy and programme development for young deaf children and their families. We provide contextual definitions of ECCE relative to Ghana and set the scene for a reflection on the narrative of the historical perspective of ECCE in Ghana.

In Chapter 5 we examine the ethical issues associated with researching childhood deafness and developing early support in the African context and explain the critical ecological research approach adopted by the project team. We review ethical issues associated with early childhood research and interventions across cultures that are discussed in the comparative and international research and discuss the implications for research into the early childhood and care of deaf children. The aims of the empirical project work

Introduction: Context, Vision, and Objectives **17**

undertaken in Ghana are discussed and we explain how we used the bioecological model in conjunction with social theory to inform our methodological approach. Throughout the chapter we draw on individual reflections among project team members to provide contextual examples of ethical dilemmas and how they were approached in project design, execution, and working practices.

Chapter 6 is the first of the case study sections of the book that draws on our research project findings to examine different aspects of deaf ECCE in Ghana including the experiences of caregivers, the language and communication development context, the role of professionals, and deaf intervention and leadership. In this chapter we focus on what was learned from the project work about caregivers' lives, their experiences of raising their deaf children, and planning for their education. The outcomes of interviews with education and health practitioners, and deaf leaders are discussed in later chapters. We briefly review the project goals, describe the methodological approach, and highlight the challenges that we experienced researching in this context. We introduce the 12 families who participated in the study. We outline the different family structures, level of education, and the employment experience, language, and communication practices and describe caregivers' experiences of having a deaf child, and of the early care and support provision and opportunities. Additionally, as for other sections of the book, deaf members of the project team have made personal contributions about their lives and experiences as young deaf children. We reflect on what can be learned from this specific context about the experiences of caregivers of deaf children in other African and global South contexts where there are similar resource, infrastructure, and inclusivity challenges.

Chapter 7 examines the communication and meaning-making strategies among deaf children and their families to illuminate the multilingual repertoires, communication strategies, and language development opportunities available in young deaf children's lives in Ghana. The chapter begins with an overview of multilingualism in Ghana and describes how different indigenous and non-indigenous languages co-exist and interact, and the roles that they play in society. The status and uses of GhSL in this multilingual context are explained. Drawing on four case studies from our project data, we extrapolate the specific language issues around the early support of children and their families and discuss the role of different professionals and the potential of community-based support. We also share reflections from three of the deaf project team members about their lives growing up in a multilingual context. In conclusion, we reflect on the relevance of the Ghanaian context for other multilingual (particularly) African contexts where there are parallel issues of caregiver agency and autonomy, stigma around deafness and the use of sign language, and insufficient resourcing that results in the cultural and linguistic minoritization of deaf children and their families.

Chapter 8 examines the role of professionals in the delivery of support services for deaf children and their caregivers in Ghana. We draw on the case study work undertaken in Ghana and report on the interviews that we conducted with 24 health and education professionals focusing on the experience of hearing health clinicians in the early identification context. We describe their working context, the objectives and drivers for their working practices, and the support that they offer for children and their families. A deaf project team member also shares his perspectives based on their lived experience of growing up as a deaf child in Ghana and current experience of supporting children and families. We review the extent of training and resources available to professionals and opportunities for collaboration. We identify the improvements needed to meet the Early Hearing Detection and Intervention 1-3-6 guidelines, increase multi-professional collaboration, and ensure the quality of early support for deaf children and their caregivers.

Chapter 9 focuses on deaf leadership in Africa and provides data from Ghana to highlight the role of deaf adults in early care and education of young deaf children and their caregivers in Ghana. In this chapter, we present data from 17 deaf adults who held different leadership roles at the district, regional, and national levels in Ghana. We report on their roles as deaf adults in supporting ECCE in Ghana for young deaf children and their caregivers. The chapter discusses the existing programmes and strategies of deaf leaders promoting equity and inclusion for young deaf children and their families. We highlight the critical roles that deaf leadership can play in supporting ECCE for young deaf children and their families. To accomplish this milestone for young deaf children and their families, we argue for the need to prioritize language and communication of the children and the support deaf leaders can offer to achieve this. Again, the chapter focusses on the roles deaf adults can play in building ECCE training infrastructure and collaborate with other practitioners in the supporting the children and their families.

The final chapter (10) explores the insights from the Ghana case study work and wider contribution of this text to understandings of the ECCE of deaf children in Africa, and other low-resource global South contexts. The new knowledge and research questions that emerge from this work are discussed in the context of international perspectives on early childhood care and education and next steps are identified for research and practice.

Drawing on the bioecological perspective that framed the original project work and the writing of this text (Bronfenbrenner & Morris 2006), we reflect on the different cultural contexts for deaf ECCE, the implications for resource and capacity building, and examine the potential for North–South learning. We review what we have learned as a project team about the external influences on ECCE provision and caregiver experience as well as the day-to-day realities of caregiving and raising a deaf child, and specific issues around language and communication. Drawing on this experience and reflecting on our journey as a cross-cultural research project and writing team, we discuss ways in which current ECCE paradigms can become more inclusive of different cultural contexts and propose workable interventions and ECCE strategies that build on local knowledge and practices.

References

Avard, D., Vallance, H., Greenberg, C., & Potter, B. (2007). Newborn screening by tandem mass spectrometry: ethical and social issues. *Canadian Journal of Public Health*, 98, 284–286.

Bronfenbrenner, U., & Morris, P. A. (2006). The bioecological model of human development. In W. Damon & R. M. Lerner (Eds.), *Handbook of child psychology: Theoretical models of human development* (pp. 793–828). New York: Wiley.

Carling, R. S., Whyte, E., John, C., Garstone, R., Goddard, P., Greenfield, T., Hogg, S., Le Masurier, C., Cowen, S., Moat, S. J. & Hopley, C. (2022). Improving harmonization and standardization of expanded newborn screening results by optimization of the legacy flow injection analysis tandem mass spectrometry methods and application of a standardized calibration approach. *Clinical Chemistry*, 68(8), 1075–1083.

Chapman, M., & Dammeyer, J. (2017). The significance of deaf identity for psychological well-being. *Journal of Deaf Studies and Deaf Education*, 22(2), 187–194.

Chataika, T., Berghs, M., Mateta, A., & Shava, K. (2015). From whose perspective anyway? The quest for African disability rights activism. In A. de Waal (Ed.), *Reclaiming activism: Western advocacy in contention* (pp. 187–211). Zed Books.

McIlroy, G., & Storbeck, C. (2011). Development of deaf identity: An ethnographic study. *Journal of Deaf Studies and Deaf Education*, 16(4), 494–511.

Skutnabb-Kangas, T. (2014). Afterword. Implications of deaf gain: Linguistic human rights for deaf citizens. In H. D. L. Bauman, & J. J. Murray (Eds.), *Deaf gain: Raising the stakes for human diversity* (pp. 492–502). University of Minnesota Press.

2
Childhood Deafness in Sub-Saharan Africa

Daniel Fobi and Derrick Asomaning

Introduction: Early Childhood Deafness in Sub-Saharan Africa

Deafness is estimated to be the fourth leading cause of disability worldwide (Cunningham & Tucci, 2017). Recent estimates on the prevalence of deafness places the figure at over 466 million people in 2018 with sub-Saharan Africa (SSA) being the third leading region after South Asia and Asia Pacific (WHO, 2018). Most infants with an early onset hearing loss are born in developing countries, specifically SSA where services are scarce and deaf awareness infrastructural support is limited (Bezuidenhout et al., 2021). Evidence indicates that 31% of cases of hearing loss can be attributed to prenatal and postnatal infections, 17% to birth-related causes, 4% to ototoxic medicines, and 8% to other causes such as substance abuse (Mulwafu, et al., 2016; WHO, 2016). The WHO (2016), reports that 60% of these cases could be averted through preventive measures. In such a context childhood deafness is often coupled with experience of poverty and poor health (Knoors et al., 2019; Stevens et al., 2013; UNICEF, 2013). The social and economic burden of childhood deafness on the individual, those close to them, and wider society is therefore significant (WHO, 2018).

Deafness in the early years of life can have a significant personal, educational, social, and economic impact on the developing child and on those who are responsible for their growth and wellbeing. Childhood deafness impacts primarily on access to spoken language and communication. In an environment where there is no access to a visual signed language and/or early access to hearing technologies, early childhood deafness disrupts opportunities for social interaction and can hinder subsequent developmental progress.

Daniel Fobi and Derrick Asomaning, *Childhood Deafness in Sub-Saharan Africa* In: *The Early Care and Education of Deaf Children in Ghana.* Edited by: Ruth Swanwick, Daniel Fobi, Yaw Offei, and Alexander Oppong, Oxford University Press.
© Daniel Fobi and Derrick Asomaning 2024. DOI: 10.1093/oso/9780192872272.003.0002

Without suitable intervention, deafness can thus become an eventual barrier to educational achievement, social participation, and autonomy (Yoshinaga-Itano et al., 2021). Unattended childhood deafness usually persists into adulthood, impacting on world knowledge, independence, and mental health (Hintermair, 2014; Yoshinaga-Itano et al., 2021).

Further, in contexts such as SSA, where negative cultural beliefs and practices can lead to discrimination and stigma, deafness can also become a cause of individual isolation, loneliness, and depression (WHO, 2016, 12). Public awareness and attitudes toward childhood deafness have been reported to be poor in general and aggravated by superstitious beliefs and customs in developing countries (Andrade & Ross, 2005; Olusanya, 2000; Stephens, et al., 2000; Swanepoel et al., 2005). A survey carried out in South Africa indicated that knowledge regarding risk factors for hearing loss was insufficient and 57% held at least one superstitious cultural belief regarding a possible cause of infant hearing loss. However, the attitudes of mothers regarding infant hearing screening were overwhelmingly positive with almost all (99%) indicating the desire to have their baby's hearing screened after birth and a very high acceptance (87%) of hearing aids as a means of intervention (Swanepoel & Almec, 2008). Nonetheless, superstitious beliefs continue to affect the caregivers of deaf children and the way they support their children since within some (often rural) communities families are stigmatized and excluded.

Early Intervention

The adverse consequences of childhood deafness can be mitigated through early identification and intervention programmes that offer sign and spoken language and technology interventions (Osei et al., 2018). When initiated by 6–9 months of age, early identification and intervention can facilitate early identification and early access to services including personal amplification and family-centred communication support (Swanepoel et al., 2009). Such measures can ensure that the developmental outcomes of deaf infants are commensurate with their hearing peers (Yoshinago-Itano, 2021).

However, most deaf children are born in low resource contexts where the early identification and management of childhood deafness is underdeveloped (Swanepoel, 2008). Olusanya et al. (2014) report that more than 90% of the estimated 718 000 infants born annually with congenital or early-onset permanent bilateral hearing loss reside in developing countries where environmental risks are more prevalent and early identification programmes are extremely uncommon. Although some progress has been made in terms of initiating pilot hearing detection and intervention programmes, these still reach very limited numbers of people (Olusanya et al., 2019; Swanepoel & Storbeck, 2008).

SSA is one of these contexts where there is limited access to objective screening methods in the early weeks of life which means that deafness is not identified, and intervention not put into place. Out of the 46 SSA countries, only two nations, South Africa and Nigeria, perform neonatal hearing screening, which are either hospital or community based (Kushalnagar et al., 2019). Kushalnagar et al. (2019) provided rank ordering of settings and procedures used in neonatal screening in both South Africa and Nigeria. In South Africa, private sector hospitals head the rank for settings offering newborn hearing screening. Newborn screening services in the private health care sector are not mandated by management but are dependent on individual initiatives from private practice audiologists (Swanepoel, et al., 2009). A telephone survey conducted by Meyer et al., (2012) indicated that newborn hearing screening was available in 53% of private health-care obstetric units in South Africa of which 14% provided universal screening. On the other hand, 7.5% of public sector hospitals nationally provide some form of infant hearing screening and less than 1% provide universal screening in South Africa (Bezuidenhout et al., 2021).

In Nigeria, the rank order of settings providing neonatal hearing screening is reversed. Community-based programmes are likely to be more common than hospital based programmes, which reflects Nigeria's birth patterns (Kushalnagar et al., 2019). According to Olusanya et al. (2019), a total of five universal neonatal hearing screening programmes, funded by a combination of public and private sources including donation or loan of equipment by manufacturers and offered at no charge to parents, have been piloted in Nigeria.

In terms of the procedures used for neonatal hearing screening in SSA, the protocol commonly used in hospital-based screenings is the two-stage screening protocol with Transient Evoked Otoacoustic Emissions (TEOAE) testing followed by Automated Auditory Brainstem Response (AABR) testing for children referred from the first-stage screen (Olusanya et al., 2021). In contrast, Meyer et al. (2012) reported that in the private health sector of South Africa, most (81%) of the healthy baby screening programmes used only OAE screening. Auditory brainstem response screening was employed by 24% of neonatal intensive care unit screening programs with only 16% repeating ABR screening during the follow-up screen. Theunissen et al. (2008) found that in public sector hospitals in South Africa, a screening OAE was used as the initial screen in seven out of 12 hospitals with a screening program, while AABR was used by only two hospitals. Diagnostic distortion product evoked otoacoustic emissions (DPOAE) tests were used by three hospitals to screen infants. Three hospitals reported using behavioral observation as part of their screening procedure although all of these reported using it in combination with objective methods. Friderichs et al. (2012) evaluated a community-based universal infant hearing screening program in the Cape Metropolitan area of South Africa over a 19-month research period. The study employed a two-stage DPOAE screening protocol was employed to reduce the burden of false positive referrals to tertiary hospital level. Friderichs et al. (2012) evaluated a community-based universal infant hearing screening program in the Cape Metropolitan area of South Africa over a 19-month research period. The study employed a two-stage DPOAE screening protocol. A two-stage screening protocol was employed to reduce the burden of false positive referrals to tertiary hospital level.

According to Kushalnagar et al. (2019), type professionals used for newborn hearing screening in SSA include non-specialists, clinic nurses, and audiologist. Olusanya et al. (2021) found that existing health-care personnel in hospital-based projects are more commonly entrusted with screening except in a few countries like Nigeria where non-specialists are recruited and specially trained to conduct screening. The use of non-specialists as screeners at primary health-care level has been found to be cost-effective while regular health workers are effective in educating parents on the program. Restricting screening to highly skilled personnel like audiologists or other ear care specialists may not serve the course of rapid spread of infant hearing screening as an important public health program due to the general dearth of such manpower (Olusanya et al., 2007). In Olusanya et al. (2008)'s cross-sectional study of community-based infant hearing screening in Lagos, Nigeria, screening personnel consisted of two full-time and two part-time staff members with no prior experience in audiological testing. They were given two weeks of focused training by the principal investigator of the study. In Friedrich et al. (2012)'s evaluation of community-based infant hearing screening in South Africa, clinic nurses served as screening personnel. Similar to the training of non- specialists in Nigeria, the nurses were trained and mentored in infant hearing screening before the service commenced. Alternatively, though, in Gauteng, South Africa, Swanepoel et al. (2007) examined a universal neonatal hearing screening program in a private health care hospital where the screening was conducted by two qualified audiologists. Data on screening personnel in public sector hospitals in South Africa was not available at time of research.

Within the SSA, the average age of diagnoses is almost two years with enrolment into intervention programmes at over two and half years (Yoshinago-Itano, 2017). In Ghana for example, deafness is typically detected at 5 years with some being identified as late as 8 years old (Fobi & Oppong, 2019; Oppong & Fobi, 2019). This inevitably leads to a delay to children starting school. The lack of early care and intervention services for deaf children and their families in SSA is attributed to restricted resources and the lack of training for audiologists and other hearing health care specialists. South Africa reports slightly better statistics in terms of early identification and intervention when compared to other countries in SSA, however, late detection and identification beyond the recommended 6–9-month window still prevails.

This situation is compounded by the inequality of resources between the public and private health care providers. Most people access public health care services that offer less resources compared to the private health care services. Although the private health care sector has state-of-the-art medical services, most of the population in SSA do not have the financial resources that will enable them to access such services. In South Africa for example (classified as an upper middle income-country) much of the population (approximately 85%) rely on the public health sector whilst the remaining minority (approximately 15%) access the private health care sector which comprises the majority of national health care expenditure (National Treasury Department, 2005). Even the intervention programmes in the private sector, which offer sophisticated and modern equipment, are unstructured and unsystematic because they depend on the initiatives of individual audiologists who are not mandated by hospital management (Bezuidenhout et al., 2021). The presence of a hospital-based screening programme does not mean every baby will be screened (Theunissen and Swanepoel, 2008).

Furthermore, as Swanepoel et al. (2009) point out, early screening and diagnosis are not useful if these processes are not systematically followed through with language, communication and hearing technology support. The high cost associated with hearing technologies and cochlear implant surgery remain obstacles in limited resource contexts such as SSA and interventions that focus on supporting visual and sign language communication among children and their families are not prioritized or even considered as an alternative (Swanepoel et al., 2007). It is not therefore surprising that caregivers become focused on the development of spoken language as a means to ensuring the inclusion of their children in their communities. Deaf children's

Social Exclusion and Marginalization

Social interaction is key to the overall development of every child. It is during the elementary school years that social behaviours and skills are initially developed, and children establish, develop and maintain friendship (Engels et al., 2002). The positive social interactions and skills such as helping others, sharing, and resolving dilemmas promote the psychological wellbeing of the child (Hiebert, 2019). Engels et al. (2002) point out that social interaction can be challenging for some children because it depends on communication, social awareness, and appropriate timing of behaviours to interact effectively. In these circumstances children require appropriate support. Deaf children are at a greater risk of being socially excluded compared to their hearing counterparts when they are not surrounded by accessible communication and lack opportunities to develop social skills and behaviours (Marschark & Hauser, 2008).

Social exclusion on a wider scale can be manifested in a range of life situations that when combined can create a vicious cycle. Barnes and Morris (2008) propose seven dimensions of the different ways in which exclusion is experienced by individuals and groups. These include the following:

1. Material dimensions: insufficient income, poor-quality housing and physical environments (Jordan, 1996).
2. Spatial exclusions: Restrictions on where people can live and on their mobility within and between places (Sibley, 1995).
3. Access to both public and private goods and services (Batsleer and Humphries, 2000).
4. Health and well-being: Poor health is both a consequence of material deprivation, and can be a source in its own right of exclusion from social participation (Banks & Purdy, 1999).
5. Cultural: Certain lifestyles are regarded as irresponsible, immoral or 'other'. Fear of the other can lead people to exclude those regarded as outsiders (Sibley, 1995; Ward, 2005).
6. Self-determination: Certain social groups: Children, people with learning difficulties, and those regarded as mentally incapacitated, are considered incapable of (and in some cases legally excluded from) taking decisions about life choices.

7. Public decision making: In spite of the expansion of participatory practices in public decision making, many of those who are most marginalised remain excluded from decision-making processes.

Barnes and Morris (2008)

We examine these dimensions within an ecological context for development as a means of illustrating the ways in which deaf children and their families might experience exclusion in the SSA context in different aspects of their lives.

Material Dimensions

The material dimensions and spatial exclusion may correspond to the microsystem which constitutes deaf children's immediate environments, such as families, community, school, and playgrounds, as well as the church. Many deaf children in SSA come from poor homes that are not equipped to attend to their material needs. In Ghana, for instance, many deaf children go to school without the appropriate learning materials, such as books, pens, and pencils. Thus, teachers often assume parenting roles by providing these materials for the children (Oppong & Fobi, 2019).

Material deprivation has a particular significance for families with children with disabilities. A majority of such families live in or on the margins of poverty (Gordon et al., 2011) and the costs of raising a child with disability have been estimated at three times that associated with raising a nondisabled child (Bahry et al., 2019). Children with disabilities, including deaf children, often live in houses and environments that are not adapted to their needs and this can have deleterious effects on their health, and on both the mental and physical health of parents (Clarke, 2006). Gendreau (2011) found that families with deaf children especially those in rural areas have inadequate resources. The issue of limited resources often affects how much longer it would take for the family to learn language and experience less stress and frustration due to not establishing a shared language in the home (Gendreau, 2011).

Limited resources on the part of deaf children and their families contribute to their exclusion at all levels of the ecological system. Many families have inadequate finances to provide their deaf children the basic necessities of life, quality education, and recreation. Barnes and Morris (2008) found that parents in their study cited low income as key to their non-use of local leisure and recreational facilities. This is particularly significant in view of the poor quality of the physical environment in which many of them live and the absence of safe space for play.

Spatial Exclusions

Deaf children are also excluded spatially and in terms of access to resources in their external environment in relation to educational provision. Valentine and Skelton (2002) posit that deaf people may become marginalized in four spaces; at home, in educational institutions, in the work place, and within deaf communities. Most countries in SSA have special schools for deaf children and some mainstream provision that is described as inclusive. The chosen and most affordable option for many families is for their deaf child to attend the mainstream school in their own communities. However, these schools lack the resources to provide the range of language, communication, and learning support that deaf children need. The only option for parents is therefore to send their children to one of the special schools for the deaf. These schools are usually located at a distance and so offer boarding facilities. Young deaf children who attend these schools are thus separated from their parents, siblings, and local community for months at a time only returning when schools are on vacation.

Spatial exclusion has health and well-being consequences. Although, there are house-parents in special schools who take care of the children's physical needs, such as washing and dressing, their emotional needs are not met: they grow up experiencing very little parental love and care, and this has been found to impact on the emotional bonds between deaf children, their parents, and siblings (Nortey, 2009). Further, the connection between the different developmental environments does not function in a way that fosters their emotional well-being. Partnerships between home and school are generally not well established (Honu-Mensah et al., 2022). Caregivers are cut off from their children's school lives due to the physical distance between homes and school and do not see their children grow and develop. Many parents do not manage to visit the school until the start of the vacation and there are also instances of parents leaving their child in a school for the deaf and never visiting the school again. In spite of the increased enrolment of deaf children in both special schools and regular schools, professionals and the deaf community have expressed concerns that students will be forgotten in classrooms without support from teachers and parents, and that their language, communication, and social needs cannot be met in a public-school environment (Innes, 1994). It is not surprising that many deaf children subsequently find the transition from dependent childhood to independent adulthood challenging (Valentine & Skelton, 2002). Their vulnerability around this period can in part be explained by the experience of marginalization that exposes them to emotional and well-being precarities (Coles, 2018).

The spatial dimension of exclusion is also evident in terms of deaf individuals' access to religious organizations and gatherings (Yate, 2017). Although, efforts are being made by some Christian churches to break down the communication barriers that hinder the deaf from participating in church activities by providing sign language interpreters, they are still unable to remedy the social isolation of its deaf members from the rest of the congregation. Reading of religious texts such as the Bible has been difficult for deaf congregants due to English being a second language to them although recent sign language translations of the Bible are improving accessibility (Yate, 2017). However, these translations are usually available online and comes with internet data cost. Thus, some deaf people do not have access because of affordability. In addition, potentially unqualified interpreters and social isolation results in poor religious experience and usually prevent deaf individuals from spiritual growth and regular church attendance. Deaf children are not able to access religion because hearing parents are not able to explain religious sermons and texts to them in a language they can understand.

Health and Wellbeing: Access to Services

Barnes and Morris (2008) include health and well-being as one of the dimensions of social exclusion experienced by individuals and groups, and for deaf people this often centres on access to hearing health and medical services. According to principles of social justice and the fundamentals of basic human rights, each person should receive fair and equal access to health care (Douglas et al., 2014). Yate (2017) highlights the significant health disparities for deaf people and indicates the need for greater awareness within the medical profession of the health needs of deaf people and accessible avenues for deaf people to seek medical aid.

Communication between deaf people and health-care professionals can be improved through the employment of professional sign language interpreters (Nortey, 2009). This comes at a high cost that tends to fall on deaf individuals or their families. Countries in SSA do not routinely cover the cost of sign language interpretation for deaf people in these situations even though there are policies that direct institutions to create inclusive access for deaf children and their families. The usual practice is for deaf individuals and their families to make their private arrangements for interpreters when accessing medical care or information in other public and private institutions. Since many deaf children come from low-resourced families, the cost of hiring professional interpreters to mediate communication between them and health-care professionals is prohibitive.

There are an increasing number of technologies that can facilitate communication among deaf people and their health-care professionals (Yate, 2017). These include Video Relay Services (VRS) and Video Remote Interpreting (VRI). VRS employs a sign language interpreter to facilitate a telephone conversation between a signing and a non-signing person who are in separate locations. The interpreter communicates with the deaf person in sign language via a video connection and with the hearing person by spoken language via a regular phone. VRI allows access to a real-time interpreter on screen for a signing and a non-signing person when an interpreter cannot be physically present with them. VRI has widespread use and is often available in hospital emergency rooms to allow for quality communication among deaf patients and their non-signing health-care professionals. Since the Covid pandemic both VRS and VRI are gradually coming into use in the SSA context.

This technology also offers the possibility of tele-intervention (TI) services for families of deaf children that can allow for the provision of support across rural and remote areas via mobile phones, through the internet using computers, or even televisions as monitors. Tele-intervention services can include health-oriented support such as screening, diagnosis, fitting, and management of amplification but also potentially offer sign language instruction for families. During the Covid-19 pandemic, TI was found to be a successful way to deliver services to families and is becoming an increasingly popular mode of delivery in some parts of the world (Behl et al., 2017; Havenga et al., 2017; Yaribakht & Movallali, 2020). However, TI direct to the home relies on a good quality internet service. Alternatively, an accessible local site can be used that has good internet access such as a school, health facility, or another public service location, such as a library.

Yate (2017) talks about the importance of cultural competence in mitigating the barriers to health care experienced by deaf people. She argues that medical professionals must understand patients' cultural background in order to provide quality care. This includes the values and beliefs, worldview, tradition, and behaviours of families and communities (Sullivan, 2015). According to Yate (2017, p. 5), 'Cultural competence includes the mind-set, actions, and standards necessary to provide medical care to patients from a different culture.').

Awareness of the importance of culturally competent practice is increasing in general but has yet to embrace deaf culture (Eckert & Rowley, 2013). This is especially true in the SSA context where many medical practitioners are unable to adapt to the communication preferences of deaf people or to increase their use of visual strategies using sign language, gestures, finger spelling, facial expressions, and other forms of embodied communication. Family members and friends of deaf individuals thus often become mediators during interactions between medical professionals and deaf individuals. However, the signing skills of family members vary. Their skills and vocabulary may not be adequate for the topic of discussion (Fobi et al., 2022; Yate, 2017), and they may inadvertently intervene in appropriate ways by speaking for the deaf person or breaking confidentiality expectations (Richardson, 2014).

The absence of cultural competence can lead to communication barriers and foster distrust between members of the deaf community and health-care professionals. Deaf patients can also become too intimidated to ask questions or explain their symptoms (McKee et al., 2013; Richardson, 2014) and this is disruptive for the development of a trusting relationship necessary for holistic care (Thorn, 2014). Unsuccessful encounters between deaf patients and medical professionals can also compound medical issues where an accurate history or report of symptoms cannot be obtained (Atkinsona & Wolla, 2012). A delayed or incorrect diagnosis can lead to an expensive hospital stay and further health risks. There is also a risk that procedures are performed without the patients' informed consent especially where consent material is provided in written English without additional support (GNAD, 2017; McKee et al., 2013; Richardson, 2014).

With repeated bad experiences, deaf patients often rely on self-diagnosis and the purchase of medication from local pharmacies, or the use of traditional healing methods. According to the Ghana National Association of the Deaf (GNAD, 2017), deaf patients will visit multiple health-care providers in search of a practitioner who they feel that they are able to communicate with.

Promoting cultural competency and awareness among health-care practitioners is a step towards reducing the health disparity among deaf individuals, promoting their access and inclusion, disrupting the cycle of distrust and improving patient outcomes (Yate, 2017).

Cultural Dimensions

Culture is defined by Parasnis (1996) as a way of life. Culture is an integrated pattern of human knowledge, beliefs, and behaviour that is acquired as a member of society. It includes the ideas, assumptions, and values of a group, and shapes all that we do (Giaouri, et al., 2022). Wald and Knutson (2000) posit that there are two different ways to view deafness: deafness as a disability and a medical pathology, or deafness as a culture with its own values, traditions, and customs. Deaf culture is passed on through social interactions and language in the deaf community. Being a member of the deaf culture is contingent on many factors, such as knowledge of the language, hearing status of family members, cultural competence, and personal identification. Being born deaf or hard of hearing does not automatically mean that one is a member of deaf culture (Giaouri et al., 2022). Deaf culture is often regarded as abnormal by the hearing populace in SSA and deaf people are often considered as outsiders, and this type of cultural exclusion can play out on several levels (Fobi et al., 2021, Valentine & Skelton (2002). Deaf people who use sign language can be marginalized by the hearing world, and deaf people who prefer spoken language communication and make use of hearing technologies can be discriminated against within the deaf community. As we have seen in the individual stories within the writing team, there are many different ways to be deaf and these binaries create inauthentic and unhelpful barriers.

Self-Determination

The dimensions of self-determination and inclusion in decision-making processes are also relevant to deaf children and adults. Generally, deaf individuals are not consulted when making decisions that concern their lives at the family, community, and national levels. Even on the personal level, sometimes their opinions are neglected. Caregivers often make decisions by themselves or consult professionals like teachers, audiologists, nurses, and psychologists in making choices related to their deaf children; however, deaf children themselves are rarely involved in the decision-making process. Caregivers of our study commented as follows:

'No one advised me to take him to that school. The inclusive, the Winneba inclusive school. I took him there myself because I had the opportunity to read special education as a general programme, introduction to special education yeah so, I was able to use that knowledge to take him to school.' (Caregiver 5)

'The psychologist encourage us to continue to keep her in a regular school and then get a special needs teacher in the school to help with the Childs progress.' (Caregiver 6)

'I look for tips from teachers. What people do in more developed countries? I print it out and give it to the teacher and explain it.' (Caregiver 9)

Deaf people are usually not involved in decision-making concerning their life because typically they are considered as illiterate, lacking the necessary skills in making appropriate decisions and choices. According to Nortey (2009), many deaf people in Ghana are excluded from family gatherings. Where they are involved in family meetings, their suggestions and advices are not taken seriously by hearing members of the family, which often leads to feelings of loneliness, neglect, disappointment, and depression.

Public Decision Making

The opinions of persons with disabilities including deaf people are rarely considered when formulating national policies that concern them. These policies are usually designed to 'satisfy' the demands of the international development sector and thus do not effectively meet the specific needs of deaf people. Moreover, such policies are ambiguous and lack specific implementation strategies, leading to social exclusion and marginalization of deaf people (Oppong & Fobi, 2019).

In order to improve the lives of deaf children and their caregivers, their inclusion in every aspect of life (education, religion, and community) needs to be facilitated by policy makers and practitioners. A key pathway to this is through the development of inclusive educational provision that has the potential to challenge societal barriers, change attitudes, and provide equal and accessible opportunities for development, participation, and autonomy.

Educational Inclusion

Educational inclusion in regular education originated in the United States in the 1970s under the terminology 'least restrictive placement' (Stone, 2019). Educational inclusion has an important role in eliminating discrimination and improving social justice (Walping, 2016). The Framework discourages segregation and encourages schools to ' ... accommodate all children regardless of their physical, intellectual, social, emotional, linguistic or other condition' (UNESCO, 1994, p.6). Thus, the Framework called on all education systems to become child-focused and to acknowledge the heterogeneity of children (Fobi, 2021). From the Framework's perspective, inclusive education took on two meanings:—how to move away from assumptions about the needs of children with disabilities being entirely impairment based (and thereby placing them into special education based largely on medical reasoning); and how to transform mainstream education systems to become aware of the learning needs of all children so as to help establish education systems that are barrier free (Kiuppis, 2014).

In spite of the increasing awareness of inclusive education, there is generally lack of clarity and consistency over the concept of inclusion (Fobi, 2021; Wapling, 2016). Hayford (2013) argues that inclusion means different things to different people, authorities, and professionals in different countries. However, the term inclusive education is more broadly understood as a reform that supports and welcomes diversity among learners (Burnett, 2009). In the Ghanaian context, inclusive education is perceived as the 'value system which holds that all persons who attend an educational institution are entitled to equal access to learning, achievement, and the pursuits of excellence in all aspects of their education, and which transcends the idea of physical location but incorporates the basic values that promote participation, friendship, and interaction' (Government of Ghana, 2015, p. 5). Inclusive education aims at eliminating exclusion that is as a consequence of negative attitude and lack of response to diversity in race, economic status, social class, ethnicity, language, religion, gender, sexual orientation, and ability (UNESCO, 2009).

Bayat (2014) and Sharma and Das (2015) note that in education analysis, the terms 'inclusion' and 'integration' are often confused and used interchangeably, although, they are not the same. Integration is largely associated with mainstreaming children with disabilities into regular classrooms but inclusion is about accommodating all children (Wapling, 2016). In other words, integration involves deaf children fitting into the school's system whereas inclusion refers to transforming the school's system to meet the learning needs of the deaf children. This lack of clarity has a profound impact on the understanding and implementation of inclusive education, leading to a lack of overall progress in improving education for children with disabilities including the deaf (Sharma & Das, 2015).

Policy and Practice

Wapling (2016) notes that the confusion around the concepts of inclusion seems to have resulted in the tendency of low- and middle-income countries (LMICs) to adopt the term education at policy level but one that in practice means integration of children in mainstream schools. Pather (2013) observed a similar trend of inclusion in Southern Africa where inclusive education models are essentially focused on the integration of children with disabilities and without considering the wider aspects of educational needs, such as poverty or ethnic status. So in reality, inclusive education is being implemented using an integration perspective which does not reflect the shift in thinking envisaged or promoted by the international development sector (Wapling, 2016). In addition, there is limited support for implementation despite the existence of a reasonably positive policy environment. Wapling (2016) described the implementation of inclusive education policies in LMICs as 'symbolic implementation'. Governments in LMICs including those in SSA seem to adopt policies that meet international priorities but pay little regard to implementation at the level of school and teachers. Thus, many inclusive education policies are ambiguous and contain little direct strategies in the way of implementation (Wapling, 2016).

Another major challenge of inclusive education in the SSA context is the lack of resources. Donohue and Bornman (2014) point out that the ambiguity of policies is linked to the lack of funding and it is intentional since polices are created to conform to international demands and norms and not as a result of locally led changes. Limited funding has led to poor implementation of inclusive education policies. A significant barrier to the effective implementation of inclusive education in South Africa (as elsewhere) is funding (Donohue & Bornman, 2014). Professionals and stakeholders responsible for the implementation of inclusive education policies are dissatisfied with the level of financing in many LMICs (Amoako, 2019; Kalyanpur, 2008; McDonald & Tufue-Dolgoy, 2013; Vorapanya & Dunlap, 2014). Funding is insufficient to cover the cost of adequately prepared inclusive education teacher costs and the provision of advisers and technical resources (McDonald & Tufue-Dolgoy, 2013). In addition, donors have too much influence and advocate for inclusive practices which are based on socio-economic contexts different from low income contexts (Kalyanpur, 2014; Le Fanu, 2014).

Wapling (2016) argues that special needs education has a role in inclusive education. Hence, the state of special education has direct impact on inclusive education. The poor state of special education in SSA countries had had adverse effects on inclusive education in those contexts. The majority of African countries show only a theoretical interest in the provision of special needs education (Itimu, 2008). A comparison of Malawi, Tanzania, and Zambia showed that all three countries have insufficient resources for special needs education; showed minimal to no inter-agency collaboration around children with disabilities; and had an urgent need to train more teachers in special needs education (Wapling 2016). Tumwesigye et al. (2009) noted that special schools themselves are often not adequately resourced to support their students and are in an already weak position when it comes to resourcing children in mainstream classes. In support, Maguvhe (2013) posits that the special education sector is ill-prepared to support inclusion of children especially those who are deaf. Other factors that affect and lead to poor inclusive education in SSA include negative attitudes, poor sign language skills among facilitators, and lack of curriculum adaptation.

Conclusion

Deafness and other experiences of disability are a leading cause of marginalization in different areas of life such as education, health, and community participation. There continues to be calls from the international development sector and disability activists to make life inclusive for all disabled people. This has led to an increasing focus on what it means to be an inclusive society and especially to provide inclusive education. In this chapter we have looked at issues of the exclusion and inclusion of deaf people in general, focusing on examples from SSA and drawing parallels with other low resource contexts. The opportunities and challenges that we have identified provide the broad policy and practice context for thinking specifically about the needs and experiences of very young deaf children growing up in African contexts. To provide a framework for our thinking on this the next chapter discusses understandings of childhood and parenting in SSA.

References

Amoako, S. F. (2019). Sixty years of deaf education in Ghana (1957–2017). *Journal of Communication Disorders, Deaf Studies and Hearing Aids, 7*(1), 1–11.

Andrade, D., & Ross, E. (2005). Benefits and practices of Black South African traditional healers regarding hearing impairment. *International Journal of Audiology, 44*, 489–499.

Atkinsona, J., & Wolla, B. (2012). The health of deaf people. *The Lancet, 379*(9833), 2239.

Bahry, N. S., Mat, A., Kori, N. L., Ali, A. M., Abdul Munir, Z., & Salleh, M. Z. M. (2019). Challenges faced by Malaysian parents in caregiving of a child with disabilities. *Bahry, NSGlobal Journal of Business Social Sciences, 7*(2), 118–124.

Banks, D., & Purdy, M. (Eds). (1999). *Health and exclusion.* London: Routledge.

Barnes, M., & Morris, K. (2008). Strategies for the prevention of social exclusion: An analysis of the children's fund. *Journal of Social Policy, 37*(2), 251–270. doi:10.1017/S0047279407001730

Batsleer, J., & Humphries, B. (Eds). (2000). *Welfare, exclusion and political agency.* London: Routledge.

Bayat, M. (2014). Global education diplomacy and inclusion in developing countries: Lessons from West Africa. *Childhood Education, 90*(4), 272–280.

Behl, D. D., Blaiser, K., Cook, G., Barrett, T., Callow-Heusser, C., Brooks, B. M., Dawson, P., Quigley, S., ... & White, K. R. (2017). A multisite study evaluating the benefits of early intervention via telepractice. *Infants & Young Children, 30*(2), 147–161.

Bezuidenhout, J. K., Khoza-Shangase, K., De Maayer, T., & Strehlau, R. (2021). Outcomes of newborn hearing screening at an academic secondary level hospital in Johannesburg, South Africa. *South African Journal of Communication Disorders, 68*(1), 741.

Burnett, N. (2009). *Policy guidelines on inclusion in education.* Paris, UNESCO.

Clark, G. M. (2006). The multiple-channel cochlear implant: the interface between sound and the central nervous system for hearing, speech, and language in deaf people—a personal perspective. *Philosophical Transactions of the Royal Society B: Biological Sciences, 361*(1469), 791–810.

Coles, B. (19972018). Vulnerable youth and processes of social exclusion: a theoretical framework, a review of recent research and suggestions for a future research agenda. In J. Bynner, L. Chisholm, & A. Furlong (Eds.), *Youth, citizenship and social change in a European context* (pp. 90–113). Ashgate, Aldershot, Hants.

Cunningham, L. L., & Tucci, D. L. (2017). Hearing loss in adults. *New England Journal of Medicine, 377*(25), 2465–2473.

Donohue, D., & Bornman, J. (2014). The challenges of realising inclusive education in South Africa. *South African Journal of Education, 34*(2), 1–14.

Douglas, M. K., Rosenkoetter, M., Pacquiao, D. F., Callister, L. C., Hattar-Pollara, M., Lauderdale, J., Milstead, J., Nardi, D., & Purnell, L. (2014). Guidelines for implementing culturally competent nursing care. *Journal of Transcultural Nursing, 25*(2), 109–121.

Eckert, R., & Rowley, A. (2013). Audism: A theory and practice of audiocentric privilege. *Humanity & Society, 37*(2), 101–130. doi: 10.1177/0160597613481731

Engels, R. C., Deković, M., & Meeus, W. (2002). Parenting practices, social skills and peer relationships in adolescence. *Social Behavior and Personality: An International Journal, 30*(1), 3–17.

Fobi, D., & Oppong, A. M. (2019). Communication approaches for educating deaf and hard of hearing (DHH) children in Ghana: historical and contemporary issues. *Deafness & Education International, 21*(4), 195–209. doi:10.1080/14643154.2018.1481594

Fobi, D. (2021). *Role of interpreting in the inclusion of deaf students in tertiary education in Ghana.* [Doctoral thesis, PhD thesis. Leeds: University of Leeds].

Fobi, D., Quarshie, E. N. B., Fobi, J., Appau, O., Honu-Mensah, C. M., Acheampong, E. K., & Abu-Sadat, R. (2021). Bullying victimisation among deaf adolescents: a school-based self-report survey in Ghana. *International Journal of Disability, Development and Education, 69*(1), 253–266. doi:10.1080/1034912X.2021.1989670

Fobi, D., Swanwick R. A., Asomaning, D., & Doku, R. (2022). Promoting deaf- adults' participation in early care and education of deaf children. *Journal of Deaf Studies and Deaf Education, 28*(2), 136–145. https://doi.org/10.1093/deafed/enac040

Gendreau, S. (2011). *A study of caregiver experiences in raising a deaf child.* Masters thesis. University of Manitoba (Canada).

Giaouri, S., Karipi, S., Alevriadou, A., Hatzopoulou, M., & Kourbetis, V. (2022). Deaf adults as role models for the hearing world: A literature review. *European Journal of Special Education Research, 8*(1), 1–24.

Gordon, K. A., Wong, D. D. E., Valero, J., Jewell, S. F., Yoo, P., & Papsin, B. C. (2011). Use it or lose it? Lessons learned from the developing brains of children who are deaf and use cochlear implants to hear. *Brain topography, 24*, 204–219.

Government of Ghana (2015). *Inclusive education policy.* Accra: Ministry of Education, Ghana.

Havenga, E., Swanepoel, D. W., Le Roux, T., & Schmid, B. (2017). Tele-intervention for children with hearing loss: A comparative pilot study. *Journal of Telemedicine and Telecare, 23*(1), 116–125.

Hayford, S. K. (2013). *Special educational needs and quality education for all.* Department of Special Education, University of Education, Winneba.

Hiebert, N. R. (2019). *Experiences of social inclusion and exclusion of deaf children.* [Western University doctoral dissertation] Electronic Thesis and Dissertation Repository. 6053

Hintermair, M. (2014). Psychosocial development in deaf and hard-of-hearing children in the twenty-first century. In M. Marschark, G. Tang, & H. Knoors (Eds.), *Bilingualism and bilingual deaf education* (pp. 152–186). Oxford University Press.

Honu-Mensah, C. M. Fobi, D., & Quansah, B. (2022). Developing an understanding of parent-teacher partnerships in schools for the deaf in Ghana. *Journal of Disability, Development and Education.* 71(2), 208–221.https://doi.org/10.1080/1034912X.2022.2092601

Innes, J. (1994). Full inclusion and the deaf student: A consumer's review of the issue. *American Annals of the Deaf*, 139, 152–156.

Itimu, A. N., & Kopetz, P. B. (2008). Malawi's special needs education (SNE): perspectives and comparisons of practice and progress. *Journal of Research in Special Educational Needs*, 8, 153–160.

Jordan, B. (1996). *A theory of poverty and social exclusion.* Cambridge: Polity.

Kalyanpur, M. (2008). Equality, quality and quantity: challenges in inclusive education policy and service provision in India. *International Journal of Inclusive Education*, 12, 243–262.

Kalyanpur, M. (2014). Distortions and dichotomies in Inclusive Education for children with disabilities in Cambodia in the context of globalisation and international development. *International Journal of Disability, Development and Education*, 61, 80–94.

Kiuppis, F. (2014). Why (not) associate the principle of inclusion with disability? Tracing connections from the start of the 'Salamanca Process'. *International Journal of Inclusive Education*, 18, 746–761.

Knoors, H., Brons, M., & Marschark, M. (2019). Deaf education beyond the western world: An Introduction. In H. Knoors, M. Brons, & M. Marschark (Eds.), *Deaf education beyond the Western world* (pp. 1–18). New York: Oxford University Press.

Kushalnagar, P., Engelman, A., & Simons, A. N. (2019). Deaf women's health: adherence to breast and cervical cancer screening recommendations. *American Journal of Preventive Medicine*, 57(3), 346–354.

Le Fanu, G. (2014). International development, disability, and education: Towards a capabilities-focused discourse and praxis. *International Journal of Educational Development*, 38, 69–79.

Maguvhe, M. (2013). Perspectives of South African special school teachers on special schools as resource centres. *Mediterranean Journal of Social Science*, 4, 711–717.

Marschark, M., & Hauser, P. C. (Eds.). (2008). *Deaf cognition: Foundations and outcomes.* Oxford: Oxford University Press.

McDonald, L., & Tufue-Dolgoy, R. (2013). Moving forwards, sideways or backwards? Inclusive education in Samoa. *International Journal of Disability, Development and Education*, 60, 270–284.

McKee, M., Schlehofer, D., & Thew, D. (2013). Ethical issues in conducting research with deaf populations. *American Journal of Public Health*, 103(12), 2174–2178.

Meyer, M. E., Swanepoel, D. W., Le Roux, T., & van der Linde, M. (2012). Early detection of infant hearing loss in the private health care sector of South Africa. *International Journal of Pediatric Otorhinolaryngology*, 76(5), 698–703.

Mulwafu, W., Kuper, H., & Ensink, R. J. (2016). Prevalence and causes of hearing impairment in Africa. *Tropical Medicine and International Health*, 21(2), 158–165.

National Treasury Department. (2005). *Intergovernmental fiscal review 2005.* Republic of South Africa. Retrieved fromhttp://www.treasury.gov.za/publications/igfr/2005/default.aspx.

Nortey, D. A. (2009). *Barriers to social participation for the deaf and hard of hearing in Ghana.* [Master's thesis, University of Bergen].

Olusanya, B. O. (2000). Hearing impairment prevention in developing countries: making things happen. *International Journal of Pediatric Otorhinolaryngology*, 55(3), 167–171.

Olusanya, B. O., Davis, A. C., & Hoffman, H. J. (2019). Hearing loss grades and the International classification of functioning, disability and health. *Bulletin of the World Health Organization*, *97*(10), 725–728. https://doi: 10.2471/BLT.19.230367

Olusanya, B. O., Neumann, K. J., & Saunders, J. E. (2014). The global burden of disabling hearing impairment: a call to action. *Bullet in of the World Health Organization*, *92*, 367–373. https://doi.org/10.2471/BLT.13.128728

Olusanya, B. O., Swanepoel, D. W., Chapchap, M. J., Castillo, S., Habib, H., Mukari, S. Z., ... & McPherson, B. (2007). Progress towards early detection services for infants with hearing loss in developing countries. *BMC Health Services Research*, *7*, 1–15.

Olusanya, B. O., Wirz, S. L., & Luxon, L. M. (2008). Community-based infant hearing screening for early detection of permanent hearing loss in Lagos, Nigeria: a cross-sectional study. *Bulletin of the World Health Organization*, *86*(12), 956–963.

Olusanya, J. O., Ubogu, O. I., Njokanma, F. O., & Olusanya, B. O. (2021). Transforming global health through equity-driven funding. *Nature Medicine*, *27*(7), 1136–1138.

Oppong, A. M., & Fobi, D. (2019). Deaf education in Ghana. In Knoors, H. Knoors, Brons, M. Brons, & Marschark, M. Marschark (Eds). *Deaf education beyond the Western world: Context, challenges and prospects for Agenda 2030* (pp. 53–72). New York: Oxford University Press. doi:10.1093/oso/9780190880514.003.0004

Osei, A. O., Larnyo, P. A., Azaglo, A., Sedzro, T. M., & Torgbenu, E. L. (2018). Screening for hearing loss among school going children. *International Journal of Pediatric Otorhinolaryngology*, *111*, 7–12. doi:10.1016/j.ijporl.2018.05.018.

Parasnis, I. (1996). *Cultural and language diversity and the deaf experience*. Cambridge, NY: Cambridge University Press.

Pather, S., & C. Nxumalo, P. (2013). Challenging understandings of inclusive education policy development in Southern Africa through comparative reflection. *International Journal of Inclusive Education*, *17*, 420–434.

Richardson, K. (2014). Deaf culture: Competencies and best practices. *The Nurse Practitioner*, *39*(5), 20–28. doi:10.1097/01.NPR.0000445956.21045.c4

Sharma, U., & Das, A. (2015). Inclusive education in India: past, present and future. *Support for Learning*, *30*, 55–68.

Sibley, D. (1995). *Geographies of exclusion*. London: Routledge.

Stephens, D., Stephens, R., & Eisenhart-Rothe, A. (2000). Attitudes toward hearing impaired children in less developed countries: a pilot study. *Audiology*, *39*, 184–191.

Stevens, G., Flaxman, S., Brunskill, E., Mascarenhas, M., Mathers, C. D., Finucane, M., & Global Burden of Disease Hearing Loss Expert Group. (2013). Global and regional hearing impairment prevalence: an analysis of 42 studies in 29 countries. *European Journal of Public Health*, *23*(1), 146–152. doi:10.1093/eurpub/ckr176.

Stone, D. H. (2019). The least restrictive environment for providing education, treatment, and community services for persons with disabilities: Rethinking the concept. *Touro Law Review*, *35*(1), 523.

Sullivan C. G. (2015). Implementing culturally competent care. *Nursing Outlook*, *63*(2), 227–229. http://dx.doi.org/10.1016/j.outlook.2015.01.008

Swanepoel, D. (2008). Infant hearing loss in developing countries—a silent health priority. *Audiology Today 20*(3), 16–24.

Swanepoel, D. W. (2009). Early detection of infant hearing loss in South Africa. *SAMJ: South African Medical Journal*, *99*(3), 158–159.

Swanepoel, D., & Almec, N. (2008). Maternal views on infant hearing loss and early intervention in a South African community. *International Journal of Audiology*, *47*, S44–S48.

Swanepoel, D., & Storbeck, C. (2008). EHDI Africa—advocating for infants with hearing loss in Africa., *International Journal of Audiology*, *47*, S1–S2.

Swanepoel, D., Delport, S., & Swart, J. G. (2007). Equal opportunities for children with hearing loss by means of early identification. *South African Family Practice, 49*, 3.

Swanepoel, D., Hugo, R., & Louw, B. (2005). Implementing infant hearing screening at maternal and child healthcare clinics: context and interactional processes. *Journal of Interdisciplinary Health Sciences, 10*, 3–15.

Theunissen, M., & Swanepoel, D. (2008). Early hearing detection and intervention services in the public health sector of South Africa. *International Journal of Audiology, 47*, 23–29.

Tumwesigye, C., Msukwa, G., Njuguna, M., Shilio, B., Courtright, P., & Lewallen, S. (2009). Inappropriate enrolment of children in schools for the visually impaired in East Africa. *Annals of Tropical Paediatrics, 29*, 135–139.

UNESCO (1994). *The Salamanca Statement and Framework for Action on Special Needs Education, World Conference on Special Needs Education: Access and Quality.* Salamanca, Spain, 7–10 June 1994.

UNESCO (2009). *Teaching children with disabilities in inclusive settings.* Bangkok, Thailand.

UNICEF (2013). *The state of the world's children, executive summary 2013: children with disabilities.* New York: United for Children, 1–26. Available: http://www.unicef.org/publications/files/SOWC2013

Valentine, G., & Skelton, T. (2002). Living on the edge: the marginalization and resistance of D/deaf youth. *Environment and Planning, 35*, 301–321. doi:10.1068/a3572.

Vorapanya, S., & Dunlap, D. (2014). Inclusive education in Thailand: practices and challenges. *International Journal of Inclusive Education, 18*, 1014–1028.

Wald, R., & Knutson, J. (2000). Deaf cultural identity of adolescents with and without cochlear implants. *Annals of Otology, Rhinology, and Laryngology, 12*(2), 87–89.

Wapling, L. (2016). *Inclusive education and children with disabilities: Quality education for all in low and middle income countries.* CBMChristian Blind Mission.

Ward, N. J. (2005). *Social exclusion and mental wellbeing: lesbian experiences.* [Ph.D. Thesis, University of Birmingham].

World Health Organization. (2015). *Hearing loss due to recreational exposure and loud sounds - A review.* Available at http//apps.who.int/iris/bitstream/10665/1/9789241508513_eng.pdf?ua=1&a=1/.

World Health Organization. (2018). *Deafness and hearing loss.* Geneva. http://www.who.int/en/news- room/fact-sheets/detail/deafness-and-hearing-loss.

World Health Organization. (2016). *Childhood hearing strategies for prevention and care.* Geneva, p. 30. Retrieved from http://www.who.int/about/licensing

Yaribakht, M., & Movallali, G. (2020). The effects of an early family-centered tele-intervention on the preverbal and listening skills of deaf children under tow years old. *Iranian Rehabilitation Journal, 18*(2), 117–124.

Yates, J. L. (2017). *Deaf access to healthcare.* [A Senior Thesis, submitted in Liberty University].

Yoshinaga-Itano, C., Mason, C. A., Wiggin, M., Grosse, S. D., Gaffney, M., & Gilley, P. M. (2021). Reading proficiency trends following newborn hearing screening implementation. *Pediatrics, 148*(4), e2020048702. https://doi.org/10.1542/peds.2020-048702

Yoshinaga-tano, C., Sedey, A. L., Wiggin, M., & Chung, W. (2017). Early hearing detection and vocabulary of children with hearing loss. *Pediatrics, 140*(2), e20162964.

Yoshinago-Itano, C. (2004). Levels of evidence: universal newborn hearing screening (UNHS) and early detection and intervention (EHDI) systems. *Journal of Communication Disorders, 37*, 451–465.

3
African Childhoods

Alexander Mills Oppong and Obed Appau

Introduction: African Children

Children in sub-Saharan Africa (SSA) are highly regarded and traditionally valued as a gift and blessing from the creator of the universe or other deities (Mhaka-Mutepfa & Maundeni, 2019). According to Aniah et al. (2014) and Fraser et al. (2015), maximization of births in indigenous African religions and social structures has been traditionally motivated by the importance attached to heritage and descent, as well as reverence for ancestors. African traditional values hold that childbearing is seen as necessary for moral virtue, material and spiritual well-being, and posterity (Mhaka-Mutepfa & Maundeni, 2019). In the more extreme interpretation of these values, childlessness and subfecundity were seen to deny the right of ancestors to be reborn and/or for the lineage to be continued, and thus they were associated with misfortune (Aniah et al., 2014; Fraser et al., 2015; Mbito & Price, 1992). The cultural value attached to children in the SSA context was also attributed to the economic power that children provide to the family: the growth of a family provided practical support for parents in the home and in their work, and the extension of kinship structures ensured security of landownership and heritage (Fraser et al., 2015).

Traditional childbearing beliefs have changed over time in SSA according to the development of societal and family economies, values, and lifestyles. Parents in SSA today still perceive a child as a gift from God but this does not influence them to have as many children as was common in the past. Many families prefer to limit the number of children to three at most in order to have adequate resources to cater for their needs (Hall & Richter, 2018). The trend of child bearing has also changed in SSA as a result of mothers extending

---

Alexander Mills Oppong and Obed Appau, *African Childhoods* In: *The Early Care and Education of Deaf Children in Ghana.*
Edited by: Ruth Swanwick, Daniel Fobi, Yaw Offei, and Alexander Oppong, Oxford University Press.
© Alexander Mills Oppong and Obed Appau 2024. DOI: 10.1093/oso/9780192872272.003.0003

their roles from housekeepers to career women, resulting in reduced time for family duties.

There is a significant difference between child bearing in rural and urban settings. Some families who stay in rural settings still embrace the tradition of giving birth to many children. Looking at the nature of work in rural areas, such as farming and trading, where people work for themselves, and the type of education (non-formal), it is not surprising that families hold fast to the beliefs of their ancestors about child bearing. However, the nature of work in the cities (being hired by an employer), desire for promotion at work, and type of education (formal) have all sharpened and moulded families' mentality on childbirth.

Families in rural settings were usually subsistence farmers who depended heavily on the cultivation of perennial crops such as cocoa and coffee, and some cash crops, such as plantain, vegetables, and root crops, including cocoyam, cassava, and yams, for a living and as such relied mainly on their own biological children to help them on their farms—hence rural couples gave birth to many children. In those days the wealth or economic standing of a family was judged by the number of children in the family (Bossard, 2016).

In many SSA cultures, the most influential driving force for children's development is the family (both nuclear and extended) (Garcia et al., 2008). The child belonged to the rural community because all members of rural communities were responsible for raising the child (Ajiboye et al., 2012).

Constructs of Parenting

A universal approach for parenting across the globe could be very difficult to achieve since parenting is mostly influenced by context and parents are always influenced by their cultural settings. Despite cultural differences, there is a consensus among some academics that the primary role of all parents is to influence, teach, and manage their children (Whitaker & Hoover-Dempsey, 2013). Parenting has also been explained as the process of raising children from childhood to adulthood with the aim of helping individuals to develop their emotional, physical, and intellectual well-being (Pullen et al., 2017).

Every parent has their ideology of parenting their children, depending on the community in which they live. Parenting in general has been identified as an aspect of people's culture (Harkness & Super, 2002). Many people have their own unique style of parenting based on their personal experiences and understanding, practices from generations, and transmission of cultural values. It is therefore not surprising that many studies have underscored the variations in parenting children in different cultural contexts (e.g. Bornstein, 1994; Bornstein et al., 1991; Hewlett et al., 2000; Hoff et al., 2002; Konner, 1991; LeVine, 1990, 1994; Super & Harkness, 1996; Weisner, 2000).

Santrock (2006) conducted a study on childrearing practices and found that parents learnt the skills of parenting learnt from their own and other parents, and some of the things learnt were either accepted or discarded. Santrock argues that when parenting style is learnt from predecessors, the possibility of learning desirable and undesirable methods is very high. Notwithstanding, studies have documented other forms of parenting that were used by mothers and fathers. Some of these forms of parenting are through story telling (folktales), the extended family, traditional rites and the mother's care, attention, and love (Darko, 2015).

There is an extensive literature that examine parenting theories and that attempt to classify parenting styles. Bee (1992), Berk (2005), (Darko, 2015), Hart et al., (2002), Nix et al., (1999), and Thompson et al., (2003) have emphasized other forms of parenting styles that were practiced throughout the world. These styles are authoritarian parenting, authoritative parenting, permissive parenting, and uninvolved parenting. Authoritarian parents expect the child to obey every rule and regulations given to them (the child) without raising any objection (Cherry, 2012). Cherry (2012), noted that authoritarian parenting style expects the child to adhere or follow the strict rules established by the parents without expressing an iota of doubt about such rules. Parents do not consider whether the child can follow the rules.

Cherry (2012) explained authoritative parenting as a style which establishes rules and guidelines that their children are expected to follow. Unlike authoritarian parents who are undemocratic, authoritative parents are democratic: they give room for the children to ask questions and listen to them. Parents who are authoritative are assertive, thus they train their children to be assertive as well (Baumrind, 1991). As the name implies, permissive parents are lenient and demand less from their children. They have relatively low expectations of maturity and self-control (Cherry, 2012). Parents who employed this parenting style normally operate as a friend to the child. Permissive parents always try to avoid confrontation with their children and do not expect the child to display any mature behaviour (Baumrind, 1991).

Uninvolved parents, according to Cherry (2012), attempt to make provision for their children's basic needs but detach themselves from the child's life. These parents hardly communicate with their child and do not bother themselves to give their children rules and regulations. In some extreme cases, uninvolved parents ignore the provision of basic needs for their children. The use of these parenting styles could be attributed to such factors as culture, personality, parental background, educational level, socio-economic status, family size, and religion (Amos, 2013).

Parenting Theories of Childrearing in Sub-Saharan Africa

Three theories of parenting that support the present chapter are 'socio-cultural norms' (Keller et al., 2003), the 'custom of collective responsibility' (Ajiboye et al., 2012) and the bioecological systems theory (Bronfenbrenner, 2005). Most SSA cultures predominantly practice socio-cultural norms of adult control of children and the children's duty of showing respect and obedience to adults (Ansong et al., 2017). Within the majority of SSA cultural settings, children are brought-up to respect and obey their elders and not question the authority or knowledge of parents, teachers, and other adults (Ansong et al., 2017, p.52; Hart et al., 2002; Nix et al., 1999; Thompson et al., 2003). Some of the notable indigenous tribes in SSA where the socio-cultural norm theory could be observed in practice are: the Akamba, Maasai, and Gabra people of Kenya in East Africa; the Ndebele of South Africa; the Bozo community of Mali; and Ashanti people of Ghana in West Africa (Andrea, 2014; Ganga & Chinyoka, 2017; Wanjohi, 2013).

The second theory that guides the present paper is the 'custom of collective responsibility' (Ajiboye et al., 2012). The theory is premised on the African proverb which states that 'it takes a whole village to raise a child' (Okafor, 2003). In the global South, particularly, in SSA, each member of the rural village community has the responsibility to contribute positively towards the upbringing of all children (whether that child is the biological, foster, or distant relation to the parents). It was, and still, it is incumbent upon each member of the village to display some love, compassion, care, and concern for all children in the village. A youth, a middle-aged person, or an elderly person who saw, and still, sees a child sauntering about alone would interrogate such a child about why and where they are going and if the answer given is unsatisfactory, the individual would ask such a child to go home or take him/her to the parents. Whenever children are left alone due to parents being busy or unforeseen circumstances, another family would take those children, sometimes with or without permission, and shower them with food and affection until the parents return (Ajiboye et al., 2012). In most SSA cultures, it is incumbent upon every person to lend a helping hand in caring for a child.

The other theory that supports the other two is bioecological systems theory (Bronfenbrenner, 2005). The bioecological theory was adopted to specifically illustrate proximal environmental factors (the microsystem, because that was the focus of our study) in order to capture the connection between parents/caregivers and the upbringing of their young deaf preschoolers (Woodhead et al., 2014).

Parenting in the SSA Context

In SSA, the ultimate goal of parenting is to help the child to be a responsible adult and imbibe the traditional laws of the land into themselves. In this context, the notion of parenting extends from raising individuals from birth through childhood and on to becoming young adults and has the aim of helping individuals assimilate their parents' socio-cultural values and norms, and to ultimately adopt a moral and healthy lifestyle. Parents are thus conceptualized as the custodians of their children's behavioural, intellectual, social, emotional, and cognitive development (Erbasi et al., 2016; Green, 2007; Mirabile et al., 2009).

Traditionally, parents in SSA were influenced by rituals and beliefs in the community in raising their children. It was not uncommon for parents to pass on their beliefs and traditions to their children. Some of the traditions that shaped and moulded parents' child rearing practices were instituted in the communities over centuries. Some of the conventional childcare practices are based on core knowledge and wisdom although others have emerged purely from intuition, superstitions, and unfounded beliefs (Kaur & Grewal, 2017).

Constructs of parenting in SSA have historically been strongly influenced by traditional concepts of patriarchy and gender. The practice of parenting in SSA was often based on seniority, age, or eldership where most of the power and right to decide and oversee family affairs was given to the men, grandfathers and other elderly in the communities. Mothers were traditionally expected to do most of the household chores such as washing, sweeping, bathing the children, and feeding the family, whilst fathers were expected to provide resources for the family that could help the mother to execute her duties. At the microsystem level, parents tended to assign household chores to their children based on their gender: vigorous work, such as weeding, farming, and lifting and carrying heavy things, for example, were mostly assigned to male individuals whilst less vigorous activities, such as cooking and washing (clothes and utensils), were mostly given to female individuals. Notwithstanding these gender divisions, parents in SSA worked together to achieve the family's goals but each person nonetheless had a distinct role, based on culture and beliefs. These practices differed between rural and urban communities and have changed in modern days. As every parent aspires for their children to receive formal education and become responsible adults, parents in collaboration with teachers have allowed their children (male or female) to be trained in ways that allow them perform any role in society, although in few instances, there are some minor divisions in roles as were practiced in the past.

Parents in SSA tend to teach their children specific behaviours and assign specific tasks to their children based on their ages. Parents intentionally taught their children how to perform some activities, such as sitting, crawling, walking, and running, knowing very well that their children would mature and develop to perform these activities (Super & Harkness, 2009). Parents in Zambia used their children to operate their day-to-day activities and to help them in farming and marketing (Jahoda, 1983), whilst parents in Ghana believed that their children could learn numeracy, counting, and understanding weight, quantity, and measurement in the process of growth and development (Adjei, 1977). Thus, parents in SSA were optimistic that their children could develop cognitively without taking them through a systematic curriculum as practiced in the global North (Bashir et al., 2018) but could develop all the required skills through the engagement of unintentional activities, such as playing, cooking, sweeping, and washing. Parents in SSA did not have specific learning goals for their children when assigning household chores to them; however, they always used such tasks to teach and promote acceptable and required behaviour. In their studies in Kenya, Harkness and Super (2002) found that parents correlate their children's ability to perform household chores such as sweeping and washing with their level of intelligence. It was obvious to parents that the ability to perform tasks or household chores was tantamount to intelligence and vice versa. This means that success in learning was based on the ability to perform practical tasks without taking into consideration the theoretical aspect of learning, such as knowledge, recall, and analysis.

Thus, children's upbringing is based on cultural priorities and parents' ideas (Le Vine et al., 1994). Though parents do not entrust siblings, uncles, aunties, and the entire community with the responsibility of imparting knowledge to their children, they expect all these stakeholders to have some impact on their children's life since they believe that the immediate family and the entire communities shared common goals, culture, and beliefs (Mbito, 2004).

Child rearing practices and beliefs in Africa contrast with those of Europe and America where parents use different strategies to teach their children. The global North intentionally employs different strategies to teach colours, numbers, counting, alphabet, and calculations during pre-school education to prepare a fertile ground for primary education. (LeVine et al., 2001).

Traditional practices have over time been influenced and changed by the shifts in educational level, socioeconomic status, and value systems of families and society (Singh & Yadav, 2001). Globalization in SSA has significantly influenced parenting styles, although these influences have not entirely erased the culture and belief systems which shaped more traditional parenting styles. Due to globalization and rural urban migration, many fathers are now more involved in rearing children in SSA. Both fathers and mothers are involved in income-generating jobs and this has resulted in shared responsibility for child rearing in the family. Currently many fathers participate in household chores such as cooking, washing, bathing the children, taking their children to school, and assisting them with their homework. Though fathers are still regarded as heads of African family systems, the level of authority that was designated to them to make unilateral decisions in the family has reduced since in most families now, each member has the right to share their views on family matters.

Globalization and rural–urban migration in SSA have shaped parenting styles in the twenty-first century. Parenting has changed in SSA countries such as Ghana as a result of urbanization, educational background and socio-economic status of parents (Sequeira et al., 2022). In Ghana, parents who live in urban settlements take a keen interest in their children's education: some of their children start formal education as young as six months. The availability of pre-school facilities in the cities and towns makes it easier for those who stay in urban rather than in rural areas to have early formal preschool education for their children. The educational background of parents in today's world has really impacted the current parenting system. Historically, many parents in Ghana did not have the opportunity to receive formal school education. The processes of child development, care giving, child-rearing skills, different parenting styles, theories of parenting, and the practice of parenting—all affected how parents perceived education in general. Studies have established that parents' knowledge about children and parenting helps the parents to behave positively towards their children (Oldershaw, 2002). It is therefore not surprising that many parents in Ghana nowadays pay more attention to their children's education than previously. Unlike those days where parents used to seek permission from teachers to take their children from school to assist them in farming and selling on market days, parents of today rather sacrifice their time to visit their children in schools to interact with their facilitators.

48 Care and Education of Deaf Children in Ghana

Also, parents are aware of and well versed in parenting styles today, so the majority of parents do not employ authoritarian and other domineering parenting styles which will adversely affect their children's psychological, emotional, and cognitive development. In particular parents with a higher educational background have been exposed to different philosophies of child rearing in the course of their education. Parents with a low-level educational background still tend to use more authoritarian styles of parenting with their children.

The socio-economic background of parents plays a vital role in today's parenting in SSA. Historically, many parents in Ghana were farmers and traders who were regarded as people of low socio-economic status. It is therefore not surprising that children were regarded as income generators for the family, thus, dignity and respect were attached to the number of children a family had. The narrative has changed today because parents of high-level socio-economic background often take good care of, and show genuine love to, their children.

Ghanaians by nature devote much of their attention to children's upbringing (National Early childhood care and development policy, 2004) and, in Ghana, early, non-formal early childhood care and education delivery has always been the responsibility of parents, caregivers, and families rather than the state (Garcia, 2008). Additionally, education of children in Ghana (which begins in the home) is considered a shared responsibility of the immediate family and, by extension, of the overall community. In this early education endeavour, the role of the father (and other adult males in the family and community) in the upbringing of the child is critical. Because this role is deeply rooted in the tradition and culture of Ghana, children in all of Ghana's cultures 'value the idea of a father or a father figure' (Garcia, 2008, p. 162). Overall, children whether non-disabled or disabled, such as deaf children, are usually taught to respect their fathers and, by extension, all men.

Men (grandfathers, uncles, step fathers, foster fathers, older brothers, cousins, and other male family friends) can therefore, play the role of father to a child (Garcia, 2008). In return, society expects that men (adult males) would be responsible for the protection of all children everywhere—i.e. in the neighbourhood, at school, on public transport, on the farm, and in the home (Garcia, 2008, p. 163). What this means is that every adult within the child's community, including friends of the family, neighbours, and other members of the community outside of the family, have a responsibility to teach, correct, reprimand, and protect any child. This implies that the care, protection, and education of children need to acknowledge the several ways by which fathers (and other adult males) can be involved in the entire lives of their children

(Garcia, 2008). In contrast, it appears that currently, in most contemporary Ghanaian societies, parents are getting less involved in designing interventions for their children with disabilities (Honu-Mensah et al., 2022). In typical Ghanaian families, fathers involve their children (including the deaf) in their trade, such as farming or hunting, during their early years. In this way fathers educate their children and imbue them with relevant skills and ethics while at the same time strengthening the bond between them. During the current, upsurge in rural–urban migration, up to eight million Ghanaians have migrated from rural to urban areas (Raturi & Cebotari, 2023) for various reasons. Therefore, fathers are working in the cities and towns and appear not to be spending much time with their children or performing their roles as much as they did before.

Parental Interaction

Traditionally, parents in SSA did not attach any great importance to parent–child interactions irrespective of past studies projecting the benefits derived from it (Amuyunzu-Nyamongo. Biddlecom et al., 2005; Mbugua, 2007; Paruk et al., 2005). However, parents did communicate with their children during activities such as farming, marketing, and household chores. The interactions that occurred were informal and unstructured. This could be as a result of the fact that early childhood curricula do not explain to parents how they can incorporate parent–child interactions and conversational turn-taking into their typical activities, such as farming, marketing, and household chores. Historically, some topics such as sex education (reproduction health education) were perceived as taboo and were not discussed during parent–child interactions. In many countries in SSA, the discussion of sex issues with young children was unacceptable. However, the prevalence of the extended family system at that time allowed grandparents to impart age-appropriate knowledge about reproduction and behaviour relevant for sexual relationships to the children (Fuglesang, 1997). Gradually, the issue of globalization, social change, and the switch from the extended family system to the nuclear system is changing the narrative in situations where parent–child interactions were not revered.

Frequent communication between parents and their children can help the children to be confident, tolerate other people's views, and also confide in their parents (Pullen et al., 2017; Vaccari & Marschark, 1997) and pre-eminently helps the child to acquire language and develop communication skills (Hammer et al., 2012; Kobosko, 2011; Mweri, 2016).

Family Structure and Caretaking

The extended family has been a widespread part of life in SSA, where in addition to the biological parents, other members such as siblings, uncles, aunties, and the community around takes a part in and influence the child's life. Studies in SSA have stressed how the caretaking role performed by extended family members helps the child to develop emotionally (Whaley et al., 2002). The early care curriculum teaches children about the existing family types in Africa; however, it does not incorporate extended family members into the instruction about language learning and development and strategies that could support children's optimal language development.

The approach to shared parenting and the extended family system emphasizes interconnection, conformity to group norms, relational harmony, and values that promote the welfare of the group. This contrasts with Western approaches that centre on smaller and nuclear arrangements where only the immediate family oversees the child's affairs in the home and where there is a greater focus on autonomy and independence, self-determination, and protection of self-interests and values that promote individual goals (Mbito, 2004). In attempts to evaluate the benefits of these contrasting family structures, debates have arisen over whether or not a structure that emphasizes the interdependent, collaborative, and consultative aspects of family life where children are socialized in groups and communities constitutes interference in a child's life, privacy, and developing autonomy. It is argued that Western family contexts are more likely to promote emotional maturity, independence, and autonomy (Markus & Kitayama, 1991; Triandis et al., 1988). In contrast, in SSA, an individual can visit other families without prior notice and would be welcomed. Any person in the community could also come to a parent and offer to provide guidance and advice to that child on specific issues (Ajiboye et al., 2012). Such parenting practices are not entertained in Western cultures. Societal relationships and socializations in SSA are unintentional whilst they are intentional in Western Europe cultures.

The family structure in Ghana tends to reflect the extended family practices, especially in rural communities. In such contexts most families live together in one family house, which has usually been built by a family member. The findings from our project revealed that many parents live in either the family house or a compound house.[1] Whether the co-habitants are part of the

---

[1] A compound house is a type of dwelling where people from different backgrounds or family connections rent different rooms in the same compound or collection of buildings. The main difference between a compound house and a family house is that a compound house can be inhabited by individuals who are either related by blood or those who are not related.

family or not, they have the mandate to help the child to grow physically, emotionally, and cognitively, and to acquire language and communication skills. Diverse models of caregiving and concepts of family structure are not unique to the Ghanaian or wider African context but are an important factor for this research.

In more urban areas, as a result of globalization and exposure to Western cultures, the practice of the extended communal family system is gradually changing. Many families in urban contexts live as smaller nuclear systems and are less likely to have an external family member living alongside and sharing the child rearing duties. Migration into the cities for work has also meant that many more nuclear families are detached from their extended family members and will not interact with them on a daily basis but gather for certain occasions such as festivals, funerals, and weddings. The cost involved in travel to and from cities has further fractured the interconnectivity of larger family communities and reduced the wider involvement of extended family members in children's upbringing.

Experiences of Parenting Children with Disability in SSA

Parenting a disabled child in SSA presents families with complex social, emotional, and financial challenges. Children with disabilities and their families in Africa are often not treated fairly or with respect (Bayat, 2014). The experience of stigmatization, marginalization, and exclusion on a number of levels (discussed in Chapter 2) is still widespread in SSA and these external factors make it difficult for parents to accept and manage the care of their disabled child.

Bayat (2014) underscored two key issues that influence the social stigma and negative ways of thinking attached to childhood disability. She argues that Western Judeo-Christian religions perceive creation as an act of perfection, hence any abnormalities in creation are perceived as caused by sin on either the part of family members or the child. Second, African indigenous religions explain the world as involving interactions between various natural spirits: sky, water, earth, air, forest, and ancestral. It is traditionally believed in Africa that any illness or disease is as a result of a conflict between natural spirits and the ancestors. Problems in life that make an individual go through pain are also considered to be a manifestation of displeasure of either the natural or ancestral spirits.

Due to these traditional indigenous beliefs in Africa, families that give birth to disabled children are often considered to be cursed and many people discriminate against them and exclude them from social and community activities. The birth of a disabled child in a family can disrupt the family relationships and structure whereby family members want to distance themselves from the association with evil spirits, and this can lead to separation and divorce (Harper et al., 2013). In Africa, individuals with disabilities are often raised by single parents. There is a strong culture of blame around the birth of a disabled child and this frequently falls on the mother. For instance, in Namibia, women are mostly accused of displeasing evil spirits as the cause of disability, hence disabled children are raised mostly by single women (Chilwalo, 2010).

In Ghana, Cote d'Ivoire, and other parts of West Africa, disabled children are sometimes referred to in derogatory terms as 'snake children'. In Ghana, it has been common to mock deaf children by hearing people putting leaves in their mouths and pretending to chew them. There is a perception that deaf individuals are animals and the act of putting leaves in the mouth reminds deaf children of their origin. What also often happens is, replacing the name of deaf people with a term signifying 'the deaf one' ('mumu' or 'mum' in Akan), which Oteng (1988) regarded as derogatory.

In the most extreme examples of discrimination, such children would not be allowed to live among the extended family community. Parents are faced with harsh choices. Many do not want the community to know that they have a child with disabilities due to the harsh perceptions they have about such children and so will hide the children or keep them indoors. In the worst cases, disabled children are abandoned (Bayat, 2014). The fears and prejudices surrounding deafness, and ensuing discriminatory behaviours, underline the importance of ensuring that caregivers have the opportunity to meet and interact with deaf adults who communicate in a range of different ways thus offering different examples of pathways to successful language learning and vocational success.

Education for Children with Disabilities

In some parts of Africa children with disabilities are excluded from the education system. Though such countries have not categorically stated that disabled individuals cannot be educated, the education system has not made any provision for such children. For instance, a study conducted by Assimwe et al. (2014) in Uganda, revealed that the education system is not fit for children with disabilities.

Studies have showed that many children with disabilities living in SSA are excluded from the educational system. Factors involved are beliefs and cultural practices, negative attitudes, an inaccessible curriculum, and lack of teaching resources for teachers.

Conclusion

Different global contexts for early development comprise diverse cultural traditions and lifestyles, family structures, and caregiving practices. The economic, geopolitical, and social environment and resources shape the different ways in which children are cared for and educated in formal and informal settings, and caregiving practices are embedded within cultural and societal values, beliefs, and traditions. Approaches to early care and education thus need to be developed with a full understanding of the sociocultural context, and knowledge about the resource dynamics of different early childhood contexts are a fundamental starting point. In Chapter 4, we focus specifically on Ghana as the site of the research study central to this book and introduce the Ghanaian context of early years support for deaf children.

References

Adjei, K. (1977). Influence of specific maternal occupation and behavior on Piagetian cognitive development. In P. R. Dasen (Ed.), *Piagetian psychology* (pp. 227–256). Gardner.

Ajiboye, E. O., Atere, A. A., & Olufunmi, A. N. (2012). Changing patterns of childrearing practices in Badagry of Lagos State: Implication for delinquent behaviors. *European Scientific Journal*, 8(5), 28–54.

Amos, P. M. (2013). Parenting and culture–Evidence from some African communities. In M. L. Seidl-de-Moura (Ed.), *Parenting in South American and African contexts*. IntechOpen. https://www.intechopen.com/chapters/45760

Amuyunzu-Nyamongo, M., Biddlecom, A. E., Ouedraogo, C., & Woog, V. (2005). *Qualitative evidence on adolescents' views of sexual and reproductive health in Sub-SaharanAfrica.* Occasional Report, 16. Alan Guttmacher Institute.

Andrea, J. (2014). *Pregnancy and childrearing practices in Africa.* Retrieved from:https://prezi.com/k6bkstmne-ly/pregnancy-child-rearing--practices-in-Africa/

Aniah, P., Aasoglenang, A. T., & Bonye, S. Z. (2014). Behind the myth: Indigenous knowledge and belief systems in natural resource conservation in North East Ghana. *International Journal of Environmental Protection and Policy*, 2(3), 104–112.

Ansong, D., Okumu, M., Bowen, G. L., Walker, A. M., & Eisensmith, S. R. (2017). The role of parent, classmate, and teacher support in student engagement: Evidence from Ghana. *International Journal of Educational Development, 54*, 51–58.

Assimwe, J. B., Ndugga, P., Mushomi, J., & Ntozi, P. M. (2014). Factors associated with modern contraceptive use among young and older women in Uganda; a comparative analysis. *BMC Public Health, 14*, 926.

Bashir, S., Lockheed, M., Ninan, E., & Tan, J. P. (2018). *Facing forward: Schooling for learning in Africa.* World Bank Publications.

Baumrind, D. (1991). The influence of parenting style on adolescent competence and substance use. *Journal of Early Adolescence, 11*(1), 56–95.

Bayat, M. (2014). Understanding views of disability in Cote d'Ivore. *Disability and Society, 52*, 30–43.

Bee, H. (1992). *The developing child* (6th ed.). Harper Collins College Publishers.

Berk, L. E. (2005). *Infants, children, and adolescents* (5th ed.). Pearson Education Inc.

Bornstein, M. H. (1994). Cross-cultural perspectives on parenting. In G. d'Ydevalle, P. Eelen, & P. Bertelson (Eds.), *International perspectives on psychological science, Vol. 2: State of the art lectures presented at the 25th International Congress of Psychology, Brussels, 1992* (pp. 539–369). Lawrence Erlbaum Associates, Inc.

Bornstein, M. H., Tal, J., & Tamis-LeMonda, C. (1991). Parenting in cross-cultural perspective: The United States, France and Japan. In M. H. Bornstein (Ed.), *Cultural approaches to parenting* (pp. 69–90). Lawrence Erlbaum Associates, Inc.

Bossard, J. H. (2016). *The large family system: An original study in the sociology of family behaviour.* University of Pennsylvania Press.

Bronfenbrenner, U. (2005). *Making human beings human: Bioecological perspectives on human development.* Sage.

Cherry, K. (2012). *Parenting styles: The four styles of parenting.* Retrieved fromhttp://psychology.about.com/od/developmentalpsychology/a/parenting-style.htm

Chilwalo, B. M. (2010). A comparative analysis on the psychosocial factors that influence the parenting styles of single mothers among the Damara, Otjiherero and San people in Gobbabis, [Unpublished master's thesis]. University of Namibia, Windhoek.

Darko, J. (2015). Mothering, faith and culture: Ghanaians discuss parenting in the diaspora. *Journal of Gender, Information and Development in Africa, 4*(1–2), 25–34.

Erbasi, E., Scarinci, N., Hickson, L., & Ching, T. Y. (2016). Parental involvement in the care and intervention of children with hearing loss. *International Journal of Audiology, 57*, S15–S26. https://doi.org/10.1080/14992027.2016.1220679

Fraser, J. A., Frausin, V., & Jarvis, A. (2015). An intergenerational transmission of sustainability? Ancestral habitus and food production in a traditional agro-ecosystem of the Upper Guinea Forest, West Africa. *Global Environmental Change, 31*, 226–238.

Fuglesang, M. (1997). Lessons for life—Past and present modes of sexuality education in Tanzanian society. *Social Science & Medicine, 44*(8), 1245–1254.

Ganga, E., & Chinyoka, K. (2017). An analysis of how contemporary African childrearing practices affect a child's self-concept and learning. *International Journal of Case Study, 6*, 3. Retrieved May 25, 2023 from SSRN: https://sspn.com/abstract=2964168

Garcia, M., Pence, A., & Evans, J. L. (Eds.) (2008). *Africa's future, Africa's challenge: Early childhood care and development in sub-Saharan Africa.* International Bank of Reconstruction and Development/The World Bank.

Green, S. E. (2007). 'We're tired, not sad': Benefits and burdens of mothering a child with a disability. *Social Science & Medicine, 64*(1), 150–163.

Hall, K., & Richter, L. (2018). Introduction: Children, families and the state. In K. Hall, L. Richter, Z. Mokomane, & L. Lake (Eds.), *South African Child Gauge* (pp. 22–31). Children's Institute, University of Cape Town.

Hammer, C. S., Komaroff, E., Rodriguez, B. L., Lopez, L. M., Scarpino, S. E., & Goldstein, B. (2012). Predicting Spanish–English bilingual children's language abilities. *Journal of Speech, Language, and Hearing Research, 55*(5), 1251–1264. https://doi.org/10.1044/1092-4388 (2012/11-0016

Harkness, S., & Super, C. M. (1992). Parental ethnotheories in action. *Parental belief systems: The psychological consequences for children, 2,* 373–392.

Harkness, S., & Super, C. M. (2002). Culture and parenting. *Handbook of parenting, 2*(2), 253–280.

Hart, C. H., Nelson, D. A., Robinson, C. C., Olsen, S. F., McNeilly-Choque, M. K. Porter, C. L., & McKee, T. R. (2002). Russian parenting styles and family processes: Linkages with sub-types of victimization and aggression. In K. A. Kerns, J. M. Contreras & A. M. Neal-Barnett (Eds.), *Family and peers: Linking two social worlds* (pp. 47–84). Praeger.

Hewlett, B. S., Lamb, M. E., Leyendecker, B., & Schoelmerich, A. (2000). Parental investment strategies among Aka foragers, Ngandu farmers, and Euro-American urban industrialists. In L. Cronk, N. Chagnon, & W. Irons (Eds.), *Adaptation and human behavior: An anthropological perspective* (pp. 155–178). de Gruyter.

Hoff, E., Laursen, B., & Tardif, T. (2002). Socioeconomic status and parenting. In M. H. Bornstein (Ed.), *Handbook of parenting, Vol. 2: Biology and ecology of parenting* (2nd ed., pp. 231–252). Lawrence Erlbaum Associates, Inc.

Honu-Mensah, C. M. Fobi, D., & Quansah, B. (2024). Developing an understanding of parent-teacher partnerships in schools for the deaf in Ghana. *International Journal of Disability, Development and Education, 71*(2), 208–221.

Jahoda, G. (1983). European 'lag' in the development of an economic concept: A study in Zimbabwe. *British Journal of Developmental Psychology, 1,* 113–120.

Kaur, M., & Grewal, M. K. (2017). A study to explore cultural child rearing practices among women in village Manakpura, Patiala. *International Journal of Science and Research, 6*(1), 346–350.

Keller, K., Williams, C., Wharton, P., Paulk, M., Bent-Williams, A., Gray, B., . . . & Zori, R. (2003). Routine cytogenetic and FISH studies for 17p11/15q11 duplications and subtelomeric rearrangement studies in children with autism spectrum disorders. *American Journal of Medical Genetics Part A, 117*(2), 105–111.

Kobosko, J. (2011). Parenting a deaf child: How hearing parents cope with the stress of having deaf children. *Journal of Hearing Science, 1*(3), 38–42. https://doi.org/10.17430/882157

Konner, M. (1991). *Childhood.* Little, Brown.

LeVine, R. A. (1990). Infant environments in psychoanalysis. A cross-cultural view. In J. W. A. Shweder, & G. Herdt (Eds.), *Cultural psychology. Essays on comparative human development* (pp. 454–474). Cambridge University Press.

LeVine, R. A. (1994). *Child care and culture: Lessons from Africa.* Cambridge University Press.

LeVine, R. A., LeVine, S. E., & Schnell, B. (2001). 'Improve the women': Mass schooling, female literacy, and worldwide social change. *Harvard Educational Review, 71,* 1–50.

Markus, H. R., & Kitayama, S. (1991). Culture and the self: Implications for cognition, emotion and motivation. *Psychological Review, 98,* 224–253.

Mbito, M. N. (2004). *Adolescence social competence in Sub-Sahara Africa: The relationship between adolescents' perceptions of parental behaviors and adolescents' self-esteem in Kenya.* Doctoral Dissertations. The University of Tennessee.

Mbito, M. N., & Price, N. L. (1992). *Cultural constraints to voluntary fertility regulation in Central Province, Kenya*. Keynote paper presented at an Overseas Development Administration Seminar, Nyeri, Kenya: Overseas Development Association of Britain/University of Wales.

Mbugua, N. (2007). Factors inhibiting educated mothers in Kenya from giving meaningful sex-education to their daughters. *Social Science and Medicine, 64*(5), 1079–1089.

Mhaka-Mutepfa, M., & Maundeni, T. (2019). The role of faith (spirituality/religion) in resilience in Sub-Saharan African children. *International Journal of Community and Social Development, 1*(3), 211–233.

Mirabile, S. P., Scaramella, L. V., Sohr-Preston, S. L., & Robison, S. D. (2009). Mothers' socialization of emotion regulation: The moderating role of children's negative emotional reactivity. *Child & Youth Care Forum, 38*(1), 19–37. doi 10.1007/s10566-008-9063-5.

Mweri, G. J. (2016). The acquisition of Kenyan sign language (KSL) and its significance as a mother tongue and medium of instruction in schools for the deaf in Kenya. *University of Nairobi Journal of Language and Linguistics, 5*, 85–100.

Nix, R. L., Pinderhughes, E. E., Dodge, K. A., Bates, J. E., Pettit, G. S., & McFadyen-Ketchum, S. (1999). The relation between mothers' hostile attribution tendencies and children's externalizing behaviour problems: The mediating role of mothers' harsh discipline practices. *Child Development, 70*, 896–909.

Okafor, C. B. (2003). Child rearing practices in Eastern Nigeria: Implications for social work in the United States. *International Journal of Global Health, 2*(2), 4–20.

Oldershaw, L. (2002). *A national survey of parents of young children: Executive summary*. Invest in Kids.

Oteng, F. S. (1988). *Give Them A Name*. Kumasi: Kumasi Catholic Press.

Paruk, Z., Petersen, I., Bhana, A., Bell, C., & McKay, M. (2005). Containment and contagion: How to strengthen families to support youth HIV prevention in South Africa. *African Journal of AIDS Research, 4*(1), 57–63.

Pullen, D., Swabey, K., Carroll, A., Heath, A., Lombard, S., & Garate, M. P. (2017). *Lifespan development in an educational context: A topical approach*. John Wiley.

Santrock, J. W. (2006). *Life-Span Development (10th ed.)*. McGraw Hill Companies, Inc.

Raturi, R., & Cebotari, V. (2023). The impact of parental migration on psychological well-being of children in Ghana. *Journal of Ethnic and Migration Studies, 49*(1), 192–211.

Sequeira, M., Singh, S., Fernandes, L., Gaikwad, L., Gupta, D., Chibanda, D., & Nadkarni, A. (2022). Adolescent Health Series: The status of adolescent mental health research, practice and policy in sub-Saharan Africa: A narrative review. *Tropical Medicine & International Health, 27*(9), 758–766.

Singh, P., & Yadav, R. J. (2001). Immunisation status of children in BIMARU states. *The Indian Journal of Pediatrics, 68*, 495–499.

Super, C. M., & Harkness, S. (2009). The developmental niche of the newborn in rural Kenya. In J. K. Nugent, B. Petrauskas, & T. B. Brazelton (Eds.), *The newborn as a person: Enabling healthy infant development worldwide* (pp. 85–97). Wiley.

Super, C. M., & Harkness, S. (1996). The cultural structuring of child development. In J. W. Berry, P. R. Dasen, & T. S. Saraswathi (Eds.), *Handbook of cross-cultural psychology. Vol. 2: Basic processes and human development* (2nd ed., pp. 1–39). Allyn & Bacon.

Thompson, A., Hollis, C., & Richards, D. (2003). Authoritarian parenting attitudes as a risk for conduct problems: Results of a British national cohort study. *European Child and Adolescent Psychiatry, 12*, 84–91.

Triandis, H. C., Bontempo, R., Villareal, M., Asai, M., & Lucca, N. (1988). Individualism and collectivism: Cross-cultural perspectives on self-ingroup relationships. *Journal of Personality and Social Psychology, 54*, 323–338.

Vaccari, C., & Marschark, M. (1997). Communication between parents and deaf children: Implications for social-emotional development. *Journal of Child Psychology and Psychiatry, 38*(7), 793–801. https://doi.org/10.1111/j.1469-7610.1997.tb01597.x

Wanjohi, A. M. (2013). *Childrearing practices in Africa.* KENPRO. https//www.kenpro.org/childrearing-practices-in-africa

Weisner, T. S. (2000). Culture, childhood, and progress in Sub-Saharan Africa. In L. E. Harrison & S. P. Huntington (Eds.), *Culture matters: How values shape human progress* (pp. 141–157). Basic Books.

Whaley, S. E., Sigman, M., Beckwith, L., Cohen, S. E., & Espinosa, M. P. (2002). Infant–caregiver interaction in Kenya and the United States: The importance of multiple caregivers and adequate comparison samples. *Journal of Cross-Cultural Psychology, 33*, 236–247.

Whitaker, M., & Hoover-Dempsey, K. (2013). School influences on parents' role beliefs. *The Elementary School Journal, 114*(1), 73–99.

Woodhead, M., Feathersone, I., Bolton, L., & Robertson, P. (2014). *Early childhood development: Delivering inter-sectoral policies, programs and services in low-resource settings.* Topic guide. Oxford, UK: Health & Education Advice & Resource Team (HEART). http://oro.open.ac.uk/

4
The Early Care and Education of Deaf Children in Ghana

Yaw Nyadu Offei and Linda Amanvida Gibbah

Introduction

Early childhood care and education (ECCE) covers the period in the life of a child 'that lays the foundation for health and wellbeing, whose benefits last a lifetime and even passed on to the next generation' (Early Childhood Care and Development Standards [0–3 years], March, 2018 p.11). Whereas, in most advanced or industrialized countries ECCE is defined to span the period from birth to age 8 years, (Essa, 1999; Wortham, 2000; UNESCO News, 2023), most countries in development define ECCE as the period from birth through to the age of 6 years (Eville-Lo & Mbugua, 2001; UNICEF, 2000). Early childhood care and education (ECCE) is defined to include 'all arrangements of providing care and education for children under compulsory school age, regardless of setting, funding, opening hours or program content' (Ackah-Jnr et al., 2022 p. 298).

In this chapter, we define ECCE based on the Ghanaian Early Childhood and Development Policy that focuses on the formulating 'comprehensive policies and programmes for children' (National Early Childhood Care and Development ECCE Policy, 2004, p. 5; UNESCO, 2023). This policy, like those in advanced or industrialized countries defines ECCE to cover infants and children from the age range from birth to 8 years, their parents and caregivers (National Early Childhood Care and Development ECCE Policy, 2004). This is also in line with UNESCO definitions (UNESCO News, 2023). According to the UNESCO 2023 report, the period (birth–8 years) is critical in the life of every child because during that period, remarkable brain development occurs. The period also represents an important window of opportunities for the education of children (UNESCO News, 2023). It is during this period that

Yaw Nyadu Offei and Linda Amanvida Gibbah, The Early Care and Education of Deaf Children in Ghana In: *The Early Care and Education of Deaf Children in Ghana.* Edited by: Ruth Swanwick, Daniel Fobi, Yaw Offei, and Alexander Oppong, Oxford University Press. © Yaw Nyadu Offei and Linda Amanvida Gibbah 2024. DOI: 10.1093/oso/9780192872272.003.0004

typically developing children develop their innate 'potentials and capabilities for the future' (Lemaire et al., 2013, p.,1). Children who are healthy, safe, and learning well in their early years are better able to attain their full developmental potential as adults and participate effectively in economic, social, and civic life (UNESCO News, 2023). This is also the period in the child's life where child-centred interactive methods are used to help children develop, and where formal teaching and caring for young children are carried out by people other than the child's own family (such as teachers and house parents) beyond the children's home (Lemaire et al., 2013).

For most deaf children within sub-Saharan Africa (SSA) contexts, their development within this critical period (0–8 years) is precarious due to late identification and lack of early appropriate interventions. Ideally early identification would pave the way for support with language and communication and hearing technologies (Yoshinaga Itano et al., 2021). However, in most SSA contexts deaf children are identified later than 12 months old (Knoors et al., 2019). In Ghana, the majority of children are not identified as deaf until they are 6 years old or more (Appiah-Thompson et al., 2020). Late identification and subsequently delayed intervention and support can result in significant developmental delays in terms of language and social development and academic achievement (Gale et al., 2021; WHO, 2018).

In this chapter, we turn our attention to the specific context of ECCE in Ghana as the site of the research study central to the book. We discuss the Ghanaian context of ECCE in general and examine how ECCE policies are enacted for deaf children.

Early Childhood Care and Education in Ghana

The Constitution of Ghana provides for the realization of basic human rights, health economy, the right to work, the right to good health care, and the right to education as well as reasonable access by all citizens to public facilities and services in accordance with the law (Constitution of the Republic of Ghana, 1992, revised in 1996). There is an obligation arising from the Constitution and existing national laws in Ghana (Early Childhood Care and Development Policy, 2004) which include:

Article 28 of the 1992 Constitution which mandates Government to ensure the rights of the child (Ghana, 1992, revised in 1996, p.21);
The Children's Act (Act 560) in 1998, which demonstrated Ghana's commitment to the promotion of the physical, mental and social well-being of the Ghanaian Child;

60 Care and Education of Deaf Children in Ghana

Bye-laws of the Metropolitan and District Assemblies to address specific child-related problems in their areas (Early Childhood Care and Development Policy, 2004).

The Government of Ghana has initiated a number of policies and programmes (Early Childhood Care and Development Policy, 2004) that directly or indirectly impact on the issues of children's welfare. Ghana is also obliged to meet the tenets of international conventions and treaties it has ratified. These include the United Nations Convention on the Rights of the Child (Ghana was the first to ratify this), International Labour Organization (ILO) Convention 182, Convention on Elimination of All Forms of Discriminations Against Women (CEDAW), Expand and improve comprehensive early childhood care and education especially for the most vulnerable and disadvantaged children (Education for All), and Declaration and Plan of Action of the World Summit for Children (p.7) (Early Childhood Care and Development Policy, 2004).

The Ministry of Education of Ghana is the arm of government responsible for formulation and coordination of education policies, setting standards, and monitoring their implementation. In 2004, Ministry of Education introduced an Early Childhood Care and Development Policy, also referred to as Early Childhood Education (ECE) Policy (Ackah-Jnr et al., 2022) to ensure that care and education services and programmes for children from birth to 8 years are provided (Government of Ghana [ECCE Policy], 2004). This policy acknowledged the interrelationships between care and education (Elliott, 2006; Vandenbroek, 2020), as well as the unity between development and learning (Ackah-Jnr et al., 2022).

Ghana's ECCE policy is largely considered as distributive, redistributive, and/or regulatory (Lowi & Ginsberg, 1994). Institutionally in Ghana, various ministries, departments and agencies have been responsible for different aspects of the early childhood care and education (ECCE) (Early childhood care and development policy, 2004). Thus, Ghana's policy implementation involves a multi-sectorial approach to providing quality care and education services for young children where 'Central government is the key stakeholder responsible for formulating and implementing or leveraging the ECCE policy' (Ackah-Jnr et al., 2022, p. 6). Government is responsible for mobilizing the necessary resources, including human, finance, material, and other facilities to ensure effective implementation: 'ECCE policy requires a well-defined institutional framework to translate its goals and objectives into actual programs, at the national, regional, district and community levels' (Ackah-Jnr et al., 2022, p.6). Therefore, the government works through its ministries and partners with other agencies to deliver ECCE services in accordance with Ghana's decentralization programme (Government of Ghana [ECCE Policy], 2004).

Specifically, ECCE responsibilities were devolved to ECCE-related Municipal and District Assemblies (Early childhood care and development policy, 2004) to ensure provision for promoting the holistic development of the child and are expected to operate under and coordinate key departments in the District Assembly system such as the Ghana Health Service, Ghana Education Service, Social Welfare Department, and Community Development (CD) (Ackah-Jnr et al., 2022). The ECCE aims to promote the survival, growth, and development of all Ghanaian children from birth to their eighth birthday. Critical to this policy is the efforts on the part of Government to recognize the importance of parental involvement and ensure that the standard of living and quality of life for families particularly parents in Ghana is improved (Early childhood care and development policy, 2004; Ackah-Jnr et al, 2022). In 2001, the Ministry of Women and Children's Affairs (now the Ministry of Gender, Children and Social Protection) was established by government and assigned the responsibility for policy making in respect to children (Early childhood care and development policy, 2004).

Formal Early Education in Ghana

The available Ghanaian literature suggests that since independence in 1957, governments have committed to the provision of quality of education for their young citizens. Public interest in early childhood development dates as far back as 1843 when Ghana was under British rule and, the Basel Missionaries first introduced day nurseries alongside their primary school classes thus, marking the beginning of formal (non-traditional) early (0–5 years) education in Ghana (Garcia, 2008; Lemaire et al. 2013).

During the early 1950s, there was a concerted effort on the part of political leadership in Ghana to expand ECCE. As part of this initiative, the United Nations Educational Scientific and Cultural Organization (UNESCO) supported the early childhood programmes of the World Organization for Early Childhood Education (an international non-governmental organization (NGO) that focused on children from age 0 to 8 years) to widen the scope of ECCE delivery in Ghana (Lemaire et al., 2013).

After 1960, the government of Ghana issued directives on early education 'in the form of acts, reports of special commissions, decrees and laws that focused more on social welfare and cognitive aspects instead of on the holistic development of young children' (Garcia, 2008, p. 163). In 1965, the Ministry of Education of Ghana established the nursery and kindergarten (KG) unit with the aim of developing pre-school provision for all. However, financial constraints stalled the development of this provision.

The early 1970s witnessed a dramatic shift in focus in early education delivery in Ghana. During this decade, international efforts to promote children's right to early education were scaled up significantly. UNESCO assumed direct involvement in pre-primary education and parent education, and by 1979 early childhood programmes had become increasingly focused on pre-formal education as part of a comprehensive approach to early childhood that fosters an environment conducive to a child's learning and self-expression. The term 'early childhood care and education' (ECCE) became part of the international parlance to describe holistic provision for pre-school children (UNESCO, 2000).

In the 1990s, the government of Ghana in partnership with private operators improved and expanded pre-school provision by setting up childcare centres such as nurseries and KGs across Ghana (Early Childhood Care and Development Policy, 2004). The dominance of private interests in the KG industry in Ghana has since risen exponentially. A significant proportion of the ECCE enrolment is run by private institutions including NGOs, churches, and local community associations. The major challenge with the private sector involvement is the focus on urban areas where populations are relatively high and there are increased possibilities of making profits. Consequently, many poor and rural settlements do not benefit directly from ECCE initiatives (Lemaire et al., 2013). Additionally, the active involvement of private business interests in KGs has impacted on the survival of public provision in Ghana: While private settings thrived, government initiatives crumbled giving the private sector an apparent monopoly of ECCE services and weakening the government's control of and support for ECCE centres (Lemaire et al., 2013).

Advocacy for implementing fully available KG began in 2006 with a directive that all primary schools in Ghana were to have a pre-school[1] by 2015. The Ministry of Gender, Children and Social Protection (formerly Ministry of Women and Children's Affairs) is responsible for the registration and maintenance of standards across all of these centers for children in collaboration with the Ghana Education Service (GES) that is responsible for curriculum development for children 3–5 years (EdQual, 2010).

During the early days of establishing ECCE centres in Ghana, the Ministry of Education of Ghana did not have any standardized curriculum for KGs,

---

[1] The education policy of Ghana provides children with two years of free and compulsory pre-primary education to ensure that children are enrolled in school for early learning. Pre-primary education consists of crèches (for children up to 3 years old), nursery schools for children 3 to 4 years old, and KG for children 4–6 years old (Ackah-Jnr et al., 2022; Ministry of Gender, Children, and Social Protection (2018). Classes in KG are divided into pre-KG for children aged 4–5 and KG for children 5–6 years old (NaCCA, 2019).

therefore, private schools followed their own curriculum and there were challenges in terms of quality and access especially in rural communities (National Statistical Office, 2008, p. 8). This fracture in provision prompted the Government to issue definitive structured policies and a curriculum for ECCE in Ghana (Lemaire et al., 2013). Currently, all KG provisions, including special provision, whether Government or privately owned, follow the same curriculum (NaCCA, 2019).

ECCE Capacity in Ghana

The ECCE initiative in Ghana requires manpower to thrive and specifically high levels of teacher education. In Ghana, the University of Education, Winneba has a Department of Early Childhood Education established in 2003/2004 that provides training for educational professionals to teach at the Pre-School and Kindergarten Level. Objectives of the ECCE programme include: to provide courses of study that focus on the developmentally appropriate care and education of children from birth through to 8 years of age. It emphasizes a child-centered approach and exposes students to the scientific knowledge base regarding: (1) development of children, (2) learning theory, and (3) appropriate educational practices as well as the opportunity to develop competence in working with parents of young children. A number of other colleges of education train teachers in ECCE in Ghana. Trainees from these institutions are appointed to teach in schools at all levels including the nursery and crèches. This initiative is supposed to target all children. However, there is no provision specifically targeted at training of professionals for deaf ECCE.

Early Years Provision for Deaf Children in Ghana

In Ghana there are an estimated 308,000 deaf people, the majority of whom are children (Ghana Statistical Service, 2021) who are living either in rural or urban communities, with very limited access to hearing devices or appropriate hearing health services (Denkyira et al., 2019; WHO, 2020), signed language interpretation services, and who are largely excluded from mainstream social activities (Fobi & Oppong, 2019). The developmental outlook for these deaf children is precarious: 90–95% of them are born to hearing parents who have very minimal previous experiences of deafness or understanding of the potential role of visual communication and sign language in their children's lives (Opoku et al., 2022).

The need for early support to deaf children and their caregivers is acute and yet this is not recognized in policy development. The policies in Ghana that support ECCE more broadly such as The Children Act 1998, The Education Act, 2008, the Disability Law (2006) Act 715, and the 1992 Constitution, all make provisions and support the right for persons with disabilities to education and address a wide range of issues that are critical to the well-being of children, their parents, and caregivers. However, all of these initiatives are much broader in scope and none specifically address issues relative to deaf children.

The practical challenges to ECCE delivery for deaf children in Ghana are significant. The first of these relates to deaf awareness in Ghana and the social and financial barriers experienced by caregivers in seeking and understanding a diagnosis of deafness. The second relates to the early years infrastructure for deaf children from the point of identification in the clinical setting. The third relates to the training and expertise of early years professionals in deaf education.

Burden on Caregivers

Deafness, like any form of disability when it appears in a family, can be met with initial shock, denial, and self-blame. In some contexts this may well be followed by a search for a cure or solutions. This kind of initial fearful reaction to having a deaf child is exacerbated by negative social attitudes towards disability in general in Ghanaian society.

Because of the fear and uncertainty attached to having a child with a disability in Ghana deaf children are often hidden from public view rather than exposed to neighbours and the wider community. Parents of deaf children sometimes do not want people to know that they have a deaf child. They may therefore be reluctant to seek a medical diagnosis. There are also financial constraints on caregivers' attendance at clinic associated with travel costs and potential loss of earnings.

Because there is no newborn hearing screening[2] in Ghana children are not identified with hearing loss until they attend a routine clinic health check or a caregiver or family member suspects a hearing loss and independently seeks advice (Appiah-Thompson et al., 2020). According to the Central Regional

---

[2] Newborn hearing screening aims to identify permanent moderate, severe, and profound deafness and hearing impairment in newborn babies. It involves the automated otoacoustic emission (AOAE) test and the automated auditory brainstem response (AABR) test.

Special Education Coordinator at the Central Regional Education office in Cape Coast, deaf children tend to be identified once in school either through teacher observation, screening processes in school, and exploratory discussions with parents. In Ghana, the age at which deafness is detected can therefore be very variable. Appiah-Thompson et al. (2020) found that deafness in some cases to be detected in children as old as 6 years or older. Once deafness is detected, the child will be referred to a health facility for further assessment, diagnosis and confirmation.

Audiological Services

Audiologists[3] are key professionals who provide early intervention and support services for caregivers of young deaf children. Audiological services are essential in maintaining and improving hearing and communication abilities (Blazer et al., 2016; Denkyira et al., 2019).

Although, thinly spread in Ghana, audiological services are available in order to provide support for families that have deaf children.

Currently, there are nine public/government and seven private owned audiological facilities in Ghana with over 80% of them located in the southern half of Ghana. The services provided include assessment of hearing acuity and language, a diagnosis of potential medical complications, an evaluation of deafness and habilitation needs and possibilities, counselling, information on approaches to communication, school placement options, and other services (Denkyira et al., 2019). At the point of identification it is expected that a multi-professional team that involves audiologists, hearing technicians, paediatric physicians, deaf educators, and primary health-care practitioners will collaborate to provide these services (Green et al., 2001).

One of the basic tenets of a successful early hearing detection and intervention programme is that children will be identified with a potential hearing loss by one month of age, that will be confirmed by three months of age to facilitate enrolment in an early intervention programme before six months of age (Störbeck & Pittman, 2008). However, without the widespread availability of newborn hearing screening the 1-3-6 month targets (Yoshinaga-Itano et al., 2020) are not realistic for most contexts in Ghana (Storbeck & Pittman, 2008).

---

[3] Audiologists are healthcare professionals who evaluate and diagnose hearing loss and also prescribe hearing aids and other amplification devices to help people hear better.

ECCE Capacity

The largest centre for audiological services in Ghana is the Korle Bu Teaching Hospital in Accra. Hearing and speech services that operate regionally provide a first port of call for families but are generally not as fully equipped as Korle Bu. For example, the Centre for Hearing and Speech Services (CHSS) at the University of Education, Winneba, identifies cases of hearing loss in a variety of ways, for example, though community and school screening exercises (Denkyirah et al., 2019), referrals from ENT (ear, nose, and throat), paediatricians, self-referrals (walk-ins), and referrals from family and friends who are aware of the existence of CHSS. Due to unavailability of objective screening[4] equipment, most identified and/or suspected cases from CHSS are referred to the Korle-Bu Teaching Hospital for further objective diagnostic tests such as auditory steady state response and auditory brainstem response (ASSR/ABR), pure tone audiometry (PTA)[5] and the use of parents' auditory questionnaires such as the LittlEARS Parents' Auditory Questionnaire.[6] Once confirmed, audiologists at CHSS have a discussion with parents/caregivers and make recommendations on possibilities available, such as school placements and hearing aids[7] use.

In Ghana, there is a low outcome in terms of technology support (use of hearing aids, diagnosis using ABRs and OAEs), which raises questions about what type of intervention is most useful, diagnosis, and the role of audiological clinics. Besides this, fewer children diagnosed with deafness late (Appiah-Thompson et al., 2020) are benefiting from hearing aids, and at such a late stage in their development it would seem more appropriate to have immediate referral to sign language communication support for the family. This is the model adopted in South Africa through the HI HOPES[8] early intervention partnership for families of deaf and hard-of-hearing babies (Storbeck & Moodley, 2011; Storbeck & Young, 2016).

---

[4] Otoacoustic emissions (OAEs; sounds recorded from the ear) and auditory brainstem response (ABR) are tests done in hospital after birth as part of newborn screening.

[5] Pure-tone test performed by audiometry to determine levels and degrees of hearing loss.

[6] A 35-item age dependent auditory questionnaire that reflect significant milestones of auditory development, based on the caregivers' observation of the child's auditory behaviours in daily life and, developed to support professionals and caregivers to monitor the auditory behaviours of young children with hearing loss.

[7] A device that amplifies sounds for individuals diagnosed with deafness but who have substantial usable reserve of hearing.

[8] Home Intervention Hearing and language Opportunities Parent Education Services

The HI HOPES programme focuses on the development environment, development, and learning opportunities for deaf children, the support for caregivers, and their communities to mitigate intersecting disadvantages of poverty and deprivation to improve outcomes for deaf children under 4. Partnership with parents is a central aspect of the HI HOPES programme as the basis for informed support from a multi-disciplinary team who are based in local communities to provide culturally appropriate education for caregivers. Through the programme families are also introduced to deaf adult mentors who act as language and cultural role models. Whilst the programme is child-centred, there is significant emphasis on the training of the parents and the wider caregiving community and on embedding expertise, resources, and practices within the local community. Along with a focus on the development of resources and capacity, there is support for caregivers to develop their understanding and the confidence needed to advocate for the needs of their children and encourage this agency among other parents. HI HOPES is a strong example of the fulfilment of ECCE policy and implementation plans that so often becomes stalled—especially for children with disabilities at the enactment stage (Boakye, 2008).

Preschool Support

At the point of identification in Ghana, decisions are made about the potential of hearing amplification for the individual child and advice is also given about school placement. For most of the caregivers, this is the first time that they have received confirmation of their child's hearing loss. In this context, educational advice is given on an audiological basis.

Children deemed to have sufficient residual hearing and able to make good use of hearing aid technologies are directed towards education in mainstream schools alongside hearing peers. In this case, an individualized intervention plan is put in place by the mainstream teacher supported by the special education coordinator, who is a teacher who has been trained in special education and assigned to district, regional and national education offices in Ghana to provide support for learners with disabilities. Their roles include screening school children for possible disabilities, referrals, counselling, and providing classroom support to mainstream teachers.

Children who are more profoundly deaf and unlikely to benefit from hearing aid technologies are more usually directed towards schools for the deaf where education is delivered through sign language and there is less focus on the development of spoken language. Children are encouraged to use hearing aids at home during the vacation to support communication, but this is unlikely to be of benefit if they have no exposure to a spoken language environment or support for listening skills for weeks at time in school. It is routine practice for most of the schools for the deaf in Ghana to request for a comprehensive audiological assessment report for each deaf child as part of requirements for new admissions to the school. Some of the special schools in Ghana (Cape Coast School for the Deaf, Jamasi School for the Deaf, and the Wa School for the Deaf) have audiological centres situated on their campuses.

If a referral is made to one of the special schools, caregivers have the opportunity to attend pre-school guidance and counselling sessions during the year before their child's entry to KG. This is only offered by the schools for the deaf. The programme that includes guidance and counselling for the parents as well as preschool education for the child is facilitated by a team of educational practitioners, a representative of the school's hearing assessment centre (if the school has one), and the headteacher. The programme takes place within the school and typically includes basic life skills training, support with social development and basic skills in literacy and numeracy. All children must attend this programme regardless of their age and it is not unusual for some deaf children to be starting the programme (designed for pre-school) at the age of 8 years.

The only other early years provision for deaf is located in the private sector. For example, the House of Grace School for the Deaf is a private school located in Ga South Municipality in Accra. Children with confirmed deafness and a supporting audiological report can enrolled in this school from the age of 4 years. The school is fee paying although the fees are heavily subsided by the NGO that supports them and does not have boarding facilities which means that families have to be local and able to travel daily. There is also a private school in Nsawam–OpareKrom in the Eastern Region of Ghana where children with special educational needs can be educated alongside their mainstream peers. The school has a crèche[9] that admits children from the age of 4 usually via referrals from the Korle-Bu Teaching Hospital ENT department.

---

[9] Mostly private initiatives (with no support from government) for early years education (0–3 years) largely patronized by working mothers who cannot take their children to their work place. Government supports only KG (4–6 years old).

Training

Teachers are major actors in ECCE delivery and are very much in demand in deaf education in Ghana (Oppong & Fobi, 2019). However, it appears there are limited numbers of special education teachers. Teachers in the schools for the deaf in Ghana are not all specialized in deaf education. Although some have been trained at teacher training college (now called colleges of education), the teachers who come straight from teacher training do not have any sign language training even though they do an introductory course in special education. Only the teachers who are specialist teachers of the deaf have basic sign language skills. One of the major findings in our research on the education of young deaf children and their caregivers was that most of the support teachers and the non-teaching staff, such as house parents, and security, kitchen, and maintenance staff are untrained, and many are volunteers. These notwithstanding, all three schools that formed part of our research offer sign language classes for the teachers and non-teaching staff. It could be concluded that, Ghana's schools for the deaf are highly under-resourced and the few who are available are overburdened (Akerele, 2020; Muhati-Nyakundi, 2023). Special schools across the country and others that create opportunities for deaf people are largely inaccessible as there are limited or no sign language interpreters (Akerele, 2020; Muhati-Nyakundi, 2023). It is necessary to have personnel to support deaf children in Ghana especially in technical and vocational education (Balfaah, 2017).

The Ministry of Education in Ghana rolled out an Early Childhood Care and Development policy, in 2014, aimed at providing care and education services and programmes to children from 0 to 8 years. The education policy provides children 2 years of free and compulsory pre-primary education for children at the KG level (4–6 years old) (Ackah-Jnr et al., 2022; NaCCA, 2019; Statista, 2023). The aim of Ghana's ECCE policy is to 'promote the survival, growth, development, and protection of young children' (Ackah et al., 2022, p. 298) and to allocate the responsibility of ECCE to government. Government is therefore required to ensure parents' continuous discharge of 'their traditional responsibilities of taking care and nurturing their children' (p. 298). Ghana's ECCE policy also places premium on the cognitive, 'affective, and psychomotor development' (p. 298) of children, expand, 'early childhood development services such as immunization, weighing and nutrition to all children' (Ackah et al., 2022, p. 298; Government of Ghana [ECCE Policy], 2004) and, to protect children's rights thus, 'enhancing the development of their cognitive, emotional, social, and physical potential (Ackah et al., 2022, p. 298). Furthermore, the policy aims to 'promote and protect young children's rights to survival, growth, and development, which are considered essential to future human resource development and nation building' (Ackah et al., 2022, p. 298).

The policy recognizes the close interconnections between care and education and the inseparability of development and learning (Elliott, 2006; Vandenbroeck, 2020). Ghana's ECCE policy aims to promote the survival, growth, development, and protection of young children. According to the policy, the government is responsible for ensuring that parents continue to discharge their traditional responsibilities of taking care and nurturing their children. Thus, the government of Ghana is mainly responsible for formulating ECCE-focused programmes and creating enabling an environment for parents, caregivers, and children as well as ECCE services and sectors to operate effectively in providing the needed care and education (Ackah et al., 2022, p. 298).

Currently, in schools for the deaf in Ghana, there is on average 3–4 staff per ECCE class to support classroom work—this includes the classroom teacher, assistant (supporting) teacher, and house-mothers who double as classroom support personnel (Telephone conversation with ECCE teacher, School for the Deaf, March, 2022).

Ideally, for a school for children with disabilities there has to be some collaboration between education and health sectors. Considering deaf children, this is the case in some of the schools for the deaf in Ghana. For example, at the Jamasi School for the Deaf there is a health centre that has a permanent health worker who is paid by the Government to render healthcare at the school from Monday to Friday. Similarly, at the Cape Coast School for the Deaf, the unit for the deaf/blind is affiliated to the Ewim Hospital in Cape Coast. This health/education collaboration is supported by the Disability Act 2006 Act 715 of Ghana which states inter alia:

> The Ministry of Health in collaboration with the Ministries responsible for Education and Social Welfare shall provide for the periodic screening of children in order to detect, prevent and manage disability.
>
> (Persons with Disability Act, 2006, Act 715 section 34 p.9).

The Act also states:

> The Ministry of Health in collaboration with District Assemblies and the Ministry responsible for Social Welfare shall establish and operate health assessment and

resource centres in each district and provide early diagnostic medical attention to mothers and infants to determine the existence or onset of disability.

(Persons with Disability Act, 2006, Act 715 section 35 p.9).

Previously, it was the practice for support teachers to be employed in ECCE classrooms in all schools including schools for the deaf. However, this practice has been stalled.

> The Ministry of Education of Ghana has stopped appointing classroom support teachers to schools for the deaf and, this has necessitated the 'recruitment' of housemothers to additional roles as support staff whose roles include cleaning children who soil themselves in class (. . . . . . .) The effect of non-posting of support teachers on teaching and learning is impacting negatively on teaching and learning.
>
> (Personal communication—Teacher of the deaf, September 2022)

Incidentally, the government's policy on ECCE is not clear about the exact number of staff that should be in a class at a time:

> Although there is a government policy regarding ECCE, the policy does not specify the number of professionals required in an ECCE classroom.
>
> (Personal communication—Teacher of the deaf, September 2022)

The dominance of poorly trained or untrained professionals as well as shortage of professionals in nurseries and crèches in Ghana and SSA has been reported in the Ghanaian. According to Oppong-Frimpong (2020), most of the classroom support staff, including ECCE teachers, do not have the requisite academic and professional qualification to work in ECCE classrooms. This view was supported and expressed in a conversation with a social welfare officer.

> During our supervision in nurseries and crèches, we observed that most private schools engaged Senior High School or Junior High School leavers to give care or taking these children through lessons without any training (. . .) they don't have any legal training or proper training to give care to them and the lessons and other things.
>
> (Personal communication with social welfare officer, September 2022)

The nurseries and crèches provide some basic training to these untrained/unqualified staff and employ (Oppong-Frimpong, 2020).

72   Care and Education of Deaf Children in Ghana

> They only pick them and ...I have completed Junior High School, I have completed Senior High School and I am idle, ok so then come and teach the kids, come and take care of these kids and then they are given some token, some token amounts of money and it's not errr (...) yielding any proper results as before because errr (.....) .... when they are well trained or they have any training re-training on how to handle those kinds it is better, that is why social welfare, we train those people.
>
> (Personal communication with social welfare officer, September 2022)

Generally, people responsible for the wellbeing of children in ECCE centres include; child care centre manager, administrator, coordinator, accountant, and teachers (Woode-Eshun, 2021). The list also includes head teachers, service managers, and teachers of the deaf, audiologists, clinical technicians, volunteers, national service personnel, support staff, and administrators.

The appointment of these personnel for crèches and nurseries is either by the management of the institution (if it is privately owned) or by the Ghana Education Service on behalf of government. Although the Department of Social Welfare organizes training for staff of the crèches and nurseries, this Department is not responsible for posting staff to the schools. According to a source at the Department, during their routine school supervisions whenever they discovered that a school did not have trained attendants or caregivers, they served the school with a warning notice and cautioned them to arrange for their staff to be trained as soon as possible.

> So when we go and your, errrr (.....) those your caregivers or day care attendants are not trained with social welfare, we serve them a warning, and tell them, ask them to quickly let them for training (....) and then or they engage those they have already trained with social welfare (.....) So, we ask private schools that we will come (...) oh, social welfare, I am operating a day care center where I have a crèche and nursery and I would like one of those that are being trained and then we link them (...) but we don't do posting and other things (....) for now that is what we do.
>
> (Interview with Liliane, Social Welfare Officer, 2nd September, 2022).

Every early childhood development centre/school operating crèche and nursery must register with the department (Interview with SWO 1).

There are significant challenges with regard to the ECCE training and expertise in Ghana. In schools for the deaf in Ghana, there are basically, two categories of teachers who are posted to those schools; (i) teachers who have undergone specialist training as teachers of the deaf (ToD) and have basic sign language skills and, (ii) teachers who are posted straight from colleges of education to schools for the deaf without any speciality in deaf education (ToD) except for an introductory course in Special Education that they took during their training. This category of teachers do not have any sign language training and therefore, have to undergo some sign language classes that are organized in the schools for the deaf for the teachers and non-teaching staff who are not proficient in the use of the sign language. Special schools across the country and those that create opportunities for deaf people, are largely inaccessible as there are limited or no sign language interpreters (Fobi, 2021). It is necessary therefore, to have personnel to support deaf children in Ghana.

Conclusion

Both hearing and deaf children have access to pre-school (birth to 3 years of age) provision and a shared curriculum before they enter KG[10] (age 4–5). However, there are significant age variations between hearing and deaf children. Whereas hearing children as part of their formal education enter formal school [KG] at age 4 (on average), most deaf children begin formal education between ages 6 and 18 years. This late enrolment is largely due to the social barriers described earlier and the precarious nature of the identification and confirmation process. Because of these issues with late confirmation of deafness children are often enrolled in schools for the deaf, without any established sign or spoken language communication. Therefore, deaf children miss out on crucial developmental support and education in the very early years of their life and caregivers are disempowered by the lack of infrastructure and holistic support in the early years. There are also critical issues of training and ECCE expertise in deaf education in Ghana.

In the following chapters we explore these issues in more depth in order to gain a fuller understanding of the experiences and perspectives of caregivers and education and health practitioners. We describe a research project that we undertook in Ghana and share the outcomes of our work with caregivers and education and health practitioners. We preface this with a discussion in the next chapter of the ethical and methodological implications of researching ECCE in this context.

---

[10] Due largely to late identification deaf children may be enrolled at the KG level in schools for the deaf as late as during their teen age years.

References

Ackah-Jnr, F. R., Appiah, J., Addo-Kissiedu, K., & Kwao, A. (2022). Early childhood education policy and practice in Ghana: Document and evidence analysis with McDonnell and Elmore's framework of policy instruments. *Multidisciplinary Journal of Educational Research*, 12(3), 295–321. http://dx.doi.org/10.447/remie.9964

Akerele, O. (2020). The decentralization of the Ghanaian mental health system through the non-profit sector: A case to improve access to care and disrupt the 'othering' of the mentally ill? *Intersect: The Stanford Journal of Science, Technology, and Society*, 13(3), 1–28.

Appiah-Thompson P., Meier J., Baiden F., Acheampong E. K., Akotey S. C., Honu-Mensah C. M., Amoo-Quaye G., & Adanusa M. (*2020);* Prevalence and determinants of hearing loss among primary school children in selected schools in the Central Region of Ghana. *Afr. J. Biomed. Res. Vol. 23; 277–281*

Balfaah, D. K. (2017). *Perception on deaf education and its effects on their livelihoods: A case study of the Wa School for the Deaf (WADEAF) in the Upper West Region of Ghana.* [PhD thesis.University of Development Studies, Tamale]

Blazer, D. G., Domnitz, S., Liverman, C. T. (Eds). (2016 Sep 6). Committee on Accessible and Affordable Hearing Health Care for Adults; Board on Health Sciences Policy; Health and Medicine Division; National Academies of Sciences, Engineering, and Medicine. Hearing Health Care for Adults: Priorities for Improving Access and Affordability. Washington (DC): National Academies Press (US); PMID: 27280276. On-Line edition. Retrieved on 8th May 2024 from: https://pubmed.ncbi.nlm.nih.gov/27280276/

Boakye, J. (2008). ECCED Policy: A comparative analysis in Ghana, Mauritius, and Namibia. In M. Garcia, A. Pence, J. L. Evans (Eds.), *Africa's Future, Africa's Challenge: Early Childhood Care and Development in Sub-Saharan Africa* (pp. 169–185). The International Bank for Reconstruction and Development the World Bank.

Bowman, B., Donovan, M. S., & Burns, S. M., (Eds.). (2001). *Eager to learn: Educating our preschoolers*. National Academy Press.

Constitution of the Republic of Ghana 1992 (Amendment Act 1996). Retrieved on 8th May, 2024from: https://www.law.cornell.edu/women-and-justice/resource/constitution_of_the_republic_of_ghana_(amendment_act1996).)

Denkyirah, A. M., Offei, Y. N., & Acheampong, E. K. (2019). Mobile hearing screening in a rural community school in Ghana. Journal of the American Academy of Special Education Professionals, *Winter 2019*, 30–40.

Early Childhood Care and Development Policy (2004). Ministry of Women and Children's Affairs. Republic of Ghana.

Early Childhood Care and Development Standards (0–3 years). (March, 2018). Republic of Ghana. Ministry of Gender Children and Social Protection.

A Framework for Education Quality (EdQual Policy Brief N.10.Noveer, 2010). A research Programme Consortium on Implementing Education Quality in Low Income Countries. Retrieved on 8th May, 2024 from https://www.edqual.org/publications/policy-briefs/edqualpb10.pdf/at_download/file.pdf

Elliott, A. (2006). *Early childhood education: Pathways to quality and equity for all children.* Australian Council for Educational Research. https://research.acer.edu.au/cgi/

Essa, E. (1999). Introduction to Early Childhood Education. *Early Childhood Education Series*, 3rd edition (Illustrated). Delmar. ISBN 0766800474, 9780766800472.

Fobi, D., & Oppong, A. M. (2019). Communication approached for educating deaf and hard of hearing (DHH) children in Ghana: historical and contemporary issues. *Deafness & Education International*, 21(4) 195–209 DOI: 10.1080/14643154.2018.1481549

Fobi, D. (2021). *Role of interpreting in the inclusion of deaf students in tertiary education in Ghana*. [PhD thesis University of Leeds]

Gale, E., Berke, M., Benedict, B., Olson, S., Putz, K., & Yoshinaga-Itano, C., (2021). Deaf adults in early intervention programs. *Deaf Education International, 23*(1), 3–24.

Garcia, M., Pence, A., & Evans, J. L. (2008). *Africa's future, Africa's challenge: Early childhood care and development in Sub-Saharan Africa*. The International Bank for Reconstruction and Development/ The World Bank.

Ghana Statistical Service (2021). Ghana 2021 Population and Housing Census (Volume 1). Preliminary Report.

Ghana's Constitution of 1992 with Amendments through 1996. Constituteproject.org. PDF generated: 04 Oct 2013, 20.33).

Green, L. A., Fryer Jr, G. E., Yawn, B. P., Lanier, D., & Dovey, S. M. (2001). The ecology of medical care revisited. *New England Journal of Medicine, 344*(26), 2021–2025.

Knoors, H., Brons, M., Marschark, M., (2019). *Deaf education beyond the western world: Context, challenges, and prospects*. Oxford University Press

Lemaire, M. B., Amoah, D. F., Ntsiful, D. K., Micah, S. A., & Bonney, E. A. (2013). Early childhood education in Ghana: Perceptions of stakeholders in the western region of Ghana. *Early Childhood Education, 4*(9), 1–13.

Lowi, T. G., & Ginsberg, B. (1994). *American Government (Brief)*. Norton

Muhati-Nyakundi, L. I. (2023). Teachers' agency and wellbeing in inclusive education: Challenges and opportunities. *Journal of Educational Studies, 2023*(si1), 365–379.

National Council for Curriculum and Assessment (NaCCA). Kindergarten Curriculum for Preschools (2019). Ministry of Education. Republic of Ghana.

Opoku, M. P., Nketsia, W., Benefo, E. B., & Mprah, W. K. (2022). Understanding the parental experiences of raising deaf children in Ghana. *Journal of Family Studies, 28*(4),1235–1254, DOI: 10.1080/13229400.2020.18155

Oppong, A. M., & Fobi, D. (2019). Deaf education in Ghana. In H. Knoors, M. Brons, & M. Marschark (Eds.), *Deaf education beyond the western world*. (pp. 135–160), Oxford University Press.

Oppong-Frimpong, S. (2020). Assessing the quality of ECE teachers in Ghana: Juxtaposing theory to practice. *European Journal of Education Studies, 7*(12), 752–770. DOI: 10.46827/ejes.v7i12.3505

Persons with Disability Law, 2006 Act 715

Störbeck, C., & Pittman, P. (2008). Early intervention in South Africa: Moving beyond hearing screening. *International Journal of Audiology, 47*(sup1), S36–S43.

UNESCO (2000). World Education Forum. Education for All 2000 Assessment, Dakar, Senegal.

UNESCO News, (2023). Why Early Childhood Care and Education Matters. World Conference on Early Childhood Care and Education, Tashkent, Uzbekistan, 14-16 November, 2022. Last Updated 20th April, 2023. Copyright@ Tuane Fernandez. Unesco.org.

UNICEF. (2002). UNICEF Annual Report 2002. New York.

Vandenbroeck, M. (2020). Early childhood care and education policies that make a difference. In R. Nieuwenhuis & W. Van Lancker (Eds.), *The Palgrave handbook of family policy* (pp. 169–191). Springer International Publishing.

Woode-Eshun, A. (2021). Effective leadership in early childhood education centres in Ghana. Munich, GRIN Verlag, https://www.grin.com/document/1153671

World Health Organization (2020). *World Report on Hearing*. Geneva, Switzerland.

World Health Organization. (2018). Addressing the rising prevalence of hearing loss. Geneva: World Health Organization.

Wortham, S. (2000). Assessment in elementary classrooms. Prentice-Hall. Retrieved June 23, 2022, from https://t-tel.org/about-us.

Yoshinaga-Itano, C., Mason, C.A., Wiggin, M., & Gilley, P.M. (2021). Reading proficiency trends following newborn hearing screening implementation. *Pediatrics*, *148* (4), e2020048702. https://doi.org/10.1542/peds.2020-048702

Yoshinaga-Itano, C., Sedey, A. L., Mason, C. A., Wiggin, M., & Chung, W. (2020). Early intervention, parent talk, andpragmatic language in children with hearing loss. *Paediatrics*, *146*(3), 270–277.

5
Researching Childhood Deafness and Early Support

Ethical and Methodological Implications

Ruth Swanwick and Joyce Fobi

Introduction

An increasing number of early childhood care and education (ECCE) intervention programmes are becoming established through the work of development organizations, research councils, non-governmental organizations and multilaterals with the goal of enabling the world's most vulnerable children (poor, disadvantaged, disabled) to reach their potential. The growth of this activity has raised questions about the ethical challenges of ECCE research and intervention in low- and middle-income countries and provoked discussed around what effective intervention should look like (Bizzego et al., 2020). The primary concerns voiced in the research relate to the provenance and assumptions of the science underpinning the research or intervention, the depth of knowledge gathered about the target population, and how this knowledge is used to inform intervention design and implementation (Robinson-Pant & Singal, 2013).

As outlined in the preceding chapters, the different global contexts for early development comprise diverse cultural traditions and lifestyles, family structures, and caregiving practices. The economic, geopolitical, and social environment and resources shape the different ways in which children are cared for and educated in formal and informal settings and caregiving practices are embedded within cultural and societal values, beliefs, and traditions. Approaches to early care and education thus need to be developed with a full understanding of the sociocultural context and knowledge about

---

Ruth Swanwick and Joyce Fobi, *Researching Childhood Deafness and Early Support* In: *The Early Care and Education of Deaf Children in Ghana*. Edited by: Ruth Swanwick, Daniel Fobi, Yaw Offei, and Alexander Oppong, Oxford University Press.
© Ruth Swanwick and Joyce Fobi 2024. DOI: 10.1093/oso/9780192872272.003.0005

and the resource dynamics of different early childhood contexts are a fundamental starting point. Intervention that is conceptualized according to Western models and standards of care, for example, is unlikely to be a fit for rural and subsistence-based societies where there is wealth insecurity. In fact, approaches to intervention and support that assume certain economic stability, mobility, and access to information overlook more than 70% of the world's population, who reside in low- and middle-income countries, where livelihoods are precarious and the basic needs for children to thrive are not met (Morelli et al., 2018).

Underpinning assumptions about approaches to parenting also need to be critiqued. Models of early support and intervention often centre on nuclear family structures and patterns of caregiving that are informed by Western understandings of attachment (see e.g. Luca, 2016). These approaches do not align with family and community parenting practices in rural, subsistence communities such as those described in previous chapters where interaction may centre less on exclusive and affective caregiver–child communication and more on talk alongside daily activities and a collective input from all caregivers (Morelli et al., 2003).

An ethical approach to ECCE research and intervention, where the basic principles of respect, beneficence, and fairness are upheld, thus entails a responsibility to inspect first assumptions. To proceed without this criticality risks the propagation of ECCE research and development work that is wasteful, potentially harmful to participants, and eventually ineffective (Guttmann, 2017).

Ethical Research Practice

To proceed ethically with research into this area requires a deep knowledge base that is built on cross-cultural communication and research approaches that enable rich description, that fully capture the dynamics of the cultural context, and that avoid propagating stereotypical views. This need for openness and an unbiased approach to enquiry is particularly pertinent to the context of deaf ECCE research, where it is important to avoid reporting one cultural view of deafness as though universally shared by society (Friedner, 2017)—whilst being deaf and using sign language is a celebrated aspect of inclusive societies (see, e.g., constructs of Deaf gain in Bauman & Murray, 2014), in certain contexts we have seen that the disclosure of childhood deafness is problematic for families and caregivers.

At the outset of our project work in Ghana we were aware of this ethical dimension of our research and the vulnerability of participating caregivers.

> In Ghana, families hardly expose their deaf children in public. We will have to keep in mind that families may have divulged information to interviewers that they otherwise wouldn't. We have to be very circumspect (...) to ensure interviewees are protected. (Yaw Offei)

The knowledge base that underpins deaf ECCE thus needs to encompass understandings of different deaf childhoods and caregiver experience that shape early support, and specifically language and communication practices. This knowledge should be situated within an appreciation of the surrounding ECCE infrastructure and resource and the wider cultural and societal understandings of deafness. For the development of deaf ECCE in an African context this involves challenging hierarchies of knowledge, and the principles and values that inform them, that are usually shaped among Western and rich, networked countries and/or English-speaking academies.

This is especially important where there is a change agenda. Transformation needs to be conceptualized in relative terms. For work around the early support of young deaf children change will most likely centre on approaches to communication and how this is supported. Changes proposed need to be consistent with the available resources among deaf children and their families and not derived from a particular view—for example—of interaction in the home—that is assumed to be universally applicable. The imperative is to build on already established multimodal and multilingual communication practices within the home and communities and traditional approaches to caregiving. Throughout our project work we were conscious of the importance of seeing and valorizing existing communication practices in the homes of deaf children and their caregivers.

> We should not be seen to be imposing specific approaches to communication to caregivers. [There is a danger that] Caregivers will accept whatever professionals propose. (Yaw Offei)

ECCE Research in Ghana

Project Aims

The goals of the empirical project undertaken in Ghana were informed by these issues. Our aim in undertaking this research was to examine the practical and theoretical problems involved in the development of contextually sensitive models of ECCE for deaf children and their caregivers in low- and middle-income countires (LMICs). Specifically, we sought to produce critical knowledge about childhood deafness and development to inform ECCE that is sensitive to the proximal and day-to-day interactions and processes surrounding early development. This includes caregivers' experience of having a deaf child within the development context, and their caregiving practices. For deaf children, this implies the language and communication environment, the different ways in which spoken and sign languages, and other forms of visual communication are used, and how languaging decisions are made.

We conceptualize these development processes as nested within distal or external influences on children and families including policy development and societal understandings, attitudes, and beliefs in relation to deafness, language, and communication. Through the examination of everyday experiences combined with this in-depth understanding of context our aim was to identify the available resources within and without the family and community for supporting children and families and to use these insights to support innovation and sustainable change in early years policy and practice. We wanted to reveal what works, and what can be replicated across different urban and rural contexts in order to plan for professional and academic capacity building in this area.

Ethical Challenges

The pursuit of these research aims in Ghana raised for us (the research team) a number of ethical issues that resonate with wider debates on research ethics in comparative and international education. One concern relates to the assumptions that underpin the international knowledge base and early support guidelines. Economically rich countries have driven the development of early hearing detection and intervention policy, and this has led to an agreed set of early intervention principles that stipulate that professional support for young deaf children and their caregivers should be a prompt and holistic process that recognizes the strengths and natural skills of the family, and supports development (Moeller et al., 2013). It is expected that this support is delivered by skilled and qualified multi-disciplinary teams that include deaf professionals (Gale et al., 2021), and that the intervention is sensitive and responsive to different family contexts, values, and cultures (Störbeck & Young, 2016). Crucially, these guidelines stress the importance of parent—child interaction as one of the main predictors of children's language outcomes and a substantial body of work in the Euro-Western literature focuses on the quality of parent—child interaction and how it can be measured (Curtin et al. 2021).

Further, there is international consensus that caregivers of deaf children need information and support that is professional and family oriented and prompt (Yoshinaga-Itano, 2003). The Early Hearing Detection and Intervention (EHDI) guidelines recommend that screening, diagnosis, and early intervention are completed by one, three and six months of age, respectively (Yoshinaga-Itano et al., 2020). In the last two decades, screening instrumentation has become increasingly sophisticated and suitable for newborns. Newborn Hearing Screening (NHS) within the first few days of a child's life has facilitated early detection. Where corresponding follow-up intervention and support is in place, screening is an effective catalyst for ECCE service provision. Most economically rich, and some middle-income contexts now have NHS near or fully in place (at least above 85% coverage). This coverage is closely correlated with average living standards and economic well-being (Neumann et al., 2019). However, the cost implications of systematic NHS and the lack of infrastructure around epidemiological reporting are a central constraint for LMICs (Olusanya et al., 2014).

The ethical issues surrounding this knowledge base centre on the precarities of borrowing or transferring systems, ideas, values and expectations for example around technological and communication support and obscuring traditional ways of knowing about deafness, child rearing and communication. The issues are threefold. Firstly, the early detection targets presuppose a level of infrastructure and economic resource that cannot be assumed for the Ghana context, and indeed most other African countries. Secondly, intervention approaches do not consider the global diversity of familial and social networks that surround children and families, and the significant role of the collective in early education and care in Ghana and other African societies. (Grech, 2011; Singal & Muthukrishna, 2014). And thirdly, the emphasis on children's language outcomes and quality interaction in the home may not fit with different caregiver communication practices, the social dynamics of interaction and local understandings of child development (Keller et al., 2009). Most of the families in our research sample have rural and subsistence lifestyles and are closely connected as a community. In these contexts, a large part of development and growing up involves learning to communicate with, and become part of, the community alongside caregivers. Morelli at al describe how this this involves 'fitting in' and 'orientating to others' rather than being a central distraction and demand (2018, p. 12).

Insights from the debates around the ethical challenges of early intervention point to the need for a more inclusive set of principles would need to take account of different cultural models of child development as well as the relevance of a strong collective culture and emphasis on community and extended family networks (Kabay et al., 2017). These principles led us to adopt the bioecological systems theory as a framework for our methodological approach.

A Bioecological Approach

The bioecological theory of child development emphasizes the complex interactions between multiple systems of influence on individuals' development including their immediate environment, their larger social context, and the interactions among these contexts (Bronfenbrenner & Morris, 2006). These influences range from biological, individual, family, peers, and media, to cultural and historical forces that impact how humans change over time (Howe, 2011). The bio-ecological model is an extension of Bronfenbrenner's original ecological systems theory (1977) developed to include the individual the centre of the ecology—their own biology and characteristics—as being an 'active' agent in their development (Hewett et al. 2017). As such this model emphasizes the importance of understanding bidirectional influences between children's development and their surrounding environment. In this model the environment is seen as a set of nested contexts that Bronfenbrenner, 2005conceptualizes as four distinct concentric systems.

The microsystem consists the young child's immediate environment in which the child is actively involved and directly experiences formal and informal learning from (e.g., the home, day-care/early childhood development setting), peers, the learning spaces, resources and the play environments. These interactions are reciprocal by nature, meaning that the interactions of the child shape the environment, and are also shaped by the environment where the child is *in situ* (Bronfenbrenner, 1994).

The mesosystem includes the interaction between factors within the microsystems; thus, a set of interrelations between two or more settings around the developing child. This system involves the relationship between the home and the schools (home—school partnership), for instance; decision making by caregivers and teachers and also coordination between different agencies (Bronfenbrenner, 1993) which could have positive or negative effect the development of the child (Bronfenbrenner, 1986).

The exosystem includes factors outside the child's immediate surroundings. That is, the linkages and processes occurring between two or more settings whereby these settings do not usually contain the developing child (child has no active role and direct interactions with the social ecology) but events that occur indirectly influence the development of the young child (Bronfenbrenner, 1993).

The macrosystem also includes the overarching patterns of micro, meso and exosystems characteristics of a given culture or subculture, structure or geographical space where child development takes place with particular reference to the belief systems, societal values, political trends and practices in a community for a child's development (Bronfenbrenner, 1993).

This model was originally developed for analysing the layers of influence on child development (e.g. Coleman 2013; Ertem 2011; Rogoff 2003), but it has also been adapted and used to examine the development environment and the context for early support. For example, Woodhead et al. (2014) adopted a bioecological perspective in their research to identify multiple potential entry points and delivery platforms for Early Child Development (ECD). They identify proximal entry points as the programmes in which young children participate and the distal entry points as inclusive of laws and regulations and social protection programmes, especially those that alter parents' capacities to support their children's development. (Woodhead et al., 2014; p. 13). Other educational researchers have used the bioecological model to analyse the proximal and distal factors that can influence inclusive early development for children with disabilities specific in cultural contexts (Ansong et al., 2017; Leonard, 2011; McLinden et al., 2018) and to examine inclusive educational practice (Anderson et al., 2014; McLinden & McCracken, 2016) recognizing that, children's external environments and the interaction between these environments, shape their inclusive experience (Tudge et al., 2009).

The Development of a Methodology

We adopted the bioecological model as a framework for our empirical work in Ghana to help us to identify and describe the interconnecting influences on the development environment of young deaf children including access to and the nature of early support, caregiver practices and decision making. This provided a framework for examining the different ways in ECCE is influenced by the day-to-day relationships among young deaf and their caregivers, close family, and community networks as well as the different home, work, school, and community contexts for development and the wider social, cultural and policy conditions. Our project involved actors from the full ecology of deaf children's lives in that we undertook a critical review of deaf education early years current policy and practice, interviewed education and health

84   Care and Education of Deaf Children in Ghana

professionals, caregivers and deaf advisors and observed the communication practices among young deaf children and their caregivers.

In addition to Bronfenbrenner's bioecological framework, we drew on Bourdieusian constructs of habitus, capital and field to interrogate the issues of power and agency that shape caregiving practices and especially communication choices in families who traditionally find themselves marginalized by the stigma of disability/deafness. The alignment of these theoretical frameworks, proposed in work by Houston (2017), allowed for critical analysis of concepts of agency and choice that infuse the early support literature to enrich our understanding of 'interplay between the person and their social context' (p. 66). This critical ecology perspective helped us to trace the consequences of the environmental context for deaf ECCE, identify the real resources available to caregivers and recognize the constraints on their actions and choices as ECCE agents in this sociocultural context.

One of our project objectives was to understand the proximal processes or activities occurring in the course of everyday activities between young deaf children and the persons, objects, and symbols in their immediate environment (Bronfenbrenner, 2005). We focused on caregivers' interactions with their young deaf children within their multilingual microsystems of the home and/or the school boarding house. We observed caregivers interacting with their children or their wards (as house parents in the schools for the deaf) to identify ways in which the interlocutors used spoken and signed language as well as other forms of visual communication. We also talked to caregivers about the influences on their communication practices and choices. This aspect of our methodology also considered the resource characteristics of caregivers, referred to by Bronfenbrenner and Morris (2006) as *liabilities and assets* (p. 812) such as their education, social and economic status, and mental resources that might influence their caregiving practices and capability to access early support services as well as their motivation and persistence (described by Bronfenbrenner and Morris (2006) as *force*) with the challenges that they faced. Specifically, we sought to understand caregivers' perspectives, attitudes, and beliefs about deafness as an important influential element in their approach to caregiving.

In his discussion of proximal processes Bronfenbrenner (2005) made a distinction between *stable* and *unstable* environments in terms of the effectiveness and relative influence on the individual. In this regard we found the bioecological framework to be wanting and insufficiently sensitive to the complexities of the lives of caregivers of very young deaf children in this context (of limited resource and societal awareness) and the extent to which they had any power or agency over their caregiving choices and practices.

The bioecological model goes some way to illuminating the multiple influences on the development environment and caregiving experiences and practices. However, these influences need to be understood from a social world perspective that acknowledges the infrastructure, policies, cultural attitudes and ideologies around deafness, language and communication. In particular, the ways in which different languages in deaf children's lives are legitimized or valorized in this society has a profound impact on caregivers' approaches to communication with their deaf children (O'Brien, 2021). Whilst we structured our investigation according to the bioecological framework we were also therefore interested in the position and agency of caregivers in the surrounding social space.

At the level of the *mesosystem,* we were interested to find out how the connections between the different environments of the deaf child were supportive of their early development and of caregivers. The link between school and home was of particular interest because of the potential for the enrichment of early care and support but at the same time the physical distance between school and home. Most deaf children are boarders during term time in the schools for deaf—it is unusual for them to return home for the weekends and caregivers cannot afford the travel costs or to engage in parent teacher meetings and school events. It is therefore difficult to forge supportive connections between special schools and caregivers. We also investigated the links between home and the clinical environment, with the audiology team, and the extent this connection was sustained to provide on-going support to caregivers.

At the exosystem level, we looked at the collaborations among practitioners and professionals which included collaborations between special schools and clinics, between special schools and community, and among schools in providing care and support to families. As part of this system, we examined the role of the deaf community and specifically deaf leaders and advocates in Ghana. Whilst the presence of deaf teachers in the schools provided a point of contact with deaf people for caregivers, we identified the role of deaf leaders to be more of an external (distal) influence that did not involve the day-to-day (proximal) processes and hands on engagement with children and families.

At the level of the *macrosystem* we investigated national policies of special, inclusive and early years education. At this level we were also interested in societal attitudes and beliefs around deafness, the use of sign languages and understandings of bi/multilingualism and the impact of these sociocultural factors on early support and caregiving. This attention to the wider cultural context required a critical stance towards the assumed authoritative nature of the Western knowledge-based and methods. Through our methods and working practices within the project team we sought to bring to the fore local and indigenous knowledge and practices with the ultimate goals of growing local ECCE expertise as well as research and development experience and networks.

Ethical Challenges

Whilst the use of a bioecological approach guided the development of culturally sensitive methodological approach, the ethical challenges of doing research in this context were present on a day-to-day basis. Members of the project team reflected on some of these issues and shared their experiences. Project team members were sometimes exercised by the information that they were gathering and how to approach interview data with an objective stance given their proximity to the educational institutions and capacity building brief of the project:

> During the interview, some schools told us that government always post general teachers instead of special teachers to the special schools. This is very true but instead of saying the same we can present the same information in a diplomatic way. This will not put any school into trouble and at the same time help the government or the ministry to reconsider the posting process. To sustain capacity building, the project team needs to work or collaborate with one of the educational institutions and recruit qualified professionals to oversee the centre. (Obed Appau)

One of our methodological aims was to gather multiple voices and perspectives from a range of professionals and adults who had caregiving roles with the children. As well as family members this included house parents in the schools for deaf children and neighbours in shared compound houses and community spaces with different language and communication preferences. Whilst we sought to adapt interview techniques according to individual preferences, we were also hampered by Covid restrictions, and this presented new ethical concerns about the inclusivity of our data collection strategies.

> (…) alternative measures of collecting data due to COVID- interviews through WhatsApp had to come in. These means of collecting data are not common or popular in the Ghanaian context. (Yaw Offei)

> When we changed the methodology due to Covid 19, we decided to collect data via phone calls and other online means, I asked myself, how will this look like … talking to someone who has not seen you before and vice versa. Will they open up? Will they provide accurate information? (Obed Appau)

The use of English language for interviewing was not the best for practitioners and participants. Though English is the official language in Ghana, people often feel comfortable using a mixture of the local language and English. (Alexander Oppong)

The engagement of participants in the project relied on informal as well as formal approaches that acknowledged the connectedness of people informally.

I think that there were two main ethical issues that I encountered as a member of the team. The first has to do with us having a position of power and familiarity with most of the participants so in our context it was difficult for people to say no even when they meant no because you were related to them so I have to explain to them that this was research and that they were not to participate if they were unwilling. (Daniel Fobi)

Recruitment involved open conversations with school and local communities about their perspectives on the project ambitions and objectives. Consent from caregivers needed to be carefully negotiated using home languages and multiple visits to schools and parent teacher association meetings to explain the nature of their involvement. A specific issue for us involved the perception of participative research and the relationship between the researchers and the researched and their expectations, for example, of remuneration.

In Ghana, many people request for money before they give out information. Going into the field with this in mind I felt that some participants may not give accurate information without giving them a token. Since research demands reliable and accurate data this became a challenge to me. (Obed Appau)

A final ethical issue relates to how the information from the project will be shared and disseminated so as to further the science of ECCE, and at the same time develop academic capacity in this field in Ghana and not further contribute to North–South knowledge inequities. Given the reliance on written outputs in the research contexts we developed mentoring and co-authorship strategies as a research team to facilitate the publication of outcomes in international journals. We also explored alternative ways in which the cultural realities of the project could be represented such as through the development of video materials in Ghanaian sign language alongside different local languages. In this research context where deaf education has been historically 'missionized', the ultimate aim of the work has been to change structures and attitudes from within rather than to impose external view of best practice in deaf ECCE (Canella & Lincoln, 2011).

Conclusion

In this chapter we have discussed the theoretical and practical difficulties of indigenizing and integrating the ethical considerations of early years research across cultural contexts and described the challenges experienced as we conducted ECCE research in the Ghanaian context. We have argued that the use of a bioecological framework to explore the research questions in this area supports an approach that is responsive to some of the ethical challenges discussed and that the application of social theory through the analysis process illuminates important sociocultural issues of agency and power in the early support context.

We have shown how the person-centred and context sensitive dimensions of the bio-ecological approach informed our methodological approach and have outlined the focus of the data gathering and analysis activities. Subsequent chapters will fully explain the details of the project methods and outcomes, and will discuss the main findings of the project work in four areas of caregiver experience, language and communication, multi-professional working, and deaf leadership.

References

Anderson, J., Boyle, C., & Deppeler, J. (2014). The ecology of inclusive education: Reconceptualising Bronfenbrenner. In H. Zhang, P. Wing, K. Chan, & C. Boyle (Eds.), *Equality in education: Fairness and inclusion* (pp. 23–34). Sense Publishers.

Ansong, D, Okumu, M, Bowen, G. L., Walker, A. M., & Eisensmith, S. R. (2017). The role of parent, classmate, and teacher support in student engagement: Evidence from Ghana. *International Journal of Educational Development, 54*, 51–58. https://doi.org/10.1016/j.ijedudev.2017.03.010

Bauman, H.-D. L., & Murray, J. J. (2014). *Deaf gain: Raising the stakes for human diversity.* U of Minnesota Press.

Bizzego, A., Lim, M., Schiavon, G., Setoh, P., Gabrieli, G., Dimitriou, D., & Esposito, G. (2020). Child disability and caregiving in low- and middle-income countries: Big data approach on open data. *Research in Developmental Disabilities, 107*, 103795.

Bronfenbrenner, U. (1977). Toward an experimental ecology of human development. *American Psychologist, 32*, 513–531.

Bronfenbrenner, U. (1979). *The ecology of human development: Experiments in nature and design.* Harvard University Press.

Bronfenbrenner, U. (1986). Ecology of the family as a context for human development: Research perspectives. *Developmental Psychology, 22*(6), 723–742.

Bronfenbrenner, U. (1993). The ecology of cognitive development: Research models and fugitive findings. In R. Wozniak & K. Fischer (Eds.), *Development in context: Acting and thinking in specific environments* (pp. 3–44). Erlbaum.

Bronfenbrenner, U. (1994). Ecological models of human development. In T. Husen & T. N. Postlethwaite (Eds.), *International Encyclopaedia of Education,* vol. 3 (2nd ed., pp. 1643–1647). Pergamon Press.

Bronfenbrenner, U. (2005). *Making human beings human: Bioecological perspectives on human development*. London: Sage.

Bronfenbrenner, U., & Morris, P. A. (2006). The bioecological model of human development. In W. Damon & R. M.Lerner (Series Eds.) & R. M. Lerner (Vol. Ed.), *Handbook of child psychology. Vol.1: Theoretical models of human development* (6th ed., pp. 793–828). John Wiley.

Canella, G. S., & Lincoln, Y. S. (2011). Ethics, research regulations and critical social science. In N. K. Denzin & Y. S. Lincoln, *The Sage Handbook of Qualitative Research* (5th ed., pp. 81–89). Sage.

Coleman, M. (2013). *Empowering family-teacher partnerships: Building connections within diverse communities*. Sage

Curtin, M., Dirks, E., Cruice, M., Herman, R., Newman, L., Rodgers, L., & Morgan, G. (2021). Assessing parent behaviours in parent–child interactions with deaf and hard of hearing infants aged 0–3 years: A systematic review. *Journal of Clinical Medicine, 10*(15), 3345.

Ertem, I. O. (2011). Monitoring and supporting early childhood development. In C. D. Rudolph, A. M. Rudolph, G E. Lister, L. First, & A. A. Gershon (Eds.), *Rudolph's paediatrics* (22nd ed., pp. 34–38). McGraw-Hill.

Friedner, M. (2017). Doing deaf studies in the Global South. In A. Kusters, M. M. de, & D. O'Brien (Eds.), *Innovations in deaf studies: The role of deaf scholars* (pp. 129–151). Oxford University Press.

Gale, E., Berke, M., Benedict, B., Olson, S., Putz, K., & Yoshinaga-Itano, C. (2021). Deaf adults in early intervention programs. *Deafness & Education International, 23*(1), 3–24.

Grech, S. (2011). Recolonising debates or perpetuated coloniality? Decentring the spaces of disability, development and community in the global South. *International Journal of Inclusive Education, 15*(1), 87–100.

Guttman, N. (2017). Ethical issues in health promotion and communication interventions. In *Oxford research encyclopaedia of communication*. Retrieved 6 May. 2024, from https://oxfordre.com/communication/view/10.1093/acrefore/9780190228613.001.0001/acrefore-9780190228613-e-118

Hewett, R., Douglas, G., McLinden, M., & Keil, S. (2017). Developing an inclusive learning environment for students with visual impairment in higher education: Progressive mutual accommodation and learner experiences in the United Kingdom. *European Journal of Special Needs Education, 32*(1), 89–109. https://doi.org/10.1080/08856257.2016.1254971.

Howe T. R. (2011). Bioecological approach to development. In S. Goldstein, & J. A. Naglieri (Eds.), *Encyclopaedia of child behaviour and development*. Springer. https://doi.org/10.1007/978-0-387-79069_346

Houston, S. (2017). Towards a critical ecology of child development in social work: aligning the theories of Bronfenbrenner and Bourdieu. *Families, Relationships and Societies, 6*(1), 53–69.

Kabay, S., Wolf, S., & Yoshikawa, H. (2017). 'So that his mind will open': Parental perceptions of early childhood education in urbanizing Ghana. *International Journal of Educational Development, 57*, 44–53.

Keller, H., Borke, J., Staufenbiel, T., Yovsi, R. D., Abels, M., Papaligoura, Z., Jensen, H., Lohaus, A., Chaudhary, N., Lo, W., & Su, Y. (2009). Distal and proximal parenting as alternative parenting strategies during infants' early months of life: A cross-cultural study. *International Journal of Behavioural Development, 33*(5), 412–420.

Leonard, W. Y. (2021). Toward an anti-racist linguistic anthropology: An Indigenous response to White supremacy. *Journal of Linguistic Anthropology, 31*(2), 218–237.

Luca, J. E. (2016). Side by side with responsive parents in the care for child development intervention. In T. Moreno (Ed.), *Early Childhood Matters: Advances in early childhood development* (pp. 64–68). Bernard van Leer Foundation.

McLinden, M., & McCracken, W. (2016). Review of the visiting teachers service for children with hearing and visual impairment in supporting inclusive educational practice in Ireland: Examining stakeholder feedback through an ecological systems theory. *European*

Journal of Special Needs Education, 31(4), 472–488. https://doi.org/10.1080/08856 257.2016.1194570

McLinden, M., Lynch, P., Soni, A., Artiles, A., Kholowa, F., Kamchedzera, E., Mbukwa, J., & Mankhwazi, M. (2018). Supporting children with disabilities in low-and middle-income countries: Promoting inclusive practice within community-based childcare centres in Malawi through a bioecological systems perspective. *International Journal of Early Childhood, 50*(2), 159–174.

Moeller, M. P., Carr, G., Seaver, L., Stredler-Brown, A., & Holzinger, D. (2013). Best practices in family-centered early intervention for children who are deaf or hard of hearing: An international consensus statement. *Journal of Deaf Studies and Deaf Education, 18*(4), 429–445. doi:10.1093/deaf ed/ent034

Morelli, G., Quinn, N., Chaudhary, N., Vicedo, M., Rosabal-Coto, M., Keller, H., Murray, M., Gottlieb, A., Scheidecker, G., & Takada, A. (2018). Ethical challenges of parenting interventions in low-to middle-income countries. *Journal of Cross-Cultural Psychology, 49*(1), 5–24.

Morelli, G. A., Rogoff, B., & Angelillo, C. (2003). Cultural variation in young children's access to work or involvement in specialised child-focused activities. *International Journal of Behavioural Development, 27*(3), 264–274.

Neumann, K., Chadha, S., Tavartkiladze, G., Bu, X., & White, K. R. (2019). Newborn and infant hearing screening facing globally growing numbers of people suffering from disabling hearing loss. *International Journal of Neonatal Screening, 5*(1), 7.

O'Brien, E. (2021). A mind stretched: The psychology of repeat consumption. *Consumer Psychology Review, 4*(1), 42–58.

Olusanya, B. O., Neumann, K. J., & Saunders, J. E. (2014). The global burden of disabling hearing impairment: A call to action. *Bulletin of the World Health Organization, 92*, 367–373.

Robinson-Pant, A., & Singal, N. (2013). Researching ethically across cultures: Issues of knowledge, power and voice. *Compare: A Journal of Comparative and International Education, 43*(4), 417–421. doi:10.1080/03057925.2013.797719

Rogoff, B. (2003). *The cultural nature of human development*. Oxford University Press.

Singal, N., & Muthukrishna, N. (2014). Education, childhood and disability in countries of the South–re-positioning the debates. *Childhood, 21*(3), 293–307.

Störbeck, C., & Young, A. (2016). Early intervention in challenging national contexts. In M. Sass-Lehrer (Ed.), *Early intervention for deaf and hard-of-hearing infants, toddlers, and their families: Interdisciplinary perspectives* (pp. 305–328). Oxford University Press.

Tudge, J. R. H., Mokrova, I., Hatfield, B. E., & Karnik, R. B. (2009). Uses and misuses of Bronfenbrenner's bioecological theory of human development. *Journal of Family Theory & Review, 1*(4), 198–210. doi:10.1111/j.1756-2589.2009.00026.x

Woodhead, M., Featherstone, I., Bolton, L., & Robertson, P. (2014). *Early childhood development: Delivering inter-sectoral policies, programmes and services in low-resource settings.* Topic guide. Oxford, UK: Health & Education Advice & Resource Team (HEART). Retrieved from http://oro.open.ac.uk/

Yoshinaga-Itano C. (2003). From screening to early identification and intervention: Discovering predictors to successful outcomes for children with significant hearing loss. *Journal of Deaf Studies and Deaf Education, 8*(1), 11–30. https://doi.org/10.1093/deafed/8.1.11

Yoshinaga-Itano, C., Sedey, A. L., Mason, C. A., Wiggin, M., & Chung, W. (2020). Early intervention, parent talk, and pragmatic language in children with hearing loss. *Paediatrics, 146*(3), 270–277.

6

The Experiences of Caregivers of Deaf Children

Ruth Swanwick and Obed Appau

Project Goals

The aim of our research project was to develop a critical understanding of the social and resource contexts of young deaf children that support the development of early childhood care and education (ECCE) and that can be replicated across different urban and rural contexts. We sought to identify and describe the existing precarities and available social and material resources surrounding early support and to identify the potential for change and development. To achieve these aims, the project team worked with schools for the deaf, hearing assessment centres, deaf communities, and families of deaf children to gather a breadth of information around the contextual and social understandings of childhood deafness and responsive caregiving. Our intention was to use these insights to identify and plan contextually sensitive ways of working with the available resources within and outside the family to mitigate the developmental precarities of childhood deafness, and to translate this knowledge into accessible support material for education and health practitioners, caregivers, families, and communities.

The project fieldwork was conducted by the Ghana-based research team. The Ghana team was led by two co-investigators who recruited three research assistants (RAs) to support the data collection and analysis. All three RAs had completed a Master of Philosophy degree in special education. Two of the RAs were sign language interpreters and teachers for the deaf and the third worked in special education supporting deaf individuals. All the RAs had experience of working directly with deaf children and young people and their caregivers in different educational contexts. There are very few people in Ghana with

Ruth Swanwick and Obed Appau, *The Experiences of Caregivers of Deaf Children* In: *The Early Care and Education of Deaf Children in Ghana*. Edited by: Ruth Swanwick, Daniel Fobi, Yaw Offei, and Alexander Oppong, Oxford University Press.
© Ruth Swanwick and Obed Appau 2024. DOI: 10.1093/oso/9780192872272.003.0006

doctoral level research experience and qualifications in the field of deaf education. The recruitment of researchers working at masters level was therefore pragmatic response to the lack of resource this field and the need to build academic experience and capacity.

Methodology

At the planning stages of the project, we contacted three schools for the deaf and two speech and hearing assessment centres from Southern, Middle, and Northern sectors of Ghana who agreed to participate and to help us to reach out to caregivers of deaf children between the ages of 5 and 15. Locating very young deaf children in this context is challenging because of the reasons of the infrastructure and social barriers discussed in earlier chapters. From the 25 approaches that were made to families through the schools, we were able to recruit 12 caregivers who agreed to participate in the study and to be contacted by us. Our first meetings with these participants involved the explanation of the project aims, a description of what would be involved, and an explanation of the choices that they had as participants. We emphasized the confidentiality and anonymity processes and discussed their rights to opt in and out of the project work at any time without consequence. To conclude these preliminary meetings, caregivers were given the opportunity to reflect on whether they wanted to be involved outside of the meeting contexts and to forward their consent in their own time. They did this via email (7) or using Whatsapp (5).

Having obtained approval and permission from the caregivers, the schools, and the clinics, our first objective was to conduct one-to-one interviews with all the caregivers. Before launching into the aspect of the project work, we spent time getting to know and establishing a friendly rapport with them. We felt it important to build trust and confidence of the caregivers as we would be talking about a sensitive aspect of their lives that is often associated with uncertainty in this context. We wanted them to feel comfortable with the interview process and able to share their experiences openly (Clarke & Braun, 2013). In order for us to observe the Covid-19 protocols, it was necessary for us to revise our plans for face-to-face interviews process and invite caregivers to talk to us over the telephone. This was possible because all the caregivers were hearing. We used mobile phones to conduct the calls and we sought permission from caregivers individually to audio record the interviews for the purposes of transcription. The RAs conducted the interviews in a team. One of the RAs talked with the caregiver, another made supplementary field notes, and the third RA monitored the recording.

We used a semi-structured interview format to explore the experiences of caregivers in raising their deaf children. This format gave caregivers freedom to narrate their experiences and allowed for some flexibility in our interactions with caregivers. We were able to be responsive to and explore topics that caregivers wanted to raise during the conversation (Flick, 2009; Smith & Osborn, 2003). The interview questions focused on the identification and confirmation of their child's hearing loss, language and communication practices in the home and surrounding environment, the caregivers' support needs and the existing support opportunities and possibilities, and the expectations that caregivers had. We also asked caregivers to describe any resources, interventions, and/or strategies that they had access to or used, and their experience of partnership and collaboration with caregivers and education and health professionals. Within these broad interview questions areas, we developed potential follow-up probes and prompts to support our understanding. We used open-ended questions and were conscious of the need to avoid leading or closed questions (Smith & Osborn, 2003). Each interview lasted between 50 and 60 minutes. After each interview, the recorded audio file was played in the presence of all the RAs to check the quality and integrity of the recording.

Ghana is a multilingual country and so the participating caregivers spoke different languages and dialects all of which were acknowledged during the interview. All the interviews were conducted in the caregiver's preferred language. At least one of the RAs could speak and write the local dialect of all the caregivers who participated in the study. Two of the RAs knew how to write, read, and speak Fante[1], and all the RAs could write, read and speak Twi[2]. Three of the interviews were conducted in spoken English, six in Twi, two in Fante, and one in blended English and Twi. Teamwork was an essential aspect of the interview process. In Ghana, an individuals' ability to speak a local dialect is not tantamount to the cultural understanding of the person. We found that there were occasions when the RAs would need to shift roles in order to reframe questions to meet the contextual understanding of caregivers and to make the conversation flow. This flexibility helped us to capture and fully understand the responses from caregivers.

The three RAs transcribed all the audio data responses from the 12 caregivers. Verbatim transcriptions in the language of the interview such as Twi and Fante were initially created and a written English translation was developed for the purposes of the cross-team analysis. Even though the transcriptions

---

[1] Fante is spoken by people of the southern coast of Ghana between Accra and Sekondi-Takoradi.
[2] Twi is spoken in southern and central Ghana mainly by the Akan people, the largest ethnic group in Ghana.

were time consuming and sometimes difficult, our aim was to create faithful records caregivers' responses and to ensure conceptually accurate translations (Temple & Young, 2004). All the recordings and transcripts (either in the local or English) language were rotated among the three RAs to crosscheck translation choices and sense and for the correction of any listening errors. Caregivers were also asked to review and verify the interview content. Following this process, the transcriptions and the audio recorded files were passed to the two Ghana-based co-investigators for a final cross-check and confirmation.

In the process of collecting the data from caregivers, the RAs faced some challenges that are not unusual for a sub-Saharan Africa (SSA) context. The first of these was that most of the caregivers had assumed that their time would be funded and expected to be financially recompensed for the interviews. As this was not in our original research design or ethical plan (an oversight on our part), we could not meet this expectation but provided thank you gestures in any way that we could. We have learned from this, and for future projects we have built in thank you vouchers for participants. Additionally, the mobile phone connectivity was problematic for some of the interviews, and this disrupted the flow of the conversations. Furthermore, some of the caregivers did not have phone battery life that was long enough to sustain the interaction for the estimated time for the interview and so we would have to complete the interview in sections. We also struggled to clearly hear some of the caregivers where they were in noisy outdoor settings. We were able to rely on the field notes to fill in these gaps.

Once we had collected and transcribed all of the interview data, a staged thematic approach was applied to the analysis that involved familiarization with the data, the data generation of initial codes, the grouping of codes into related themes, and the organization and naming of the themes in a meaningful way (Braun & Clarke, 2006). To mediate cross-cultural interpretations of the data, the project team worked together to build a coding instrument. For this process we worked with the notion of a code as a label that captures some content or essence of a portion of data (Saldana, 2009). Our initial approach to assigning codes was to use colour coding on the transcripts and the surface themes that were responsive to our project aims and ecological approach in the first instance. This was an iterative process that involved small group and whole team meetings to review, discuss, and contextualize different interpretations of interview extracts and to agree thematic areas. Each team member independently reviewed the interview transcripts and decided on the initial coding individually in the first instance. We then met as a team to discuss the codes that we had identified. In organizing the themes, we discussed how each of the coded themes are related to each other and how each can recast and organize under a suitable theme. We tried to understand where the experiences of caregivers occur and how their experiences were intertwined and influenced with their immediate environment, community, and policies.

To conceptualize these processes and interconnecting influences on early development, care, and support, we used Bronfenbrenner's bioecological framework (Bronfenbrenner & Morris, 2006) to assign and organize main themes according to the microsystem, mesosystem, exosystem, and macrosystem. For example, we assigned influences relating to the characteristics of the individual, the home, or family or community setting to the microsystem. We identified influences relating to the interaction between different aspects of child's developmental environment (such as links between home and school, or home and clinic) as relating to the mesosystem. The influence of external factors, such as the education or health systems, processes and policies, we assigned to the exosystem. Influence relating more widely to social and cultural context, beliefs, attitudes, and expectations, we assigned to the macrosystem.

Our discussions around these themes were a crucial part of the analysis process. As cross-cultural research team, it was important for us to have a forum for challenging one another's perspectives, enabling all team members to add contextual information so that we could zoom closer into the lives of the participants and the cultural context of the data. From the integration of these perspectives, a coding handbook was developed. This was used to mark-up transcripts individually before full team cross-checking on the main themes and the emergence of any new themes and sub-themes.

Project Participants

We interviewed 12 caregivers of young deaf children in total. We collected brief biographical information about each caregiver including details of their education and employment. Caregivers were living in both urban and rural areas of Ghana, and all their children were in school. Nine of the caregivers had two or more children, and three of the caregivers had only a child in the family at the time of gathering data. Eleven of the caregivers in the study had only one deaf child in the family whilst only one caregiver had two deaf children. Caregivers of males were the primary participants ($n = 11$), and this might be explained by the fact that there has been a tradition bias towards education for boys that is now slowly changing. There were more male deaf children than female as formal education historically used to be male dominated (Chilisa

& Ntseane, 2014). However, with the introduction of Free Compulsory Universal Basic Education (FCUBE; Salifu et al., 2018) and Girl Education (William, 2021), there has been a balance in education between male and female children. Having more male than female deaf children participating in our study was due to that fact that they were the participants whose parents consented to the study.

Despite the varying socio-economic backgrounds of caregivers, all their young deaf children were in either special schools for the deaf or inclusive local mainstream schools. All the special schools were residential and involved the children travelling—sometimes long distances—from the family home.

Some of the caregivers were living in rented houses or apartments, owned house, or family house, and others in compound houses. The caregivers' living arrangements were contingent on their different economic situations. Some of the caregivers were self-employed (traders, food sellers, hairdressers), private and public sectors. Table 6.1 provides a summary of the caregiver participants and the age ranges of the children in their care.

Table 6.1 Participant overview

Caregivers	$n = 12$	
Relationship with child	Mother	8
	Father	3
	Grandmother	1
Age of deaf child	5–10	9
	11–15	4
Sex of deaf child	Male	11
	Female	2
Location	Ashanti region	3
	Central region	4
	Greater Accra region	4
	Eastern region	1
Education	No formal education	1
	Basic level (primary and junior school)	7
	Secondary	1
	Tertiary	3
Employment	Trader	4
	Semi-professional	5
	Professional	3

Caregiver Experiences

Caregivers were asked about their experience of caring for a deaf child, focusing on identification and diagnosis, language and communication, support needs and possibilities, and expectations. One of the themes that emerged from the analysis of the interview data centred on the experience and processes around identification and confirmation of deafness and the issue of late identification.

Identification and Confirmation of Deafness

Caregivers' experience of having a deaf child was significantly shaped by the way in which they learned about their child's deafness and the delay experienced in the formal process of identification and confirmation. As discussed in earlier chapters, caregivers in this context do not experience the recommended screening and diagnosis in the first few months of life (Yoshinaga-Itano et al., 2020) that is in place in most economically rich, and some middle-income contexts (Olusanya, 2012). The issue of late identification was therefore common to all 12 caregivers. Without newborn screening, the early identification of childhood deafness can be dependent on family or community knowledge and experience. Without a screening process identification relies on caregivers acting on their early observations and suspicions or intervention from health practitioners. All caregivers in the study who suspected their child might have hearing loss took them to hospitals, clinics, and assessments for regular check-ups.

> (...) but from there we still noticed that he was still delaying to talk. We decided to go 'GEE' [Komfo Anokye Teaching Hospital] to check whether he was sick or if there was something under his tongue. We kept on going to GEE to be examined but still no positive result. (Mother 1)

> I took him to municipal hospital and they gave some drugs. I also took him to speech and hearing assessment centre at south campus and they also referred us to Interbeton [Cape Coast Teaching Hospital]. At Interbeton, they also gave him some drugs. After taking the drugs we went back to the assessment centre at south campus and the audiologist advised me to purchase a hearing aid for him. So, I bought two and he lost one. (Mother 2)

Two of our respondents reported the discovery their child's deafness as a result of someone in the community noticing a difference in the child's responses

98   Care and Education of Deaf Children in Ghana

to sound or speech. For some caregivers, the first indication was the lack of speech, but these signs are not necessarily associated with hearing loss.

> When she finally walked and we expected her to talk, it also delayed. I conferred with elders in the family and I was told not to worry because children experience delay in speech. (Father 11)

Most caregivers who went with their children to the hospital were given medications usually antibiotics and pain killers. This is common practice since most of the attending physicians are not ENT specialists but general practitioners. Caregivers also took their children to community leaders who they think they are experienced and knowledgeable in caregiving. Grandparents, chiefs, political leaders such as assembly men and women, head of schools, and religious leaders are mostly regarded as community leaders in Ghana and considered to be knowledgeable about raising children.

Some of the caregivers took their children to pastors for check-ups. Most Ghanaians have a strong Christian faith and have confidence in people who are religious leaders (pastors or priests) and their capacity to bring about a cure for their child's deafness. Some pastors do provide prayers and other related services to caregivers and their children who come to them at either the church premises or their private homes.

> We also went to see a Pastor at Kasoa[3] and the pastor told us that my child's hearing disability was from my family and the father's family members were also part of his condition. (Mother 3)

In a context where stigma is attached to any form of disability, action was problematic for caregivers who feared being open about their child's deafness. For some the inaccessibility of the health services was a barrier. Some of the caregivers did not take their children to hospitals or assessment centres irrespective of suspecting hearing loss preferring to confide in the grandparents, external family, and community members for advice and support. Consequently, children were not enrolled in an educational context with support for their deafness until beyond the start of school age and were thus starting pre-school as late as seven or eight years of age.

> He was six to seven years when we took him to the school. We were going to the school every month for training for a year before he was finally admitted into the school. (Father 2)

---

[3] Kasoa is town in the Central Region of Ghana.

The first deaf child was six or five and half years when he went to the school for the deaf. (Mother 1)

Communication

Central to caregiver concerns were anxieties about language and communication and how to interact with their deaf child. All the caregivers were hearing and were also living in communities of mainly hearing people. Of the 12 caregivers, three were learning to use sign language and had some basic skills. The other nine caregivers are aware of sign language. On learning that their child was deaf, they were interested and keen to learn the sign language to facilitate communication in with their deaf children, but they were unable to access training due to their own work schedules, travel issues, and the lack of local provision. Some of the caregivers said that they had the opportunity to learn sign language in their children' school during parents teacher association (PTA) meetings, but this was available once every term (every 4 months) and not frequent enough to support the development of skills that caregivers needed.

> I wish I can get someone to teach me sign language. The school organize some for us. It is done in the middle of every term when we go for PTA. The time they use is small, about 30 minutes. I always forget because is not continuous. (Mother 9)

> The sign language is difficult to learn. When we for PTA and the teachers teach us, I struggle to learn. They teach us only three times in a year. (Mother 10)

Caregivers talked about using their own 'home signs' in their communication with their child. This term describes gestural communication systems developed by deaf children and their families who are not familiar with a conventional signed language (Blose & Joseph, 2017). Home signs allow for communication and interaction to take place, but caregivers appreciated that there is a difference between these spontaneous signs and the sign language of the deaf community.

> I developed our own unique sign language we use to communicate. We didn't conform to the normal sign language, we included everything together, but they still understood me. (Mother 7)

The caregivers in the study knew that their children were deaf, but they still wanted their children to use speech. Caregivers did not want to send their

100   Care and Education of Deaf Children in Ghana

children to schools for the deaf because they thought that would make them loose their speech.

> (…) my husband was not too happy about the idea of him using sign language because there was no one else around who was using sign language how communicating with, he will just ask grandma, grandma, how he was going to communicate. He tried using sign language in addition to the speech and we did figure spelling at a point. He was interested but was more interested in being like speaking like everybody else. Some of them advised us to withdraw from the normal school and take him to the school for the deaf but we knew he would speak so we did not listen to them. (Mother 3)

> I have not heard of any organizations that supports deaf children. I decided to send him to deaf school. But am a bit disturbed because I was told if I send him to deaf school, he might lose the little speech he has because the schools for the deaf only use sign language and gesture as their mode of communication but I also want my son to talk. (Mother 4)

Caregivers that we spoke to reported using other visual strategies to communicate with their deaf children. Some caregivers described using demonstration and gestures. In doing so, they demonstrate their understanding of the need to adjust their communication, to engage their child's attention, and to establish eye contact. They described ways in which they blend spoken language with home signs to make meaning but expressed doubt about the use of their own sign systems, as not being a recognized or a 'proper' sign language.

> I interact with him always. Sometimes when I don't get what he is saying, I take him outside for him to show me what he wants. (Mother 4)

> The used of writing and drawing were also prominent in their communication. He uses sign language but when I am not getting him well, he writes on a paper to tell me what he meant. (Mother 10)

Though some caregivers knew that their deaf children could not hear, they continued to use spoken language in the home to talk to and instruct their deaf children, usually in addition with pointing or nodding towards the object.

> So I will just use my hand to do something he will understand. If he is not getting the particular thing, that is when I will use my hand to sign something little. (Father 5)

Caregivers described pretending to understand their deaf children's gestures in order not to make them feel bad. A lot of miscommunication and misinterpretation occurs between caregivers and their deaf children during these interactions.

> He rather uses gestures and other actions to understand what the child signs. Sometimes when my deaf child tries to communicate with his father and the father is not able to understand him, he ignores the father and comes to me. Whether I understand him or not, I try to give a nod to indicate that I have understood him; if not he will get angry with me. (Mother 1)

> One challenge is he easily gets angry when he is not able to get what he asks for. He will cry and I become sad because we are not able to understand what he says to provide what he needs. (Grandmother 12)

Support Opportunities

Many children with disabilities in Africa in Ghana are excluded from receiving support services that can help them benefit from education, health, and other systems that are crucial for their social, emotional, and cognitive development. The few caregivers who do try access the support available face several challenges. Caregivers in this context reflected on the different opportunities for formal and informal support and articulated their hopes and expectations for their deaf children. Following identification, none of the caregivers had received any early professional support, outside of routine clinic visits for hearing tests and hearing aids, and most were trepidatious about disclosing to others that they have a deaf child.

> I don't get any support from the church because I don't usually talk to people about my deaf child (…) I don't personally talk to people that I need support or help for my child. (Mother 4)

For two of the caregivers, there were opportunities for support in connection with the schools for the deaf, but because of late identification this was not available until their child was of school age. The support infrastructure through the schools' PTA meetings and contact with other parents is nonetheless a potential resource that could be expanded to include other family and community members. Caregivers talked about the emotional support that they get from schools, in terms of acceptance and expectations.

> Through school they have been introduced to examples of prominent and successful people who were deaf and are encouraged that their child would also attain such distinguished positions. (Mother 8)

Two of the parents talked about support from the church where sign language is available. They refer specifically to the Jehovah's Witness group who understand and communicate in sign language.

One of their main concerns was the financial implications of the educational support needed. Caregivers expressed concern about paying for hearing aids, school fees, and materials. Although this is available through municipal and local social welfare agencies, caregivers are often unaware of the resources or find difficult to access them. In addition to school resources, caregivers worry about the cost of hearing technologies.

> We are always with him everywhere we go just that his schooling is a bit problematic because we don't have the money to take him to school for the deaf so he attends the same hearing government school here and he plays together with children in the school. (Grandmother 12)

> We have deaf association here. A crippled woman registered my son into the association. I was paying my dues and everything but was not getting any help from them so I stopped and asked my son to also stop the association. I was told it was from the government that every month, we will be given some money but I never receive anything from the district assembly. (Mother 10)

For most, the cost of hearing aids, and especially modern and digital technologies, was prohibitive. They talked about the insecurity of their finances and the use of loans and the need for permanent work and spoke about other ways in which they have sought financial support including via philanthropic organizations. However, there is stigma associated with asking for support and the risk of their situation and their needs being exposed more publicly.

> I have no intention of seeking for help from other authorities because sometimes they will go on radio stations and discuss you that this person came to me for help. So I don't want to go to any person. I have to work hard and care for him myself. (Mother 10)

Personal Responses to Having a Deaf Child

Of the 12 caregivers that we spoke to, only two had previous experience of deafness in the family, and those with no prior experience described the experience of being in unfamiliar territory and encountering new decisions. They found it difficult to accept and believe that their child would always be deaf f irrespective of the assessment processes.

> (…) sometimes I don't really believed and accept that he is deaf. I want to interact with my child through spoken language as I see other parents communicating with their children in spoken language. So, I don't accept that he is deaf and can't hear or talk. (Mother 4)

They talked about the process of accepting their child's deafness and dealing with their personal feelings of sadness, grief, and guilt. This response was usually linked to their concerns over communication and feelings of shame and guilt.

> So, I don't accept that he is deaf and can't hear or talk (…) sometimes I become discouraged and sad for giving birth to a child like this. (Mother 4)

Difficulties with acceptance sometimes resulted in denial where caregivers eschewed opportunities to engage with the schools for the deaf and to support the development of the child's sign language hoping that they would eventually learn to speak. Most of the caregivers associated the use of sign language with the loss of opportunities to learn to use spoken language.

> If I had sent the child to a deaf school at that early age the child would have had language if not speak therefore it would not delay her academic performance but because I kept working at it will come it will come and I kept hoping that my case will be different. Acceptance was difficult. I was not ready to accept that child was deaf. At the end of the day, it delayed the child language sign. What I have learned is that if we are able to accept it we will be to deal with the situation and the early intervention will help. (Mother 6)

Waiting and hoping for change often led to late enrolment in schools for the deaf.

104   Care and Education of Deaf Children in Ghana

> He was taken through investigation process and confirmed to me that he was having hearing loss. They even suggested to me to take him to a deaf school but he was too young. I declined that advice and felt I should let him mature in age before I would take him to the deaf school. I doubted and had the belief that the speech would come later on. That was my childish thought at the time. I initially didn't accept that the children had that disability. It was upon persistent persuasion that I finally accepted their condition and decided to heed the advice of other people. (Mother 7)

Team Member Reflections

Communication

In this study, the decision making, and day-to-day experiences of caregivers were largely influenced by the external environment where caregivers encounter inhospitable and negative attitudes to deafness and distrust in relation to the use of sign language. This was most marked in caregivers' responses about communication and in their expression of anxiety about the use of sign language in their children's lives. Most of the caregivers expressed their hope that their child will use spoken language and considered having a place in society to be contingent on being able to speak. They thus demonstrated only a partial understanding of the language and communication issues and tended to adopt a polarized view of sign and spoken language possibilities, and a generally negative view of sign language.

We asked our deaf colleagues on the project team and some deaf mentors about their experience of these issues in their own childhoods. Linda who became deaf at eight years old describes the difficulties that she experienced in a hearing family who did not know any sign language.

> My parents are hearing. Since becoming deaf my parents communicated to me through spoken language, thus, made it difficult for me to interact with them. When struggling to understand my parents, they at times put their thoughts in written form for me. My immediate family use different strategies such as lip reading, spoken language, and writing to communicate with me.

Emmanuel is a young man who is deaf in the University of Education, Winneba, Ghana. He is a level 4 student who is reading Special Education. He is well respected in society due to his achievement in terms of education. His medium of learning is through sign language interpreting services. Emmanuel, who became deaf at the age of 10 years describes his parents efforts to cure his deafness and the subsequent delayed entry to the school for the deaf and eventual encounter with sign language.

> My parents did everything thus, sending me to hospitals, prayer camps, and fetish priests in order to make me hear again, but to no avail. (. . .). My father heard about a school for the deaf and made me stop the regular school in order to enroll me in the special school.

> Even with that it took my parents 6 years to send me to the school for the deaf. Due to this I was placed in class two at the age of 17 years. Also, at age 17 I did not know how to communicate in sign language because my immediate family always used spoken language to interact with me. I started learning Ghanaian sign language at the age of 17 years.

The systemic experience of stigma that created a barrier for the caregivers in the study was also reiterated by deaf colleagues on our project team. Linda describes her experience of being marginalized and excluded in the school environment.

> I received a lot of insults from my peers and teachers due to my deafness. When my peers and teachers call me via spoken language, and I do not respond they tease and laugh at me. With the exception of cultural dance, I was excluded from many academic activities due to my deafness. My classmates were not opening up to me. The community used to call me names in an insulting manner such as 'mumu' (she is deaf). The community I grew in had a perception that deaf people cannot achieve their goals (academic and social) in life. I always feel that I am unable to explore and use my potential due to how the community perceived deafness. They will never give you the opportunity as a deaf person.

Emmanuel talks about his experience of being ignored and marginalized as an adult in the community.

> The community I found myself in never had any trust for deaf people. They see deaf people as useless with no hope. Always when there is a community meeting, they ignore deaf people. Even if they invite you to a meeting, they don't take suggestions from deaf people.

Stigma of this nature, associated with disability, is reportedly lower in urban contexts where there is a higher level of education, better access to the media, education, and health centres, and to the informal community support networks around caregivers. However, almost half of Ghana's population (and the majority of people with disabilities) live in rural areas that lack these facilities. In these contexts where communal living is common, stigma is more pronounced and more difficult to avoid (Dassah et al., 2018). Linda reflected on what this means for education and employment prospects as a deaf person.

> My experience has taught me that to be a deaf person in Ghana, the only job available is teaching which mostly is unfavourable for us, thus you will never be given opportunity to work in banks, health sectors, and other related places.

In this context it is hoped that the increased visibility of deaf people in society–as leaders, role models, and advocates—will change social narratives of deafness and mediate discriminatory beliefs and behaviours. Deaf-led organizations such as GNAD are thus crucial advocates for deaf awareness and sign language recognition and access to a bilingual education and therefore key collaborators in the development of ECCE.

Conclusion

The experiences of this small sample of caregivers highlight the importance of understanding the full influence of the environment on building on caregiver's experience of raising a deaf child. Our research with caregivers revealed the precarities that they experience in dealing with the new experience of parenting, unfamiliar decisions about communication options and schooling, with additional financial burdens and the challenges of societal discrimination. These are adverse and impoverished conditions for shaping development opportunities for deaf children that are relevant to many other low-resource contexts in the global South.

The development of ECCE in such a context needs to be mindful of cultural and societal attitudes and beliefs but at the same time responsive to the expectations and hopes of caregivers for their deaf child in terms of becoming a respected member of the community and society. The start of this process is early education and the means through which children are expected to develop collective behaviours and a sense of community (Ngaujah & Dirks, 2003; Nsamenang, 2008) as well as the independent abilities to participate in society. Caregivers' expectations and hopes for their deaf children and their own relationships with the educational and school context provide a further important steer for the development of ECCE. Whilst these early experiences are hugely valued, caregivers are disempowered by a lack of balanced and timely information and confused by communication choices. They eventually lack confidence to take steps to support their children's learning. Much could be done by education and health professionals to ensure that caregivers are informed and have agency over educational choices. Upskilling the education and health workforce around the language and communication needs of young deaf children and their caregivers in this context would provide a first step towards sustainable ECCE. To achieve this, a greater understanding is needed of the context for language and communication development that in a multilingual context such as Ghana bears little resemblance to template on which the international guidelines for early intervention have been developed. This language and communication context is the focus of Chapter 7.

References

Blose, Z., M., & Joseph, L., M. (2017). The reality of everyday communication for a deaf child using sign language in a developing country. *African Health Sciences, 17*(4), 1149–1159.

Braun, V., & Clarke, V. (2006). Using thematic analysis in psychology. *Qualitative Research in Psychology, 3*(2), 77–101.

Bronfenbrenner, U., & Morris, P. A. (2006). The bioecological model of human development. In W. Damon & R. M. Lerner (Eds.), *Handbook of child psychology: Theoretical models of human development* (pp. 793–828). Wiley.

Chilisa, B., & Ntseane, G. (2014). Resisting dominant discourses: Implications of indigenous, African feminist theory and methods for gender and education research. In J. Ringrose (Ed.), *Rethinking gendered regulations and resistances in education* (pp. 23–38). Routledge.

Clarke, V., & Braun, V. (2013). Teaching thematic analysis: Overcoming challenges and developing strategies for effective learning. *The Psychologist, 26*(2), 120–123.

Dassah, E., Aldersey, H. M., McColl, M. A., & Davison, C. (2018). 'When I don't have money to buy the drugs, I just manage.'—Exploring the lived experience of persons with physical disabilities in accessing primary health care services in rural Ghana. *Social Science & Medicine, 214*, 83–90.

Flick, U. (2009). *An introduction to qualitative research* (4th ed.). Sage.

Ngaujah, D. E., & Dirks, D. H. (2003). An eco-cultural and social paradigm for understanding human development: A (West African) context. *Graduate Seminar Paper (supervised by Dr Dennis H. Dirks), Biola University, CA.*

Nsamenang, A. B. (2008). Agency in early childhood learning and development in Cameroon. *Contemporary Issues in Early Childhood, 9*(3), 211–223.

Olusanya, B. O. (2012). Neonatal hearing screening and intervention in resource-limited settings: An overview. *Archives of Disease in Childhood* 97(7), 654–659. doi:10.1136/archdischild-2012-301786.

Saldana, J. (2009). *The coding manual for qualitative researchers.* Sage Publications.

Salifu, I., Boateng, J. K., & Kunduzore, S. S. (2018). Achieving free compulsory universal basic education through school feeding programme: Evidence from a deprived rural community in northern Ghana. *Cogent Education, 5*(1), 1509429.

Smith, J. A. & Osborn, M. (2003) Interpretative phenomenological analysis. In J. A. Smith (Ed.), *Qualitative psychology: A practical guide to research methods* (pp. 51–80). Sage Publications.

Temple, B., & Young, A. (2004). Qualitative research and translation dilemmas. *Qualitative Research, 4*(2), 161–178. doi:10.1177/1468794104044430

Williams, T. M. (2021). Girl-child, health, and education in Africa. In O. Yacob-Haliso, & T. Falola (Eds.), *The Palgrave handbook of African women's studies* (pp. 2409–2423). Springer International Publishing.

Yoshinaga-Itano, C., Sedey, A. L., Mason, C. A. Wiggin, M. & Chung, W. (2020). Early intervention, parent talk, and pragmatic language in children with hearing loss. *Paediatrics 146*(3): S270–S277. doi:10.1542/peds.2020-0242F.

7

The Multilingual Context of ECCE for Deaf Children and their Families in Ghana

Ruth Swanwick and Joyce Fobi

Introduction

As discussed in Chapter 1, globally, the prevalence of childhood deafness is highest in sub-Saharan Africa and in South and Southeast Asia (WHO, 2018). These regions of the world are linguistically and culturally diverse and the use of many languages, dialects, and local or regional languages for inter-community interaction is the norm. Most deaf children therefore grow up in historically multilingual societies with a long tradition of multilingual communication and within families and communities who speak multiple languages as part of their normal daily lives.

The early care and education of a deaf child centres on language and communication skills and specifically the need for the establishment of a strong primary language, whether this is signed or spoken—as a basis for conceptual development, cognitive growth, and literacy development (Yoshinago-Itano, 2003 2014). However, much of the published research into the early support of multilingual deaf children pertains to economically rich contexts where there are established deaf education resources, early identification and support infrastructures, and professional health and education communities who are academically networked (Brons et al., 2019; Collyer, 2018). In the scoping review carried out by Cannon and Marx (2023), 76% of all studies were from the United States and Australia. This research neglects underrepresented socio-cultural contexts and minorities who have a rich history of multilingualism. Missing from this research is also an appreciation of the different patterns of language socialization in multilingual societies and the global diversity of familial and social networks that surround children and families.

Ruth Swanwick and Joyce Fobi, *The Multilingual Context of ECCE for Deaf Children and their Families in Ghana* In: *The Early Care and Education of Deaf Children in Ghana*. Edited by: Ruth Swanwick, Daniel Fobi, Yaw Offei, and Alexander Oppong, Oxford University Press. © Ruth Swanwick and Joyce Fobi 2024. DOI: 10.1093/oso/9780192872272.003.0007

Specifically, Western models of support emphasis child–parent dyads and a nuclear family structure. Little attention is given to societies that are organized around communal relationships and livelihoods (Kabay et al., 2017; Singal & Muthukrishna, 2014). The Euro-Western focus of the research also overlooks families in contexts where the use of sign language and certain local languages is stigmatized (Ndiribe & Aboh, 2022).

As a basis for the development of context-sensitive and evidence-based ECCE, research is needed into the multilingual language practices and choices of caregivers that takes account of different cultural contexts, communal intergenerational childrearing practices, and the influential role of society and community language ideologies. In this chapter, we seek to highlight the opportunities and precarities of being a deaf multilingual learner in Ghana in terms of language outcomes, cultural identity, and access to support (Cannon et al., 2022; Crowe & Guiberson, 2019). We distinguish between growing up in a multilingual environment and having opportunities to develop multilingual skills (Marshall & Moore, 2018), and we draw on our project case study material to exemplify this distinction. By seeking to understand different patterns of language socialization in this multilingual context and the complexity of individual heteroglossic life worlds (Bourdieu, 1991), this chapter makes a broader contribution to the science of ECCE by shifting the flow of knowledge from South to North and extending the language and communication perspective and possibilities of ECCE.

The Multilingual Context of Ghana

Ghana is a multilingual nation, and in the average Ghanaian household, every member speaks or understands two or more spoken languages as their first or second language. Ghana, with a population of approximately 32 million (Ghana Statistical Services, 2021), has approximately 81 living languages (Eberhard et al., 2020). Of these, 73 are indigenous and 8 are non-indigenous (including English, Hausa, and Arabic). Thirteen of these languages are described as institutional (e.g. French, Latin, Hausa, English, Arabic, Akan) in that they are used in education, media, and cooperative institutions, and are supported by both government and non-government organizations (Akoto, 2018). A large proportion of Ghana's languages (46) are in the process of development, meaning they are active languages but have limited standardization. Fourteen of these are deemed robust because they are utilized for intergenerational face-to-face communication in a sustainable manner, six are classified as endangered, and two are dying out (Eberhard et al., 2020).

English, which was inherited from the colonial period, is the official language and lingua franca in Ghana, with 9.8 million people using English as a second language in addition to their native or indigenous language (Ghana Statistical Services, 2021). Governmental and business affairs are conducted primarily in English: it is utilized in legal and administrative procedures and documents, in Ghanaian politics, and across the media. English is also the language of instruction in Ghana's educational system and one of the subjects taught in Ghanaian schools (Guerini, 2008).

Though English as the official language is a unifying factor, Ghana's multilingualism has facilitated communication among speakers of various native languages. Arabic and Hausa are also widely used by the country's northern Muslim community. Most Muslim children in Ghana attend an Islamic school popularly known as 'Makaranta' where they learn to read and write in Arabic.

Indigenous Spoken and Written Languages in Ghana

Each of Ghana's more than 70 ethnic groups has its own distinct language. Akans, Dagbani, Ewe, Ga-Adangbe, Gurma, Fulani, Guan, Gurunsi, and Bissa/Mande are the largest ethnic groups in Ghana. Typically, languages of the same ethnic group are mutually intelligible. For instance, the Frafra and Waali languages of Ghana's Upper West Region and the Dagbanli and Mampelle languages of the Northern Region share the same ethnicity of Mole-Dagbani (Kluge, 2000) and are mutually intelligible. Among all the indigenous languages, the Akan language (which is comprised of the following local dialects: Fante, Asante Twi, Akuapem Twi, Brong, Nzema, Ahafo, Denkyira, Kwawu, Asen, and Agona) is the most widely spoken indigenous language in Ghana and has a rich cultural heritage (Ghana Statistical Service, 2021). About 47% of Ghana's 32 million people speak Akan as their native or first language, and approximately 53% of Ghanaians speak Akan as a second or third language (Ghana Statistical Services, 2021).

Ghanaian Sign Languages

Three sign languages have been linguistically documented in Ghana (Nyst, 2010). These are Adamorobe Sign Language, Nanabin Sign Language, and Ghanaian Sign Language (GhSL). Adamorobe Sign Language is an indigenous village sign language used by the deaf residents of the Adamorobe community in the Eastern Region of Ghana; it is used by around 40 deaf people (adults and youngsters) in a community of about 3,000 people, representing 1.3% of the total population (Edward, 2021; Kusters, 2015). Nanabin Sign Language emerged from a family that was known for its high incidence of deafness in Nanabin, Ekumfi, in the Central Region of Ghana (Nyst, 2010); it is believed to be the first sign language in Ghana, with about 25–30 users. GhSL is recognized as the main sign language in Ghana among rural and urban deaf communities, and it is the language of instruction in the schools for the deaf. At this time, GhSL is not officially recognized as one of the languages of Ghana, but there is increasing awareness of its use supported by advocacy initiatives among deaf organizations and the deaf community, and through the media. Such efforts to raise the profile of GhSL will ultimately support caregivers of deaf children who may use multiple spoken languages in their daily lives, but have little or no previous experience of sign language communication.

Language Policy and Use

In this diverse multi-ethnic and multilingual context, the language and communication possibilities for deaf children and their families are shaped by the different ways in which the languages of Ghana are used in different contexts, including the use of GhSL.

Spoken and Written Language Policies

In the mainstream educational context, there is Ministry of Education support for the use of one or more of the 15 selected indigenous local languages as the medium of instruction (e.g. Gonja, Ga, Akan, Ewe, or Dagbani) from preschool to lower primary levels 1–3. English then becomes the medium of instruction in the upper primary levels and beyond (Education Ministry, Ghana, 2004, pp. 27–28).

The Ministry of Health in Ghana does not have such a clearly defined policy regarding language use in healthcare delivery. Clinics and hospitals throughout Ghana's 16 regions use the local languages according to the location, particularly in rural communities. In more urban areas, local languages and English are more usually combined to provide healthcare services in hospitals and clinics.

In terms of governance, English is the official language used by the executive, the judiciary, and the legislature in their business and correspondence, as well as at official ceremonies. The Ghanaian Constitution of 1969 stipulated that all members of parliament must speak, read, and comprehend English. However, in an effort to increase 'grassroots participation' in government and to encourage non-English speakers to run for elective office, the 1992 Constitution Consultative Assembly on the Constitution recommended removing this requirement. Consequently, local languages are currently permitted and used alongside the English language in parliamentary proceedings and can also be used in court with the assistance of a translator or an interpreter (Reilly et al., 2022). At the highest levels of government and private industries, companies, banks, and other corporate institutions, English is used for formal discussions and presentations at meetings. However, local languages are used with customers who have limited English proficiency. Staff members use local languages, such as Akan, Ewe, and Ga, in informal situations and unofficial transactions in the workplace.

Religious meetings and events in rural communities (Christian, Islamic, and traditional) groups tend to be conducted in local or indigenous whereas in urban areas, the local languages are more often used alongside English. Traditional and cultural gatherings, celebrations, and ceremonies such as marriages and festivals usually take place within communities, and so local languages common to the majority would be used.

Both English and local languages are used in the media. However, many people rely on the indigenous language radio stations across all the 16 regions in Ghana as their primary source of information. Akan languages are the most prevalent on Ghanaian radio, and they have assumed national significance. All printed media is produced in English.

Sign Language Policy

There has been a constitutional commitment in place in Ghana to protect the rights of people with disabilities, including deaf individuals, since 1992 (Article 29 Section 6 of the Constitution of Ghana) (Ocran, 2019), and the Persons with Disability Act (Act 715) was established in June 2006 that aims to improve the lives of people with disabilities, including deaf people, to enable them to be part of mainstream society (Asante & Sasu, 2015). Additionally, Ghana ratified the 2012 United Nations Convention on the Rights of Persons with Disabilities (UNCRPD) (Opoku-Amankwa, 2009), which highlights the right to use sign language in education, Articles 24 and 24(3) (b) and (c) also require state parties to ensure the full and equal participation of deaf people by promoting the linguistic identity of the deaf community and facilitating the learning of sign language.

Despite these commitments, no formal measures have been taken in Ghana to safeguard the rights of deaf people, specifically to support sign language learning, and promote the linguistic rights and identities of deaf communities. Ghana's official language policy, which encourages early education in children's mother tongue (their own or first language L1), does not therefore embrace the needs of young deaf children or the role of sign language in the early years (Ministry of Education, Ghana, 2004, pp. 27–28). There are no policy guidelines on the use of Ghanaian sign language as part of the curriculum in either inclusive mainstream settings or in special schools for the deaf.

The lack of resources available to research and document sign languages in use in Ghana including regional variations and local sign languages (such as the Adamorobe sign language and the Nanabin sign language) means that the rich language heritage of deaf people in Ghana is not celebrated or harnessed to promote diversity and inclusion. Deaf people in Ghana thus encounter significant barriers to participation in society. They experience difficulties in accessing quality education, employment, and healthcare in the country, and continued stigmatization, marginalization, and linguistic discrimination (Edward & Perniss, 2019). The Ghana National Association of the Deaf has urged the government to legally recognize GhSL as the official language of deaf people and to incorporate it into the Basic Education level curricula in order to promote educational inclusion and provide opportunities for young deaf children to learn in an environment where all sign language is valorized alongside other home languages.

The Multilingual Lives of Four Families

In bioecological terms, we have set out the broad (macro) multilingual context of Ghana and drawn the social and political landscape. Using this framework, we are able to see the external (exo) influences on language use and communication practices in society, and more specifically in the contexts of education, health, and among local communities (Bronfenbrenner, 2005; Bronfenbrenner & Morris, 2006). To understand the implications of this socio-cultural context for the early care and support of deaf children, and specifically family language choices and communication practices requires an insight into the daily lives and interactions of families. We have selected four case studies from our project data in order to explore the realities of this complex multilingual context for families and reflect on the language and communication challenges and opportunities for ECCE. For each of the cases, we seek to identify proximal and distal influences on multilingual language development and use. We also provide an analysis of the infrastructure, policies, cultural attitudes, and ideologies around deafness, language, and communication that shape multilingual practice, including the ways in which the use of different local spoken languages and sign languages in society are legitimized (Bourdieu 1990, 1991; Salö, 2018).

The Owusu Family (Yaw and Kofi)

The Owusu family (Yaw and Kofi) are from the Ashanti Region, which is located in the south of Ghana and shares borders with 4 of the country's 16 political regions: Brong-Ahafo to the North, the Eastern region to the east, the Central region to the south, and the Western region to the south west. The Ashanti region includes individuals from all the regions of Ghana, as well as all ethnic groups, including Akan, Ewe, Mole-Dagbane, Ga-Adangbe, and Guan. People from the other 15 regions of Ghana migrate to Ashanti to look for affordable living and work, so the region is also home to nearly all of Ghana's languages. The Akan languages (Asante Twi, Fante, and Akuapem Twi) are the dominant indigenous languages, but Asante Twi is widely spoken and primarily used for traditional events, church services, and other ceremonial purposes, and is the medium of instruction from preschool through lower primary 1–3 in government schools. The English language is used as the medium of instruction at the upper primary, junior high, and senior high school levels, and Asante Twi is then taught as a subject.

The family resides in an urban community in the Ashanti region where the vast majority of residents are Asantes (natives of the Ashanti Region) and where Asante Twi is the predominant language used for day-to-day economic and business activities. The other minority groups in the region (who may speak Fante, Ewe, Dagomba, Frafra, Hausa, or Ga) learn Twi in order to participate in these activities but will use their respective local languages among family, local, and community encounters.

Family Owusu consists of three boys (ages 17, 15, and 11), two of whom are deaf (ages 15 and 11), respectively, and the hearing caregivers—the mother and father. In the home, Asante Twi is the spoken language used by the caregivers and other family members. Before their deaf children, Yaw and Kofi, were admitted to the school for the deaf, the mother learned some basics in GhSL with the help of the school, and she describes how this has helped

116   Care and Education of Deaf Children in Ghana

their communication. This knowledge of sign language has enabled mutual understanding.

> For instance, if the child comes home on vacation, he might ask for his towel, shoes, soap, etc., so we were taught all these things, and I also learned some of them. I am not very educated, but I could sign and understand some of the signs. So, when he comes home and asks for a towel, rice, or banku[1], I understand and fulfil his request. (Mother 1)

When communicating with their deaf children, the parents also point to things and demonstrate what they want their children to do. They also told us that when sending the deaf child on an errand, they would give them a written list in English of what they wanted the children to buy, and that this strategy worked very well for them.

> Because I don't know all the sign language, I sometimes communicate with him through gestures or actions. For instance, when he asks for a towel in sign language, I am able to show him a towel. Again, I make a sign to him if I want him to buy pepper, tomatoes, or onions for me, and he also understands me. Sometimes I try to give him an example of the item I want him to buy for me, but he will refuse that and rather prefer to write the name of the item on paper. (Mother 1)

The mother explained that when she has difficulty understanding one of her children, she sometimes pretends using gestures that she understands to give her time to think about what the child is really saying and to protect him from feeling isolated or angry. She describes how she uses this strategy to smooth communication frustrations between the children and the father, who does not know any sign language.

> Sometimes, when my deaf child tries to communicate with his father and the father is not able to understand him, he ignores the father and comes to me. Whether I understand him or not, I try to give a nod to indicate that I have understood him; if not, he will get angry with me. So that is how we communicate in the house. (Mother 1)

Despite the communication difficulties that the mother describes, she said that seeing Yaw and Kofi communicate in sign language brings her joy and she

---

[1] Banku is a traditional Ghanaian dish made from fermented maize and cassava dough.

is happy that other people in the community engage with her deaf children even though they do not know sign language.

> I get excited to see the two of them communicating in sign language. A lot of people in the community also sent him on an errand to buy water and other things through gestures or actions, but not his school's sign. (Mother 1)

The main concern that the mother shares is the need to improve her own and the family's signing skills to facilitate more successful communication and ensure that Yaw and Kofi's time at home from school is happy. She acknowledges that they need external help with this.

> I am not good enough at sign language to communicate well with the children. If we can get someone who will teach all my family members sign language so that when they come from school, we can also communicate with them effectively, it is not helpful if we are not able to communicate well with our deaf children. They will also not be happy if they cannot communicate with family members when they come back from school. (Mother 1)

This complex, multilingual situation presents challenges for the caregivers as well as the deaf children. There is the potential to establish a supportive language environment in that sign language is valorized in the context of the school for the deaf, and the mother has been able to benefit from some intervention. However, sign language support is not consistently available from the school, it has not reached other family members, and there is no other access to sign language tuition and support. The school and home communication environments are very estranged. Schools for the deaf in Ghana use GhSL, and written English for teaching purposes, although different local languages may be used among the teaching and caregiving staff outside the classroom depending on the region. This family speaks the dominant and administrative language of the region at home, which the children do not learn at school, and although they use written English for some of their communication with Yaw and Kofi, this use is minimal. The mother recognizes that her children may feel isolated when returning home at the weekend and in school holidays because the family and community do not know their 'school signs'.

Families of deaf children do not have the agency to solve these issues in their day-to-day interactions. The problems reside with the enactment of the disability legislation and inclusive education policy that would enhance the visibility of GhSL and the availability of GhSL tuition to caregivers. Further, the language policy in schools for the deaf (GhSL and English) is at odds with the language policy in mainstream schools, where local languages are supported and valorized at least in the primary stages. GhSL thus has limited social capital outside of the school for the deaf environment, and the children's home languages used by their parents and siblings are not valorized within the school for the deaf environment. This is a disempowering situation for all family members, and isolating for the deaf children.

The Dazie Family (Ato)

The Dazie family is from the Central region, which is one of Ghana's 16 administrative regions and is bordered by the Ashanti and Eastern regions to the North, the Western region to the west, Greater Accra to the east, and the Gulf of Guinea to the south. The Central region has the third-highest population and includes people from all 16 regions and all ethnic groups in Ghana, including the Akan, Ewe, Mole-Dagbane, Ga-Adangbe, and Guan.

The Dazie family lives in an urban community where Fante and Effutu are the dominant spoken languages, but where a number of other minority languages are used (including Twi, Ewe, Dagomba, Frafa, Hausa Ga, and English). Fante is one of the most commonly used Akan languages (Asante Twi, Akuapem Twi, and Fante) and the most widely spoken language in this community. Effutu is more commonly spoken in coastal areas among fishing communities. Both Fante and Effutu are the predominant languages used for day-to-day economic and social activities by the majority, who will switch to their local language (Twi, Ewe, Dagomba, Frafra, Hausa Ga, among others) as appropriate in family and community encounters. In the government schools, Fante is the medium of instruction from preschool to lower primary 1–3, after which time English becomes the medium of instruction and Fante is taught as a subject.

The family comprises a mother who is hearing and three children (ages 3, 7, and 10 years), the oldest of whom is deaf. The deaf child, Ato, is enrolled in an inclusive school in the community where they live, which accommodates deaf children by providing an inclusive curriculum and sign language interpreters. Ato is a day student who walks 10–15 minutes every day from home to school.

In this household, both Fante and Effutu languages are spoken. Effutu is the primary language at home, and the family members switch to Fante in the presence of a third party who does not speak Effutu. The majority of people in this community can speak and understand Fante. The mother learned some sign language from a local church and frequently combines GhSL signs with spoken Fante, but as she explains, she is the only family member who signs.

> I was lucky to get a white man who is a Jehovah's Witness at town hall to teach me some sign language, but not all. So, I am able to communicate with him in sign language. He corrects me with the right signs when I make mistakes. But his siblings are not able to communicate with him in sign language. They play and talk to him as a hearing person. (Mother 2)

The mother reports that when she does not understand some of the things that her son signs, he will write down in English what he is trying to say. She finds this very helpful.

> He uses sign language, but when I am not understanding him well, he writes on a piece of paper to tell me what he meant. (Mother 2)

She also uses gestures and demonstrations to make herself understood.

> Sometimes I give him the broom, and he will understand that he has to sweep. (Mother 2)

> The surrounding community communicates with Ato using spoken language and does not accommodate his deafness in any way. The mother must therefore act as a mediator to ensure mutual understanding. (Mother 2)

> The community communicates with him in the same way as it communicates with hearing people (spoken language), but he asks me for clarification when he does not understand what they are saying to him." For instance, if they shout and call his name (Ato), he will turn and ask me what they are saying if he doesn't hear them. (Mother 2)

The main carer in this family is a single mother who is separated from the father of the deaf child. In Ghana, it is common for caregivers to be single parents, either as a result of teenage pregnancy, the death of a spouse, health issues, or external family and/or tribal issues and disputes. This creates challenges for the sole carer, such as those experienced by this mother. One of these challenges relates to the financial burden of caring for her child on a precarious income derived from petty trading and with only occasional financial assistance from the father.

A second issue is that of moral education, which in Ghana is assumed to come from the father for boys and the mother for girls. The heavily gendered roles associated with childcare and the running of a house extend to responsibilities for discipline (father) and for household chores (mother). This may be why the mother experiences difficulties managing the behaviour of her child in the absence of a male authoritative figure.

Ato is profoundly deaf and not able to access the spoken languages of the home (Fante or Effutu). Sign language is his preferred mode of communication, and he and his mother had the opportunity to learn the GhSL through the Jehovah's Witness church before he started school. In Ghana, the church is an important aspect of people's lives, and as well as offering spiritual guidance, the church also seeks to provide physical and emotional support to community members. For this reason, the Jehovah's Witnesses and other churches, such as the Church of Christ, have made a commitment to ensuring that deaf people can fully participate in church life through GhSL and have made it their mandate to train their members to act as sign language interpreters for the deaf. The Jehovah's Witness church has an established practice of offering GhSL support to deaf individuals and their families as part of their mission to spread the gospel. This support has facilitated smooth communication between Ato and his mother.

In school, Ato uses GhSL and other gestures to communicate, though the school has access to the Fante, Effutu, and English languages. The school does not include Ato during class hours for the learning and writing of the Fante language in the school because his deafness will not permit him to hear the sounds of the Fante language. He has a trained sign language interpreter paid by the government to ensure his educational inclusion. The sign language interpreter also trains the hearing people in the school so that they can interact with Ato in GhSL in the school. Some of the teachers in the schools are already special educators and could communicate in GhSL with Ato. This has made Ato's being in an inclusive school not a challenging situation for him at all.

The Boateng Family (David)

The family Boateng (David) is from the Greater Accra region of Ghana, which is one of the most populous regions in Ghana, along with Ashanti, and is home to people from all 16 regions and all ethnic groups in Ghana. The primary indigenous languages spoken in Greater Accra are Ga and Dangme, but the region is home to nearly all of the country's spoken languages. (This has made the Ga language gain popularity as a second language among some Ghanaians, as traders use it for business and communication).

This family resides in an urban community in Greater Accra where Asante Twi, and Ga are the primary spoken languages for day-to-day economic activities. Other spoken languages (Fante, Frafra, Hausa, Nzema, and Dagaree, among others) are used with other speakers in family and local community encounters. During festivals and traditional events, Ga or Dangme are spoken. The medium of instruction from preschool through lower primary 1–3 in government schools is Ga or Dangme, depending on the ethnic group of a community, until upper primary level, when English becomes the medium of instruction and Ga or Dangme are taught as subjects.

The family comprises two hearing parents and three children (ages 17, 12, and 8), the eldest of whom (David) is deaf. David has some residual hearing, so he can hear and use speech in some situations, but he does not have full access to spoken language and is learning sign language at school. David attends a school for the deaf in Ghana, therefore, the main language used in the school is GhSL among students and staff; however, among teaching and non-teaching staff, English, Asante Twi, Ewe, and Ga, among any of the indigenous languages, are used for communicating. Because it is a special school for the deaf, none of the indigenous languages are taught and written as a subject in the school, with the exception of English. The family uses Asante Twi and English to communicate at home. No one has learned any sign language, and it is not used in the home. David and his mother interact in both Twi and English, using gestures, demonstrations, and pointing to facilitate understanding.

> We have been talking the normal way. Sometimes, when you talk, he hears what you are saying. And David himself can sometimes say something that we hear in the house. He can call Afia, the senior sister, and Ama, but it's just communication like this that he can't do, though he does hear some of the words. (Mother 3)

The family also uses gestures, pointing, and written English to make themselves understood, as well as tapping or hand waving to attract attention. When they send David on an errand or want to provide him with a description of something, they write in English or draw a few items on paper. When David does not understand certain words spoken in the Twi language, the family switches to English or vice versa.

> We don't sign, but we do talk to him. So, if he doesn't understand, he wants us to write. Sometimes he himself, when he wants to tell me something, will just bring a pen and paper and write it down, and then I will know that he said this or that. (Mother 3)

122   Care and Education of Deaf Children in Ghana

Also, David imitates his mother's actions and behaviour to do the same or gives responses based on the actions of the other family members.

> He'll sit there and watch us. When we are laughing, he will also laugh. He doesn't hear what we are saying. (Mother 3)

Although David has some residual hearing, he is enrolled in one of the schools for the deaf in the Eastern Region of Ghana, and he can communicate in GhSL. His family members do not have an interest in learning the GhSL. Their experience is that David was hearing and communicating in spoken language in his early years, and they continue to hope and pray to God that he will be able to do so again. They communicate with him in Asante Twi, with the addition of pointing, gestures, and the use of written English. As a result of this mixed exposure, David is developing multilingual and multimodal ways of communicating (GhSL, spoken language Asante Twi, and gestures) with a range of people.

The Opoku Family (Dora)

The Opoku family is from the Eastern region of Ghana, which is one of Ghana's 16 administrative regions and borders on Lake Volta to the east, Bono East Region and Ashanti Region to the north, Ashanti Region to the west, and South-Central Region and Greater Accra Region to the south. It is one of the most populous regions after Greater Accra and Ashanti. Akans are the predominant and indigenous inhabitants of the Eastern region. The Akan languages (Asante Twi, Akuapem Twi), as well as Ewe, Krobo, Hausa, Anum, and English, are spoken in this region, as are Fante, Dagomba, Frafra Hausa, and Ga. Twi, Krobo, and Anum are the most widely spoken languages in churches, during traditional activities, and in day-to-day business activities.

The family resides in an urban community in the Eastern region where Asante Twi is the predominant language used for social and economic activities on a daily basis and Akuapem Twi is used as the medium of instruction in government schools from preschool to lower primary 1–3, when English is used as the medium of instruction and Akuapem Twi is taught as a subject.

The family consists of a mother and father who are hearing and two children (5 and 9 years old), one of whom is deaf: Dora, who is 9 years old. Dora goes to a mainstream school in the local community. In the family home, Asante Twi is spoken by all the family members. None of the members of the family use GhSL. All family members communicate with Dora at home using spoken Asante Twi accompanied by gestures (pointing, actions, and air drawings) and have developed strategies to establish attention. To communicate with Dora, they also use gestures, demonstrations, pointing, or drawing. Dora has picked up some spoken Twi and tries to repeat certain words and names of some family members in the house, though her speech is not very intelligible. The father describes how communication takes place.

> When you speak and she looks attentively at your face, she is able to understand what you are conveying to her. At times, when you speak, she is able to say the words after you, but they may not come out clearly. When she is facing you and you point at her to bring you something, she is able to undertake such tasks. She is able to call out the names of the children in the house, the mother, and myself. Though they may not come out clearly, you will see she is calling out names. (Father 1).

The family members are keen that Dora learns to use spoken language but acknowledge the use of manual signs—such as drawing pictures in the air—to support communication, albeit not the 'prescribed sign language'.

> She plays with friends. She plays 'ampe' most often. She knows when it's her turn in the 'ampe' to move forward and compete with the opposing friend. At times, the friends use unorthodox signs to communicate with her. (Father 1)

The father shared his concern over not being able to communicate with Dora and his wish for ease of communication with her.

> For now, it's my desire that there will be smooth communication between us, understanding each other well, but it is not so. (Father 1).

He is particularly keen that if she learns sign language, her the spoken language skills that she is developing will not be eroded.

> My prayer is that she doesn't lose the few words she is able to speak on her return from school. If she signs to Kwame and Akwasi who are her siblings, I would not know what she means. (Father 1).

The caregivers believe that Dora's use of single spoken words and names of family members is an indication that she will eventually be able to communicate fully in spoken language. They therefore prefer to continue to use Asante Twi with her and encourage others to do the same to support her language development. The caregivers do not see the need to enrol Dora in a school for the deaf or for her to learn GhSL, believing that she could even lose the spoken language that she has by doing so. Though the father does incorporate the use of gesture, demonstration, pointing, or drawing in his communication with Dora, his preference is to encourage her use of spoken language (Asante Twi). This approach is common among many families of deaf children in Ghana who are unsure about the role and use of GhSL and are perhaps ill informed about the consequences of this, and who, although they use multimodal strategies, do not always recognize their value and potential for the support of spoken and sign language development.

Reflections on Family Experience

These case studies provide rich examples of the multilingual context of ECCE for deaf children in Ghana and bring specific sociolinguistic issues to the fore. Deaf children in Ghana are born into a multilingual culture where, at home and in the surrounding community, multiple spoken languages are used alongside spoken and written English. There is clearly a need in a country like Ghana, where a number of different languages are in use, for information about early childhood deafness and support and intervention processes to be available in different languages and in different formats, such as on paper or digitally on websites that can be accessed through mobile phones or computers.

Most deaf children are born to hearing parents who usually speak more than one indigenous language in the home and community context and who also use spoken and written English with their deaf children alongside different forms of visual communication. For most, this comprises a combination of individual GhSL signs, home signs, writing, drawing, gestures (pointing, actions, mime, demonstration), and touch. Early support in this context needs to centre on visual communication and specifically on enhancing and legitimizing the resources and strategies that caregivers already intuitively deploy in communication with their deaf children.

Deaf children and their hearing caregivers only encounter GhSL in connection with the school for the deaf context, and this is sometimes not until their child is primary school age, 6 years old or more, because most of the deaf children in Ghana are identified late, which delays their enrolment in school. (However, age 4 years is the ideal age for both hearing and deaf children to be in primary school). Beyond this context, there are no fluent models of GhSL in the home or the wider community, very limited access to GhSL, and the indigenous languages of the home are not used in the school context. Whilst deaf children are born into a rich multilingual culture, they thus experience an impoverished language learning experience where they are excluded from the multilingual communication practices of family and community. Caregivers are physically and culturally disconnected from the school for the deaf and do not benefit from supportive partnerships with deaf adult role models, mentors, and other professionals.

In developing early support in this context, there is a need for a full understanding of the different written and spoken languages in play in deaf children's lives and an analysis of the most accessible and practicable communication possibilities as fitting with the family language practices and needs of the child. This has to be undertaken with an awareness of the wider social–cultural dynamics surrounding language use and deafness, where sign language is seen as separate from the multilingual culture of the society and associated with minoritized individuals and communities. Whilst there are increasing initiatives to legitimize and valorize local languages, this does not extend to GhSL. In this context, families have limited choice or agency about their language or communication approach. Models of early support that assume family agency in 'inviting families to examine and potentially transform their own language ideologies' (Mitchiner & Batamula, 2021) are therefore not contextually relevant.

The day-to-day or proximal communication issues for families can be seen as a product of more macros, societal structures around language, education, disability, and inclusion. We might view these interrelated factors in Bourdieusian terms, taking his notion of 'field' to denote the infrastructure, policies, cultural attitudes, and ideologies around deafness, language, and communication that become socialized in 'habitus', that is a way of thinking and being—and in this case, approaches to caregiving—that is the result of social conditioning (Bourdieu, 1990, 1991). There is an interaction here. Caregivers are disempowered by the disjuncture between home and school communication but at the same time propagate the separate 'linguistic markets' of home, where the use of sign language is not valorized, and school, where its use is legitimized (O'Brien, 2021). That said, caregivers do not have the agency themselves to bring sign language into the multilingual repertoire of their homes and communities. This would require a change at a macro or societal level in the way in which disability in general and deafness specifically are viewed in society and recognition of GhSL in educational policy.

Reflection on these case studies and analysis of the day-to-day and wider contextual realities point to ways in which current guidelines and recommendations around deaf ECCE need to stretch and reconfigure to include different global multilingual and low- and middle-income countries contexts, such as Ghana. Specifically, an understanding of the extent to which multilingualism for these families is shaped by societal and cultural structures and ideologies would shift the emphasis from purely 'lingual' interventions to the wider social actions that legitimize sign language use as part of local multilingual language practices.

Adult Reflections on Growing Up in a Multilingual Context

When we asked our deaf colleagues about their experience of growing up with a hearing loss in such a multilingual society, their reflections echoed the fact of a rich spoken language environment, the difficulties of access to this as well as the dissonance between the home and school language environments, and the global difficulties of access to communication and sign language support and recognition. **Linda** talks about her experience of the use of three spoken languages in her life before encountering and learning sign language at high school.

Being born into a typical Ghanaian home where communication mainly depends on our local language, it was a wonderful experience being able to converse freely with people, whether in school, at special events, or at home. Losing my hearing at the age of 8 through an illness indeed put a toll on the family as they strived harder to ensure I received the required education and support. In the home, Twi and Fante are the two local dialects spoken among us, with a bit of fluency. My everyday conversations depend on lip-reading and written texts. After a clinical diagnosis determined I was profoundly deaf in both ears, it was one of the most difficult moments for me. Close family contacts were my speech translators. It was very frustrating for them as well because they had to double-pronounce words for me before I could comprehend their meaning.

Within the school environment, speaking English was compulsory, so anyone found using a vernacular language would be punished. During those times, I was enrolled in a normal basic school before my hearing loss incident occurred; however, my family had no idea there existed a special school for the deaf and hard of hearing, so I was encouraged to continue from there until I completed basic six. Classroom instruction was challenging, and I had to struggle to level up with my peers in academics. I used gestures and speeches in every conversation I engaged in in the classroom and outside.

After completing Junior high school, I chanced upon the opportunity to learn sign language before getting enrolled at the school for the deaf in 2018. That is where I felt included in being part of a community that has used a similar form of communication until now. In the community setting where I usually mingle with various individuals with whom I am familiar, I engage them in one-on-one conversations, which often assist me in pronunciation or slips of the tongue. While in the deaf community, I use sign language.

Richard also used four different spoken languages before he lost his hearing and describes the issues of having access to sign language interpreting in different language communities. He talks about the benefits as well as the challenges of living in a multilingual community as a deaf person.

I lost my hearing when I was 17 years old. Before then, I could already speak four local (Ghanaian) languages. The local language I used the most was the Ga language instead of the Ewe language, being my mother tongue. However, when I lost my hearing, I felt completely excluded due to communication barriers.

First, I was not, and even today, I am not, a good lip reader. I had on several occasions attempted to practice lip reading, but with no success. The issue was that lip movement by people differs from person to person. On top of this, I find it challenging to look directly into people's faces for a long time. Beside this, on many occasions, I reiterate the person's spoken words wrongly. For instance, the words 'spoon and sponge'. While the speaker says 'spoon' I often misread the lip as 'sponge'. Sometimes, some people do not see this as a challenge on my part. They would laugh so loudly that I would get pissed off, and I felt it would be better off not trying lip reading at all.

Secondly, my degree of hearing loss was clinically diagnosed as profound (above 80DbHl in both ears). I have had several tests at many places, and all the audiologists commented that the cochlear implant is my last solution. As a result, I do not benefit from hearing aids. Within multilingual communities, one of my biggest challenges is accessing sign language interpreters for a specific language at a time. For instance, my family speaks the Ewe language. The available sign language interpreters within the community where I live are either Akan or Akuapem speaking people. There was a time when I had to contact an sign language interpreter from another region after a total of over 13 hours of travelling just to assist me at a family meeting. Some people have argued that when we deaf people gather to create a community of deaf people, we are contributing to social segregation. Living in a hearing community has its own positive side. Living in a multilingual community improves not only one's social inclusion but also improves opportunities and the ability to perform various functions such as access to employment, education,

128   Care and Education of Deaf Children in Ghana

and quality health care. Nonetheless, there are times when I perform the function of a sign language interpreter, interpreting sign language into spoken languages. Having an extensive knowledge of sign language and other oral linguistic skills, I do not, at times, see myself as having a disability within a multilingual community because I'm able to share my opinions without hindrance.

Derrick also talks about the experience of growing up using multiple languages and how he has developed different multimodal strategies to communicate with different members of the family, and in the community. Whilst he prefers to use spoken languages with hearing people, he emphasizes the importance of text and visual communication, including gestures, to facilitate successful interaction.

I use multimodal communication due to the multilingual and cultural contexts in which I live. My father is an Akyem, and my mother is an Assin. My wife is a Fante. I lived with my grandparents in Akim Soabe in the Kwaebibirem Municipality in the Eastern Region during my childhood years. I had my junior high education in Accra, where we lived among Ga people. Thus, I can speak three languages: Twi, English, and Ga. Therefore, the people I interact with on a daily basis come from different cultural and linguistic backgrounds. Thus, I employ different communication modes depending on whom I am communicating with and the circumstances. I communicate with my wife through simultaneous communication; we sign and speak at the same time. I always communicate with my daughter through speech, although I sometimes teach her simple GhSL vocabulary. I also communicate with my parents and in-laws through speech. When I visit my uncles and aunts, we use speech and writing to communicate.

I use speech as expressive communication, writing and lip-reading as receptive communication. I use the same method when I visit offices, such as the bank. My lip reading is not always accurate, especially when I meet new people whose lip movements, I am unfamiliar with. I use gestures too, especially when buying items or using public transport. Since I speak normally, as hearing people do, I have no problem with expression; the difficulty lies in reception. When I ask about the price of an item, I am sometimes able to lip-read the amount quoted by the seller. In cases where I am not able to understand what they say, I ask them to use their fingers to indicate the amount. For example, raising all five fingers to indicate GHC5 [GHC is the abbreviation of Ghanaian cedi, the official currency of the Republic of Ghana] or closing all the left and right fingers together to indicate GHC10 Sometimes, a seller would show me a sample of the money that corresponds to the amount of the item. For example, a seller may show me GHC50 (to mean that the item costs the same amount) or show me GHC50 and then gesture 'two' with his fingers to show that the item costs GHC100 (2 times GHC50). I am currently teaching at a regular school. I use speech during lessons and lip-read responses from my students. Where I am unable to get what they say, I ask them to write their responses or questions. I communicate with colleague teachers through speech and writing. I use the same method of communication at church. In the larger community, I use speech and lip-reading. At the university, where sign language interpreters are readily available, I use them when going to offices or talking to lecturers who do not know sign language. I always use sign language when I am in the company of deaf people, such as when I meet deaf friends, visit the Ghana National Association of the Deaf office, or a school for the deaf.

Reflections on Individual Experience

These reflections highlight the complexities involved in navigating the cultural and sometimes political influences on the use of local and official spoken languages that are experienced by deaf people in a multilingual country such as Ghana. Their comments also demonstrate the value placed on the local languages in family and social life and indicate the personal importance of connection to these languages.

The different and multiple ways of engaging in deaf–hearing communication that are described by Linda, Richard, and Derrick illustrate the communication flexibility and language awareness that they have had to deploy in all aspects of their daily lives. It is worth noting that both Derrick and Linda became deaf in their early adult lives, which is why they have been able to continue to confidently use spoken language. Their communication dexterity and the successful interaction that this has afforded in their lives underline the importance of maximizing the visual aspect of spoken communication (speech-reading) and the accessibility to communication provided by the use of co-speech gestures, signs, and text.

Evident from each of these reflections is that the onus to make communication work in social and formal settings (such as booking a sign language interpreter for a local language) is on the individual deaf person, the family, and sometimes the community. The communication challenges experienced by Linda, Richard, and Derrick would have been less individually burdensome in a context where access is viewed as a societal responsibility that is supported by the appropriate infrastructure, resources, and legislation.

As observed in the comments from families, the language world of the school for the deaf is at once fully inclusive and facilitative in that it provides a sense of belonging and community and access to easy communication with other deaf-signing people. At the same time, this is an exclusive experience in that it is not easily shared by hearing families and friends. This dilemma is heightened in this context where the language landscapes of mainstream and special schools do not match (local languages are not used in special schools for the deaf and sign languages are not used in mainstream schools) and where wider opportunities for exposure to sign language use and tuition are limited beyond the provision offered by local deaf community and the church, which in larger cities sometimes takes on the role of family.

Conclusion

ECCE programming, that has as its core focus the development of language and communication, needs to be sensitive to and inclusive of the social, cultural, and linguistic practices of multilingual societies. What we learn from this work is that the ways in which different languages, including sign languages, are either valorized or marginalized in deaf children's lives impact interaction at the proximal level (home, family, community) on a daily basis as well as on education, employment, and wider opportunities for participation and autonomy in society. This implies the need to revisit guidelines and models of 'best ECCE practice' that assume the presence of one spoken language that is consistent and non-contested across home, school, and wider social contexts and to further the science of ECCE to include multilingual communities and minorities. Most importantly, a shift in the flow of knowledge around ECCE, that has traditionally been from North to South, is required to drive the development of contextually appropriate methodologies, research questions, and theoretical perspectives.

References

Akoto, O. Y. (2018). Language choice and institutional identity: a study of the mottos of Ghanaian educational institutions, *WORD, 64*(3), 177–190. doi:10.1080/00437956.2018.1490421

Asante, L. A., & Sasu, A. (2015). The Persons with Disability Act, 2006 (Act 715) of the Republic of Ghana: The law, omissions and recommendations. *Journal of Law, Policy and Globalization 36*:62–68.

Bourdieu, P. (1990). *The logic of practice*. Stanford University Press.

Bourdieu, P. (1991). *Language and symbolic power*. Harvard University Press.

Bronfenbrenner, U. (2005). *Making human beings human: Bioecological perspectives on human development*. Sage.

Bronfenbrenner, U., & Morris, P. A. (2006). The bioecological model of human development. In W. Damon & R. M. Lerner (Eds.), *Handbook of child psychology: Theoretical models of human development* (pp. 793–828). Wiley.

Brons, M., Knoors, H., & Marschark, M. (2019). Deaf education beyond the Western World: Knowledge exchange, best practices, and challenges. In H. Knoors, M. Brons, & M. Marschark (Eds.), *Deaf education beyond the Western World* (pp. 399–448). Oxford University Press.

Cannon, J. E., Guardino, C., & Paul, P. V. (Eds.). (2022). *Deaf and hard of hearing multilingual learners: Foundations, strategies, and resources*. Routledge

Cannon, J., & Marx, N. (2023). Scoping review of methodologies across language studies with children. In *Critical perspectives on plurilingualism in deaf education* (pp. 195–216). Multilingual Matters.

Collyer, F. M. (2018). Global patterns in the publishing of academic knowledge: Global North, global South. *Current Sociology, 66*(1), 56–73.

Crowe, K., & Guiberson, M. (2019). Evidence-based interventions for learners who are deafand/or multilingual: A systematic quality review. *American Journal of Speech-Language Pathology, 28*(3), 964–983.

Eberhard, D. M., Simons, G. F., & Fennig, C. D. (Eds.). (2020) *Ethnologue: Languages of the World*. 23rd edition. SIL International. Online version: http://www.ethnologue.com.

Edward, M., & Akanlig-Pare, G. (2021). Sign language research in Ghana: An overview of indigenous and foreign-based sign languages. *Journal of African Languages and Literatures* (2), 114–137.

Edward, M., & Perniss, P. (2019). *Comparing Ghanaian (GSL) and Adamorobe (AdaSL) Sign Languages* Presentation at the 13th Theoretical Issues in Sign Language Studies (Hamburg, 27 September 2019).

Ghana Statistical Service (2021), *2021 Population and Housing Census: National Analytical Report*. Ghana Statistical Service.

Guerini, F. (2008) *Language alternation strategies in multilingual settings. A case study: Ghanaian immigrants in northern Italy*. Peter Lang.

Kabay, S., Wolf, S., & Yoshikawa, H. (2017). 'So that his mind will open': Parental perceptions of early childhood education in urbanizing Ghana. *International Journal of Educational Development, 57*, 44–53.

Kluge, A., (2000). The Gbe language varieties of West Africa: A quantitative analysis of lexical and grammatical features. [MA thesis] Cardiff University.

Kusters, A. (2015). *Deaf space in Adamorobe*: An ethnographic study of a village in Ghana: Gallaudet University Press.

Marshall, S., & Moore, D. (2018). Plurilingualism amid the panoply of lingualisms: Addressing critiques and misconceptions in education. *International Journal of Multilingualism, 15*(1), 19–34.

Ministry of Education, Ghana. (2004). *White paper on the report of the education reform review committee* (pp. 27–28). Accra: Government of Ghana.

Ministry of Education, Ghana. (2004). *White paper on the report of the education reform review committee*. Accra: Government of Ghana.

Mitchiner, J., & Batamula, C. (2021). Family language policy and planning: Families with deaf children. In K. Snoddon & J. C. Weber (Eds.), *Critical perspectives on plurilingualism in deaf education* (pp. 195–216). Multilingual Matters.

Ndiribe, M. O., & Aboh, S. C. (2022). Multilingualism and marginalisation: A Nigeria diversity approach. *International Journal of Multilingualism, 19*(1), 1–15.

Nyst, V. (2010). Sign language varieties in West Africa In D. Brentari (Ed.), *Sign languages* (pp.405–432). Cambridge University Press

O'Brien, D. (2021). Bourdieu, plurilingualism and sign languages in the UK. In K. Snoddon & J. C. Weber (Eds.), *Critical perspectives on plurilingualism in deaf education* (pp. 60–80). Multilingual Matters.

Ocran, J. (2019) Exposing the protected: Ghana's disability laws and the rights of disabled people. *Disability & Society, 34*(4), 663–668, DOI:10.1080/09687599.2018.1556491

Opoku-Amankwa, K. (2009). English-only language-in-education policy in multilingual classrooms in Ghana. *Language, Culture and Curriculum, 22*(2), 121–135.

Reilly, C., ResCue, E. & Chavula, J.J. (2022), Language policy in Ghana and Malawi: Differing approaches to multilingualism in education. *Journal of the British Academy,10*(s4): 69–95. https://doi.org/10.5871/jba/010s4.069

Republic of Ghana. (1992). *1992 Constitution of the Republic of Ghana*. Accra, Ghana:Republic of Ghana.

Republic of Ghana. (2006). *Persons with Disability Act (Act 715)*. Accra: Republic of Ghana.

Salö, L. (2018). Thinking about language with Bourdieu: Pointers for social theory in the language sciences. *Sociolinguistic Studies, 12*(3-4), 523–543.

Singal, N., & Muthukrishna, N. (2014). Education, childhood and disability in countries of the South–Re-positioning the debates. *Childhood, 21*(3), 293–307.

UN General Assembly, *Convention on the Rights of Persons with Disabilities*, 13 December2006, A/RES/61/106, Annex I.

World Health Organization. (2018). *Deafness and hearing loss*. Geneva. http://www.who.int/en/news- room/fact-sheets/detail/deafness-and-hearing-loss.

Yoshinaga-Itano, C. (2003). From screening to early identification and intervention: Discovering predictors to successful outcomes for children with significant hearing loss. *Journal of Deaf Studies and Deaf Education, 8*(1), 11–30.

Yoshinaga-Itano, C. (2014). Principles and guidelines for early intervention after confirmation that a child is deaf or hard of hearing. *Journal of Deaf Studies and Deaf Education, 19*(2), 143–175.

8
The Role of Professionals

Yaw Nyadu Offei and Linda Amanvida Gibbah

Introduction

Multi-professional collaboration in the early care and education of deaf children is essential for ensuring better overall development outcomes for deaf children and the well-being of their caregivers (Störbeck & Young, 2016). Effective partnerships among professionals are also critical in building strong communities that can enable deaf children to grow up into autonomous citizens who can fully participate in society (Alexa et al., 2016).

In this chapter, we discuss multi-professionals' involvement and collaboration in the early care and education of young deaf children and how these partnerships impact the provision of support services for the children in Ghana. We draw on interviews that we undertook with 24 clinicians as part of the research project work and discuss the insights gained from these data in terms of the role of hearing health practitioners and the influences on their practice. We discuss the opportunities and constraints of collaboration in this context, and the implications for the development of quality early childhood care and education (ECCE) for deaf children and their families in Ghana.

We define 'clinician' as a member of staff from either of the health centres that participated our study: the Centre for Hearing and Speech Services (CHSS) at the University of Education, Winneba and the Salvation Army Rehabilitation Centre at Agona Duakwa.

To provide further perspectives on multi-professional support we include the reflections of one deaf team members and a contributor to the project, Linda. She shared her lived experience of growing up as a deaf

---

Yaw Nyadu Offei and Linda Amanvida Gibbah, *The Role of Professionals* In: *The Early Care and Education of Deaf Children in Ghana*. Edited by: Ruth Swanwick, Daniel Fobi, Yaw Offei, and Alexander Oppong, Oxford University Press. © Yaw Nyadu Offei and Linda Amanvida Gibbah 2024. DOI: 10.1093/oso/9780192872272.003.0008

child in Ghana and her educational journey by providing a signed story that she translated herself. She also reflects on her current role as a mentor who is supporting deaf children and their families in Ghana and showing leadership by demonstrating the potential of deaf participation and leadership in ECCE.

The chapter concludes with a discussion of the implications of what has been learned from the project work about the potential of multi-professional early support and intervention. We propose ways in which this aspect of early support can be developed to improve support practices in Ghana and other African contexts with parallel early support issues and priorities.

Early identification, appropriate and timely intervention, and parental support are understood to be essential for the successful educational outcomes for young deaf children and the well-being of caregivers (Bredekamp, 2020; Moeller et al., 2013). The authors stressed the need for a multi-disciplinary approach to service delivery for young deaf children and their families. Importantly, the start of the process must be initiated by the parents and as we found from our interviews with caregivers (Chapter 6), this is problematic and burdensome given the costs associated with visits to clinics and lack of confidence on the part of parents to disclose deafness in the family and engage with the clinical context.

The Research Context

We have established in earlier sections of the book that Ghana has a developing infrastructure for coordinated education and health services for deaf people. Further, Ghana has a developing sign language (GhSL) and an active association of the deaf (GNAD) that campaigns to reduce the social isolation and marginalization of deaf people (Kusters, 2015; Nyst, 2012). However, the early support of young deaf children and their caregivers is an unmet need (Oppong & Fobi, 2019). Ghana does not have a national newborn hearing screening programme and, this has contributed significantly to late diagnosis of childhood deafness. Children are often identified with a hearing loss as late as 8 years old (Oppong and Fobi, 2019). Additionally, there are no early years (0–4 years old), programmes for deaf children although there are schools in Ghana that offer language and communication support to families. Many parents, particularly those living in rural and remote communities are not sufficiently informed about the kinds and levels of support available for their deaf children (Blazer et al., 2016).

The Research Project

Participants

Twenty-four professional participants agreed to participate in interviews as part of our ECCE research activities in Ghana (see Table 8.1). This comprised 13 males and 11 females selected from two health facilities and three educational settings. Our participants included head teachers, service managers, teachers of the deaf, audiologists, clinical technicians, volunteers, national service personnel,[1] support staff, and administrators. Of the nine clinicians that took part in the interviews, six were from the CHSS of the University of Education Winneba, and three were from the Salvation Army Rehabilitation Centre at Agona Duakwa. All the clinical participants were hearing. Of the 15 educators that took part in the interviews, five teachers including the head teacher were from the Demonstration School for the Deaf at Mampong-Akuapem, seven teachers including the head teachers were from the Ashanti School for the Deaf, Jamasi, and three teachers including the head teacher were from Savelugu School for the Deaf. All the teachers interviewed were teachers of the deaf from kindergarten one to lower primary. Three of the teachers (one from each school) were deaf.

Methodology

The original project plan was to engage participants in focus group interviews and to interview managers on a one-to-one basis. However, we adjusted our plan as a result of the Covid-19 pandemic in order to ensure compliance with national and international travel restrictions and social distancing requirements. In order to keep the research team and participants safe, we interviewed our participants online, or face-to-face on a one-on-one basis in accordance with Covid safety protocols. To achieve this, we hired conference call facilities and provided additional internet connectivity bundles for both the researchers and participants. This made it possible for mobile phone calls and WhatsApp messaging to be used for setting up, carrying out, and recording our interviews. Deaf participants were initially contacted via

---

[1] National Service is a one-year mandatory service for recent graduates of tertiary institutions in Ghana. This service provides graduates with work experience in public and private sectors, as part of their civic responsibilities. They are usually paid a non-taxable allowance at the end of every month as approved by the Ministry of Finance.

136   Care and Education of Deaf Children in Ghana

Table 8.1 Health and education participants, their roles, and work places

Participant (Clinicians and educators)	Health and Education Contexts
Part time audiologist	Centre for Hearing and Speech Services
Clinical assistant	Centre for Hearing and Speech Services
Audiologist and University Lecturer	Centre for Hearing and Speech Services
Volunteer support staff	Centre for Hearing and Speech Services
Volunteer support staff	Centre for Hearing and Speech Services
National service support staff	Centre for Hearing and Speech Services
Kindergarten (KG) 1 teacher	Mampong Demonstration School for the Deaf
Assistant head teacher	Mampong Demonstration School for the Deaf
Teacher of the deaf and house parent	Mampong Demonstration School for the Deaf
Teacher of the deaf KG2[a]	Mampong Demonstration School for the Deaf
Deaf teacher	Mampong Demonstration School for the Deaf
Head teacher	Savelugu school for the Deaf
Teacher of the deaf KG2	Savelugu school for the Deaf
Deaf teacher	Savelugu school for the Deaf
Teacher of the deaf KG2	Ashanti School for the Deaf
Head of KG department and teacher	Ashanti School for the Deaf
Teacher of the deaf	Ashanti School for the Deaf
Teacher of the deaf	Ashanti School for the Deaf
Head teacher	Ashanti School for the Deaf
Teacher and senior house parent	Ashanti School for the Deaf
Deaf teacher	Ashanti School for the Deaf
Administrator	Salvation Army Rehabilitation Centre
Rehabilitation officer and support staff	Salvation Army Rehabilitation Centre
Prosthestist [b] and support staff	Salvation Army Rehabilitation Centre

[a] In schools for the deaf, many children of 6 or 7 years of age are still in KG due to late identification and reporting.

[b] A healthcare professional who makes artificial limbs (prostheses) for people with disabilities.

text messages and WhatsApp video call and asked for their interview preference (whether face-to-face or on-line). Deaf participants in the Southern and Middle sectors opted for face to face interviews through their respective sign language interpreters and in full compliance with international Covid-19 safety protocols. We negotiated interview data and times and we provided participants with the project information sheet and consent form via email or WhatsApp as preferred. We did this at least three days before the interview schedule.

On the day of the interview, we made phone calls and/or text messages to remind the participants at least an hour prior to the planned call. During the interviews one research assistant made the phone conference call, introduced the participants and the other research assistants. We took the consent of the participants either verbally or via audio recording as appropriate. Again, we allowed time for questioning and clarifications from our participants after which the main interview itself was conducted. Each of the interviews lasted between 30–60 minutes.

Data Analysis

As for other aspects of the project we took a bioecological approach to the analysis of our interview data with practitioners. This involved a four-stage coding process and the development of a coding handbook. Our coding system was structured around the four nested systems of influence that inter-relate to affect early development, care that we have outlined in earlier chapters (Bronfrenbrenner, 2005; Bronfrenbrenner & Morris, 2006). The analysis of our data involved four stages that were completed over a six-month period. During this time, weekly meetings involving research assistants and the whole team took place on-line to review interview material and develop consensus around the interpretation of participant responses, the assignment of themes, and the identification of main and sub-themes.

Our data shows that there is a primary connect between education and health centres on the early assessment and identification of hearing loss that then opens access to educational placement that is normally in special schools. However, due to the lack of newborn screening for children in Ghana the start of the process is typically initiated by the caregivers when they suspect their children show signs of a hearing loss.

Project Findings

The Working Context of Clinicians

In our study clinicians were asked to talk to their roles when it comes to providing support for young deaf children and their parents. The clinicians stated that as part of their role, they give general advice to parents about communication and in doing so emphasize 'difference' and not 'deficiency'. Additionally, the clinicians emphasize the benefits that the use of sign language with their children will give them.

> We try to educate the parent on the need to learn the sign language so that he or
> she can communicate with the child. Because we always tell them that, the child
> will be very glad. (Clinician-Audiologist)

Clinicians also talked extensively about providing counselling and the emotional support to parents and their caregivers. Their comments underline the emphasis that they give to 'acceptance' and 'hope' and the importance of having high expectations for their child. Caregivers need this emotional support. They often arrive in clinic seeking answers having first of all sought traditional herbal treatment and support from faith organizations but with little understanding of rehabilitation and educational possibilities for their child. For many parents meeting with the clinician is their first experience of talking to someone who understands deafness and the options that are available to them. Clinicians often find themselves having to provide encouragement to parents to work with their child's needs and to be positive:

> We tell them they (the child) can attain any goal that they want to achieve whatever
> they want to be life (...) we always advise the parent they should always provide.
> This is the time the child needs them most. They should make sure they take the
> child's education very seriously, with that the child can also get to the highest level.
> (Clinician-Audiologist)

In our research the clinicians talked about the resources available to them for the clinical assessment of deaf children. They describe how their work in the clinics is hampered by lack of resources and a stable workforce. The clinicians talk about outdated and non-functional basic equipment such as audiometers tympanometers,[2] oto acoustic emission equipment, and otoscopes. They also worry about the lack of permanent trained skilled staff, the inadequacy of in-service training and their reliance on volunteers with limited training. Neither of the centres has a speech and language therapist. The resource challenges that they identified centred on the resources needed for much earlier identification and for delivering consistent intervention programmes following identification.

> Currently we do not have a speech therapist; however, from time to time we get
> volunteers, speech therapist volunteers from Germany and USA who come around
> to attend to some of the children. (Clinician)

---

[2] A tympanometer is a diagnostic tool used by hearing care professionals to test the health of the tympanic membrane (ear drum) and middle ear.

Their expression of the need for more specialized early intervention professionals and an improved identification infrastructure is echoed across sub-Saharan Africa literature (Wonkam-Tingang et al., 2021). Olusanya (2008) identifies scarce human resource as a main challenge confronting countries in the sub-Saharan context referring to the acute shortage of health workers in all specialties, against the backdrop of the fact that most of the population live in rural areas (Olusanya, 2008, p.S10).

The need for outreach services for families who are unable to travel from rural and remote communities to the clinics that are situated mainly in the cities and big towns was indeed identified as pressing issue in our research. It is in response to this need that, CHSS, has a mobile audiology ambulance— (the Hearing Assessment and Research Klinic (HARK)–which is purposefully designed for hearing screening in remote communities. Although CHSS has used the ambulance to check the hearing of about 50,000 children living in deprived areas of Ghana, there are still many communities that have not yet been reached. As supplement to the HARK, there are audiology ambulances also, at other centres in Ghana such as at the Audiology centre at the Komfo-Anokye Teaching Hospital in Kumasi and at the Korle-Bu Teaching hospital in Accra that also focus on reaching out to communities within the middle and upper parts of Ghana with hearing and ear care.

Parent–Professional Partnerships

For successful upbringing of young deaf children, a strong and mutually respectful relationship between health and education professionals and caregivers is essential (Knoors et al., 2019; Moeller et al., 2013). This first connection is usually triggered by the assessment and identification of hearing loss. Caregivers who spend most time with the child (grandparents, house helps, and friends) are usually the first to suspect hearing loss. Whilst this can confirmed by the professionals, the expertise about their own child that parents bring to the clinical provides critical pointers to ongoing habilitation plans.

However, we found parents to be trepidatious and uncertain about engaging with the clinics and unsure as to the sequence of events and what should be expected of them. For caregivers to confidently navigate education and health environments required the establishment of trust and positive working relationships between professionals and families, and the provision of adequate interpreting and mediating support. The emphasis on trusting and empathetic relationships has been found to be especially important in engaging with traditionally marginalized families (Swanwick et al., 2019). The professionals that we interviewed made efforts to facilitate parent–parent support, and sought to build connections between parents and deaf adults.

> We tell them that all hope is not lost. They can achieve all that they want to achieve in life. Because we admit students who are deaf in the university, University of Education Winneba, we always use them as an example that we are having some students who are deaf, and they have gone through the basic education and climbed to the tertiary level and doing so well. Even some of the parent sometimes meet the students who are deaf and will be communicating so in seeing them, they will even be happy seeing them. (Clinician)

Getting as far as the clinic for a medical assessment of a hearing loss is recognized as a significant hurdle for parents, but once this connection is made clinicians also seek to build parents' expectations for their child. For some parents this will be the first connection with people who know about and understand childhood deafness and who can explain what is possible. Clinicians are often instrumental in getting parents to send their children to school and start learning sign language.

> When they are able to get to know that some deaf can also attend school event at the university level they are delighted. Some are willing to learn the sign as well to take the children to schools. (Clinician)

Where possible clinicians facilitate parent–parent support, and they try to enable parents to meet interns who are deaf. Their advice and support focuses strongly on expectations.

Clinicians also comment on the need for more engagement from parents and describe the precarious lives of deaf children in contexts where their deafness is not understood. They see themselves as a vital link in the support system.

> Support from parents is difficult, you have few parents who understand and are ready to go all out to support their kids but for some of them without us the children would have been dumped elsewhere. So that is the challenge. (Clinician)

Collaboration among Professionals

The importance of multi-professional involvement and collaboration has been documented in the literature (Epstein, 2018). In our study we found that successful connections are made between professionals through the clinic system where audiologists will refer patients out of clinic for example to speech and language therapists, neurologists, counsellors, and ear nose and throat (ENT) surgeons. For example, the CHSS works closely with ENT doctors at various large teaching hospitals in Accra and Cape Coast Teaching Hospital and other hospitals in Accra, and it is actively involved in clinical training at the University of Education, Winneba. We also found the system of undergraduate work-based placements offered to medical students to provide a crucial connection between health and education.

> The final year students of the University of Ghana Medical School come here in batches. That is their outreach programme, they go out to visit special schools to find out about their sanitation, means by which they give first aid, the washrooms and all sort of things. (Educator)

We also found the involvement of and collaboration with non-governmental organizations (NGOs) and non-profit organizations to be supportive of the delivery of ECCE services for young deaf children and their families. NGOs and non-profit organizations (such as the Salvation Army) are active in the provision of hearing aids and their accessories and also provide financial support for the set-up of audiology centres and clinical training. These collaborations not only facilitate the donation of resources but are also important for raising societal awareness of childhood deafness, the educational requirements, and conditions. One of our school-based participants talked about the benefits of NGOs.

> So, this school has sponsors like the ATP [American Technical Powers] (. . .) individuals, churches, alumni in schools. So even when you come to the school, there are facilities put up by other organizations and churches. (Educator)

The Salvation Army, established in 1922 in Ghana by a British missionary, is particularly active in Ghana in their support of children and adults with disabilities. They collaborate with the Rehabilitation Centre at Agona Duakwa and CHSS to provide support to parents and deaf children. They support caregivers with referrals to relevant professionals, transportation costs, fees for diagnosis, and provide equipment. They also run a Community Based Rehabilitation Centre at Agona Duakwa, to provide rehabilitation services to children with physical disabilities. This centre also facilitates the assessment of young deaf children for school placement and helps with the acquisition of hearing aids. Part of their strategy involves recruiting student interns from the

University of Education, Winneba deaf education programme on year-long voluntary placement to work with children and families in different centres. The Salvation Army also facilitates supportive connections between other NGOs, schools, and clinics (such as Ghana Health Service and Christian Health Association of Ghana). For example, their collaboration with the Samuel Wellington Botwey Foundation based in Accra facilitates the provision of funding to support deaf children's education.

The Liliane Foundation (LF) based in the Netherlands provided funding via the Roman Catholic Parish, Winneba, during a collaboration with CHSS that lasted for over a decade, and it supported single and disadvantaged parents of children with disabilities by paying for school tuition fees, uniforms, and stationery, and providing financial support for parents to start up small businesses. This foundation has also supported young deaf adults financially to learn trades, and provided them with start-up equipment (tools, sewing machines, hair dryers).

In early 2000s, CHSS had a collaboration with Insituut voor Doven IVD, a Dutch-based educational institution (now Royal Dutch Kentalis) that provided training modules in early intervention. The training targeted deaf teachers selected from schools for deaf people all over Ghana, audiology clinical staff (CHSS), and peripatetic officers in district education offices in Ghana. The training that spanned over a period of 5 years (2–4 weeks per year) was hosted in CHSS, Winneba, and included modules in techniques in basic audiological assessment. As part of this collaboration, CHSS were also provided with a permanent ear mould laboratory and a hearing aid repair facility. In addition, LF sourced for funding from the Rotary Foundation and CORDAID to support the training of an audiologist (the author of this chapter) in London UK to pursue a 1 year MSc in Audiological Sciences. This was at a time in the history of Ghana when there were just three practicing audiology professionals in a country with a population of 17 million and not a single training programme for audiologists available in institutions in Ghana.

As a result of this collaboration and training opportunity links between UK and Ghana charities and Rotary clubs were made that provided for audiological equipment and a mobile ambulance (the HARK) to facilitate the early identification and intervention of deaf children. Similar collaborations with Starkey Group of Companies (an NGO) have facilitated the provision of hearing aids, spare batteries, and repairs, and supported public education programmes about deafness and types of intervention.

These supportive connections that exist between NGOs, schools, and clinics are generally formal. Collaboration between the parties involved is underpinned by contractual arrangements and a memorandum of agreement. That

Role of Professionals 143

these connections exist is of benefit to children and caregivers, but the provision is not systematic and equally available. The reliance of these forms of support highlights the impoverished nature of the infrastructure surrounding young deaf children and their families.

In the next section we present the story of a deaf mentor, who was part of the research team and shares her experiences as a deaf child growing up in Ghana.

Deaf Adults Perspectives

A deaf adult, Linda shares her perspectives. Linda talks about her experience of growing up as a deaf child in Ghana. Linda's story begins with a brief history about her early childhood.

> I am native of a village in the Ashanti region of Ghana called Obuasi, and I was under the care of someone (not my real parents). I lived at Obuasi as a street/ homeless child. I never had the opportunity to get enrolled in a school and my biological parents wouldn't take care of me because I am deaf. I have two biological siblings (a brother and sister) who are hearing normally; unsurprisingly, my biological parents paid much more attention to them and neglected me

Linda further reflects on how her hopes of receiving education was frustrated resulting in her living in the streets for her livelihood.

> One day, a man named Mr. A (real name withheld) who hails from the USA came to Obuasi on a working visit and a philanthropist as he is he chanced on me and expressed the need to adopt me. Fortunately, he adopted me and took me to Takoradi (a city in the Western region of Ghana) where he resided. A few months later, I started school at the Sekondi School for the Deaf, where I was left in the care of my adoptive mother. A few months later Mr. A left for the US but ensured that remittances were available for my upkeep. He kept communicating with me so I know what was going on.
>
> When Mr A left for the USA, I was mistreated harshly by my adoptive mother. She hardly catered for me even though my adoptive father continued to support me financially. These cruel treatments prompted me to leave the school and return to the streets for my survival, where I did petty trading and odd jobs just to survive. I could not stand the pain of separation. Upon his return from the US, I was declared missing so he reported to the police and lo and behold, I was found. He warned my adoptive mother to never ever neglect me. But she repeated the same mistakes again when Mr A returned to the US. What to do? My adoptive mother's

144   Care and Education of Deaf Children in Ghana

sister decided to take care of me instead, but there were some disagreements between the two sisters which again prompted him (Mr A) to fly back to Ghana. Upon
returning, he fell seriously ill and died after a short illness. I was so heartbroken.
I didn't know whom to turn to again. This greatly affected my studies in school.

A few months after his death, I was sent to Accra to learn a trade as a hair-
dresser (which is quite common in Ghana) under the apprenticeship of a deaf lady.
Unfortunately, living with her was the worst for me. She never took me to school
although she had hearing children. I would do all the household chores and they
(family) treated me as a housemaid. It really hurt to go through all these troubles
all over again.

Linda continues to narrate how her hopes came alive again after several
painful years as a growing deaf individual.

However, one fateful Sunday, my deaf mother took me along to church at Circle
(surburb of Accra), where some members of her church noticed how badly she
treated me and called me for chat. After discussions, they realized that all my life,
I had not been properly cared for or given a home or schooling that would help me.
Subsequently, an elder at the church took upon the role of finally adopting me,
staying with and staying with his family has been the best part of my life. My new
adoptive parents are very supportive, and I have gained some skills as a caterer
where my adoptive mum owns her business. Currently, I am a graduate student at a
University in Ghana and I work with the National Association for the Deaf.

We also asked Linda to share her views on the experiences of young deaf children in the context of family and community life. She talked about the ways in
which deaf children are sometimes marginalized.

Most children who are deaf don't get the chance of taking part in family and community life because those around them feel they have nothing to contribute or
offer. They are devoid of love and care as many families see them as a burden
when they hardly understood their needs. Others too feel, including a deaf child
in a family or social gatherings will destroy the mood and embarrass them in some
way for example, making strange noises as they try to talk or being shouted at for
not doing something right. So whenever family members are attending a party or
a programme, the deaf child is told to stay at home and be a watchdog. This is not
only a form of discrimination but it also reduces the self-confidence of the child.

She also corroborated the position of some of the professionals that we
interviewed in the Ghana study that some parents were trepidatious about

disclosing that they had a deaf child because of the level of societal stigma and shame that they experienced.

> Some parents don't want others to know they have a child who is deaf because they are afraid of being laughed at. Some too would go to the extent of taking the child to a pastor or fetish priest for miracles. Others too would pay huge sums to get the child a cochlear implant and force them to talk because they feel it is a burden to learn sign language or explain things to them all the time. Again some parents also don't want to be mocked for what happened in their youth; for example; they may have made fun of a deaf person during their time back which they are afraid others may know it was the reason they birthed a deaf child.

This personal story and perspective painfully underlines the general lack of understanding and knowledge about deafness in this context and how this lack of societal awareness influences the responses and behaviours of some caregivers. Caregivers do not always understand the nature of deafness and what it means for their child because they are not properly informed or supported, and furthermore they are vulnerable to stigma.

Professionals who are the first to meet caregivers of deaf children have an important role to play in providing balanced information, building trust and confidence at the first point of contact with caregivers. Without early screening, this can become a game of catch up as caregivers rarely arrive in clinical setting within the first few months of their child's life when they most need this information. This delay hinders the start of habilitation and early education and compounds low expectations and negative experience. We saw from our interviews that clinicians who meet caregivers first do what they can to mitigate these delays and provide encouragement and support to caregivers. However, their efforts are hampered by impoverished resources and a depleted workforce. Furthermore, they are operating in a societal contexts where the public education about deafness, language, and communication is wanting.

Conclusion

A multi-professional team that collaborates to provide support for deaf children and their caregivers is critical in building a successful inclusive environment aimed at ensuring that deaf children succeed in the classroom and in their overall well-being.

In Ghana, clinicians such as audiologists, rehabilitation professionals, administrators, and educators work with deaf people to bring understanding about language and communication to their work. These professionals (audiologists, rehabilitation professionals, administrators, and educators) have a robust training infrastructure and experiences that constitute their understanding about language and communication. However, there are insufficient resources to reach and equip all families, especially in rural areas, with the technology and habilitative support that they need. Given the insufficient resources at their disposal, they rely extensively on support from NGOs and other not profit organizations. Even with this external support the existing arrangements fall significantly short of meeting the Early Hearing Detection and Intervention 1-3-6 guidelines (hearing screening by 1 month, identification of hearing loss by 3 months, and receiving intervention by 6 months of age) that most high resourced countries have achieved, or can realistically strive to achieve (Moeller et al., 2013; Yoshinago-Itano et al., 2020).

The primary connection between the education and hearing-health contexts in Ghana focuses on the assessment and identification of hearing loss that then triggers access to special school. Thus, at the professional level, there is a commitment to connect health and education services and good connections between the schools and the clinics. There are also outreach services to include children whose families are unable to travel to the clinics. For example, CHSS has a mobile audiology van that is purposefully designed for hearing screening in remote communities. In these communities, there are often several people who otherwise would never have the prospect of getting their hearing assessed.

Furthermore, there are connections between other professionals through the clinic system where audiologists will refer patients out of clinic, for example, to speech and language therapists, neurologists, counsellors, and ENT surgeons. Additionally, supportive connections exist between NGOs, schools, and clinics. These relationships facilitate the donation of resources, such as play equipment, and are important for raising societal awareness of childhood deafness and the educational implications and needs.

The professionals that we interviewed were able to provide some insights into the day-to-day contexts of deaf children's early lives and the relationships and interactions within that context that influence early care and support. They also provided some insights into the overarching societal influences on early care and support in terms of institutional and policy influence, societal infrastructure, ways of life, culture, belief systems, and resource dynamics. As professionals they are less directly influenced, or hampered, by issues of stigma and marginalization. One of the key findings from this aspect of the project work and highlighted by the contributions from deaf team members is the need for caregivers' peer support and contact with deaf adults at a much earlier state of their child's life (Gale et al., 2021). This is a theme that we examine in more detail as part of the project work and discuss in Chapter 9.

References

Alexa K., Fellinger, P., & Fellinger, J., (2016). Health care access among deaf people, Journal of Deaf Studies and Deaf Education, *21*(1), 1–10. https://doi.org/10.1093/deafed/env042

Blazer, D.G., Domnitz, S., & Liverman, C.T. (Eds.). (2016). Hearing health care for adults: Priorities for improving access and affordability. *National Academies Press.*

Bredekamp, S. (2020). *Effective practices in early childhood education: Building a foundation.* (4th ed.). Pearson Education Inc.

Bronfenbrenner, U., & Morris, P. A. (2006). The bioecological model of human development, In R. M. Lerner & W. Damon (Eds.), *Handbook of child psychology: Theoretical models of human development*, Vol. 1 (pp. 793–828). John Wiley.

Bronfenbrenner, U. (2005). *Making human beings human: Bioecological perspectives on human development,* SAGE Publications.

Epstein, J. L. (2018). *School, family, and community partnerships: Preparing educators and improving schools.* Routledge.

Gale, E., Berke, M., Benedict, B., Olson, S., Putz, K., & Yoshinaga-Itano, C. (2021). Deaf adults in early intervention programs. *Deafness & Education International*, *23*(1), 3–24.

Knoors, H., Brons, M., & Marschark, M. (2019). Deaf education beyond the western world: An introduction. In H. Knoors, M. Brons, & M. Marschark (Eds.), *Deaf education beyond the western world* (pp. 1–18). Oxford University Press.

Kusters, A. (2015). *Deaf space in Adamorobe: An ethnographic study of a village in Ghana.* Gallaudet University Press.

Moeller, M. P., Carr, G., Seaver, L., Stredler-Brown, A., & Holzinger, D. (2013). Best practices in family-centered early intervention for children who are deaf or hard of hearing: An international consensus statement. *Journal of Deaf Studies and Deaf Education*, *18*(4), 429–445.

Nyst, V. (2012). Shared sign languages. In R. Pfau, M. Steinbech, & B. Woll (Eds.), *Sign language: An international handbook* (pp. 552–574). Mouton de Gruyter.

Olusanya, B. O. (2008). Priorities for early hearing detection and intervention in sub-Saharan Africa. *International Journal of Audiology* (Suppl. 1): S3–S13.

Olusanya, B. O., Wirz, S. L., & Luxton, L. M. (2008). Community-based infant hearing screening for early detection of permanent hearing loss in Lagos, Nigeria: a cross-sectional study. *Bulletin of the World Health Organization, 86*, 956–963

Oppong, A. M., & Fobi, D. (2019), Deaf education in Ghana, in H. Knoors, M. Brons, & M. Marschark (Eds.), *Deaf education beyond the Western World: Context, challenges, and prospects* (pp. 53–73). Oxford University Press.

Störbeck, C., & Young, A. (2016). Early intervention in challenging national contexts. In M. Sass-Lehrer (Ed.), *Early intervention for deaf and hard-of-hearing infants, toddlers, and their families: Interdisciplinary perspectives* (pp. 305–328). Oxford University Press.

Swanwick, R., Elmore, J., & Salter, J. (2019). Educational inclusion of children who are deaf or hard of hearing and from migrant Roma families: Implications for multi-professionals working. *Deafness & Education International*, *23*(1), 25–42. DOI: 10.1080/14643154.2019.1685756

Wonkam-Tingang, E., Kamga, K. K., Adadey, S. M., Nguefack, S., De Kock, C., Munung, N. S., & Wonkam, A (2021). Knowledge and challenges associated with hearing impairment in affected individuals from Cameroon (sub-Saharan Africa). *Frontiers in Rehabiltation Sciences*, 2, Article 726761.

Yoshinaga-Itano, C., Sedey, A. L., Mason, C. A., Wiggin, M., & Chung, W. (2020). Early intervention, parent talk, and pragmatic language in children with hearing loss. *Paediatrics*, *146*(3), 270–277.

9

Deaf Adult Participation and Leadership in ECCE

Daniel Fobi, Derrick Asomaning, and Richard Doku

Introduction

Deaf leadership refers to the leadership and representation of deaf individuals in various aspects of society, including education, employment, politics, and community organizations. Deaf leadership recognizes the unique perspectives, experiences, and talents of deaf individuals, and seeks to empower them to be agents of change in their communities. Deaf leadership has become increasingly recognized as an important factor in promoting positive outcomes for the deaf community. In particular, deaf leaders have the potential to play a critical role in supporting the early care and education of young deaf children. Deaf leaders bring unique experiences and perspectives that can inform culturally and linguistically responsive practices, promote advocacy and mentorship for deaf children and families, and collaborate with other practitioners to ensure that young deaf children have access to high-quality care and education.

Deafness as a hidden disability needs to be identified very early, preferably within the first three months after birth, so that early support and intervention can be given to deaf children and their families. The quality of life for any child born deaf hinges on early identification and subsequent interventions and supports provided for the child and his/her families (Deaf Federation of South Africa, 2006; Yoshinaga-Itano, 2021). Vijaylaxmi (2009) points out that deaf children and their families need formal support from professionals, such as audiologists, speech and language therapists, counsellors, and special education teachers who may also be deaf.

Daniel Fobi, Derrick Asomaning, and Richard Doku, *Deaf Adult Participation and Leadership in ECCE* In: *The Early Care and Education of Deaf Children in Ghana*. Edited by: Ruth Swanwick, Daniel Fobi, Yaw Offei, and Alexander Oppong, Oxford University Press. © Daniel Fobi, Derrick Asomaning, and Richard Doku 2024.
DOI: 10.1093/oso/9780192872272.003.0009

They also need informal support from immediate family members such as parents, siblings, grandparents, and other members of the community in which deaf children live (see Chapter 8 for multi-professional collaboration in supporting early childhood care and education (ECCE) of young deaf children). However, many of these caregivers, especially parents and other immediate family members, find it difficult to effectively support deaf children because most of them are hearing and have no prior knowledge or experience of deafness. Research indicates that over 90% of deaf children are born to hearing parents, many of whom are unprepared for the consequences of deafness (Marschark, 1997; Ross et al., 2004;). Vijaylaxmi (2009) posits that developing alternative forms of communication with their deaf children, making correct decisions regarding educational options, and for maintaining consistency in parenting can be stressful to parents.

One way in which parents and other caregivers can be helped to understand the ECCE of young deaf children is through deaf leadership. Deaf leadership involves deaf adults and mentors providing diverse supports, guidance, and services to deaf children and their families with the aim of improving their lives holistically.

Constructs of Deaf Leadership

The history of deaf leadership can be traced back to the early nineteenth century when the first schools for the deaf were established in Europe and North America. One of the key figures during this time was Thomas Hopkins Gallaudet, who founded the first American school for the deaf in Hartford, Connecticut in 1817. Gallaudet's work helped to establish the foundation for deaf education in the United States and laid the groundwork for deaf leadership in the years to come. Throughout the nineteenth century, deaf leadership emerged as a prominent force in the deaf community, with deaf individuals assuming leadership roles in deaf organizations and advocating for deaf rights. This role of deaf adults has shaped the narrative of ECCE of young deaf children and their families and has supported many families in the language and communication of young deaf children (Gale et al., 2021). One notable organization that emerged from the deaf community during this time was the National Association of the Deaf, which was founded in the United States in 1880. The National Association of the Deaf became a powerful force for deaf advocacy, promoting the use of American Sign Language, supporting families with deaf children learn sign language and pushing for the recognition of the deaf community as a linguistic and cultural minority.

In the early twentieth century, deaf leadership continued to evolve and expand, with the establishment of more deaf organizations and the emergence of prominent deaf leaders. One such leader was George Veditz, who served as the president of the National Association of the Deaf in the 1910s and is perhaps best known for his 1913 film 'The Preservation of the Sign Language', which is now considered a cultural treasure. The mid-twentieth century saw the emergence of deaf civil rights movements, which were largely inspired by the broader civil rights movements of the time. In the United States, the 1960s and 1970s saw the establishment of organizations such as the National Black Deaf Advocates and the National Hispanic Council of the Deaf and Hard of Hearing, which aimed to address the intersectional challenges faced by deaf people of colour. In more recent years, deaf leadership has continued to evolve and expand, with the emergence of new organizations, movements, and leaders. Deaf Leadership International Alliance is one of such leadership of deaf people whose main aim is to have cross-national conversations of how the language and communication of young deaf children and their families across the globe can be supported, and which strategies and working well in different countries. One other notable movement is the Deafhood movement, which seeks to reclaim and celebrate deaf culture and identity. Another prominent organization is the World Federation of the Deaf, which represents over 70 million deaf people worldwide and advocates for their rights on a global scale.

Until the mid to late 1960s, hearing individuals dominated formal leadership of deaf education. Training programmes about ways to teach and lead deaf people in deaf education abounded in the 1960s; however, these were for hearing individuals as deaf people were not considered even to be admissible until the late 1960s (Moores, 2007). In spite of these inequalities and discrimination in formal leadership of deaf education, Moores (2007) states that there was a strong movement of organizations operating for and by deaf people such as the National Association of the Deaf and the World Federation of the Deaf. Yet, the occurrence of deaf leaders in mainstream leadership was rare (Kam-Larew & Lamkin, 2008). This was due to the pathological view of deafness, which perpetuates the idea of deficit on the part of deaf individuals. Thus, deaf people were conceived by the hearing community as those who need help and assistance and not those who need to help and assist others (Napier & Leeson, 2016). In other words, the predominantly hearing perspective was that deaf people should be followers and not leaders. In addition, Kamm-Larew and Lamkin (2008) point out that spoken language dominated deaf education in the 1940s; hence, deaf individuals rarely had a place in leadership. Since deaf leadership was affected during this era, equally their participation in ECCE was also affected. Buchanan (1999) identified language, identity, schooling, and the general status of deaf adults to be inextricably linked to the success or failure of deaf workers and educators. Over the years, the gatekeepers of identity and leadership tended to be the dominant hearing society (Kam-Larew & Lamkin, 2008). Breivik (2005) states that the influence created by the hearing-normative concept of deficit created in the deaf identity often results in identity confusion for many deaf individuals. Thus, 'it appears that being deaf in and of itself is enough to create barriers to achievement to educational and vocational goals' (Doe, 1999, p. 283). However, in reality, the deficit view is a construct of a hearing normative society. The true barriers are socially constructed (Kam-Larew & Lamkin, 2008). In contrast, there are professional organizations in countries such as the United States that provide services to families and deaf children and adults have established committees of deaf professionals, such as the American Academy of Audiology and Association of Medical Professionals with Hearing Loss.

Deaf Leadership in Education

Davis (2007) asserts that 'over the past 30 or so years, the status of deaf people has changed in important ways, as deaf activists and scholars have reshaped the idea of deafness, using the civil-rights movement as a model for the struggle to form deaf identity' (p. 6). Davis (2007) continues to state that in the past, it was the hearing people who set up 'the barriers and checkpoints'; however, now, segments of the deaf community has declared themselves as the gatekeepers. Currently, there are calls for a new definition for the skills required to lead within the deaf community (Kam-Larew & Lamkin, 2008). Professionals and social workers who provide services, intervention, and supports to deaf children are required to be knowledgeable about deafness and be familiar with deaf culture because the quality of the services they provide would depend on their understanding of the beneficiaries of such services. The Family Centred Early Intervention (FCEI) and the Joint Committee on Infant Hearing recommend service providers to connect with and infuse deaf adults and leaders in early intervention programmes for deaf children due to the benefits they bring to such programmes, such as language and communication support, educational information, and role modelling as well as counselling. The infusion of deaf adults and leaders involves the description of deaf adults as part of the entire early intervention system steeped into the fabric at all levels that may include collaboration, connecting, leadership, partnering, or engaging in all levels of decision-making and service provision' (Gale et al., 2021, p. 4).

The FCEI principles 4 and 8 specifically relate to connecting with deaf adults and leaders in the provision of early intervention services to deaf children and their families. Principle 4 of the FCEI deals with family social and emotional support and states that service providers should 'support connections between families and adult role models who are D/HH (deaf and hard of hearing)' as well as 'provide social and emotional supports to promote the well-being of parents and siblings. Inform parents about and refer them to professional mental health services, if considered appropriate. Recognize the importance of family well-being for child development' (Moeller et al., 2013, p. 435). The purpose is to enable families to 'accrue the necessary knowledge and experiences that can enable them to function effectively on behalf of their deaf children' (Moeller et al., 2013, p. 435). Hintermair (2000) explained that when parents contact deaf adults they show a strong sense of competence with regards to their deaf child's upbringing. Therefore, the opportunity for parents to connect with deaf adults and mentors is very important for families with deaf children (Jackson, 2011).

Principle eight of the FCEI focuses on collaborative teamwork and recommends that the early intervention team should include 'individuals who are deaf (role models/mentors)' in order to develop 'an optimal team that focuses on the family and includes professionals with experience in promoting early development of children who are D/HH' (Moeller et al., 2013, p. 440). It was further recommended that early intervention teams offer families opportunities for meaningful interactions with adults who are deaf:

(a) Deaf adults can serve as role models, consultants, and/or mentors to families, offering information and resources and demonstrate enriching language experiences.
(b) Involve deaf community members on the team in culturally and linguistically sensitive ways (Moeller et al., 2013, p. 441).

Connecting with deaf adults and mentors enables parents to understand the capabilities of their children (Rogers & Young, 2011), and help in promoting language and communication development (Watkins et al., 1998). According to Gale et al. (2021), the consensus published by the FCEI was influenced by the recommendations published by the Joint Committee on Infant Hearing (JCIH), 'which was established in 1969 to make recommendations regarding early identification for children with, or at risk for hearing loss and newborn hearing screening in the United States' (p. 7). The JCIH has explicitly recommended including deaf adults in their position statements since 1995 (JCIH, 1995; JCIH, 2000; JCIH, 2007; Muse et al., 2013). These recommendations can be found in the JCIH Goals 3, 10, and 11 respectively.

JCIH Goal 3 emphasizes ensuring deaf adults as stakeholders with the goal for families and their young deaf children to 'have early intervention providers who have the professional qualifications and core knowledge and skills to optimize the child's development and child/family wellbeing' (Muse et al., 2013, p. e1328). Goal 3a specifically recommends deaf adults as collaborative partners in teaching sign language to deaf children and families because 'intervention services to teach ASL [American Sign Language] will be provided by professionals who have native or fluent skills and are trained to teach parents/families and young children' (Muse et al., 2013, p. e1329). Goal 10 also recommend that deaf adults be active participants in the development and implementation of early hearing detection and intervention (EHDI) systems at the national, state/territory, and local levels (Gale et al., 2021). The goal is that 'their participation will be an expected and integral component of the EHDI systems' (Muse et al., 2013, p. e1337). The rationale is that language and communication are the heart of the support services and that it is critical (Gale et al., 2021) to include 'individuals who are deaf [because they] know what works to meet their language and communication needs in a way that people who are hearing cannot' (Muse et al., 2013, p. e1337). Finally, Goal 11 by JCIH is an explicit goal which recommend deaf adults supporting, mentoring and guiding young deaf children and their families for the purpose of ensuring that 'all children who are D/HH and their families have access to support, mentorship, and guidance from individuals who are D/HH' (Muse et al., 2013, p. e1338).

The above discussion reveals that there are numerous calls to infuse deaf adults and leaders in early intervention programmes serving deaf children and their families. According to Wax (2019), due to the continuous shortage of qualified deaf mental health professionals with expertise in deafness, a potentially cost-effective way of enhancing access of existing mental health services to deaf clients may be to train recognized leaders of the deaf community to serve as liaisons—bridges—between the two systems (mental health providers and the deaf community).

Kamm-Larew and Lamkin (2008) surveyed leadership programmes operating for and by the deaf community in the United States. They identified three categories of leadership programmes operating for deaf and hard of hearing individuals:

Youth leadership programmes
Special interest mentoring groups
Formal leadership training programmes

The youth leadership programmes focus on deaf youths. An example is the National Association of the Deaf Youth Leadership Camp, which advocates for 'scholarship, leadership and citizenship' and states that it provides campers with opportunities to 'discover self-identity, develop self-esteem and confidence, and build leadership and teamwork skills through hands-on-activities' (Kamm-Larew & Lamkin, 2008).

The special interest mentoring groups provide leadership training and support to deaf individuals based on ethnicity, gender, and profession. Kamm-Larew and Lamkin (2008) point out that 'within the deaf community, leadership training seemed to take place within the context of role models and empowerment through identity association with special interest groups'. An ethnic-based leadership group in the United Sates is 'the National Black Deaf Advocates organization, which hosts leadership training at its biannual conferences. Another is the Deaf People of Color, which exists to dispel the hearing hegemonic misconceptions and provide role models to underserved deaf individuals' (Kamm-Larew & Lamkin, 2008). Kamm-Larew and Lamkin (2008) found out that there was 'a trend of leadership initiatives based on subcultures within the deaf community, for example, Nation Deaf Black Advocates (NDBA). This organization provides leadership and support to a wide range of those whose identities intertwine with its own through its Youth Empowerment Summit and Black Deaf Senior Citizens and Family Network programs' (Kamm-Larew & Lamkin, 2008). A gender-based leadership programme within the deaf community is the Deaf Women's Leadership Programme, which emphasizes empowerment through professional advancement and development (Kamm-Larew & Lamkin, 2008). 'There are also professional and social networks whose main mission is to provide mentoring to those with similar identities' such as the Deaf Attorney Network.

Under the formal leadership training programmes, Kamm-Larew and Lamkin (2008) identified the Gallaudet Leadership Institute (GLI), which hosts and supports many of the youth and special interest leadership groups. Another unique training programme, Pennsylvania Society of Advancement for the Deaf (PSAD), places emphasis on empowerment, professional development, and decision making skills (Kamm-Larew & Lamkin, 2008).

In addition to the above leadership programmes and activities for and by the deaf community, there are several early deaf leadership programmes and activities in the area of early care and education of deaf children. These include deaf leadership in different domains such as health, education, and community support. These deaf professionals often work with families in early years

Care and Education of Deaf Children in Ghana

to prove care and support the deaf children and their families. However, most of these kinds of activism and development are driven by Western theories and context. Very few of these systems are inclusive of deaf leadership and support for ECCE of young deaf children in the global South. In the next section, deaf leadership in Africa and Ghana is discussed.

Deaf Leadership in Africa and Ghana

Traditionally, people with disabilities (PWDs) including those who are deaf in Africa were discriminated against, stigmatized, neglected, and even rejected. Although the status and condition of PWDs have drastically changed positively over the years, poor treatment and negative attitude toward PWDs still persist in some cultures on the continent. This change was, in part, due to the influence of Christian missionaries who came to Africa. Fundamentally, Christianity emphasizes charity toward humanity. Thus, PWDs were accepted and taught to be independent and responsible people in society. The Christian missionaries established schools and taught deaf people (both adults and children) sign language. This was a way of showing charity to humanity and a means of spreading the gospel.

Therefore, deaf leadership in Africa could be said to begin with the emergent of deaf education on the continent. A notable missionary who have had great influence in deaf education and leadership is Reverend Andrew Jackson Foster (1927–1987). Foster was a deaf African American graduate from Gallaudet College, now Gallaudet University. He came as a missionary to Africa, specifically Accra in 1957, the year Ghana gained its independence (Oppong & Fobi, 2019). Foster discovered that many deaf children in Africa were illiterate, had no language, and were isolated (Moore & Panera, 1996). Ghana itself then had no programmes, schools, or teachers for the deaf. Thus, Foster established a school for the deaf in Ghana, which was the first to use manual communication in the region. He also introduced American Sign Language and English-based signs (Kiyaga & Moores, 2003; Oppong & Fobi, 2019). Researchers have not agreed how many schools for the deaf were established by Foster nor on the number of countries in Africa where those schools were found. Carroll and Marther (1997) point out that Foster established 31 schools for the deaf (nine in Ghana) in 17 African countries. However, Eleweke et al. (2015) opine that Foster started 32 mission schools for the deaf in 13 African countries. In addition, he established training centres in Nigeria and Kenya by 1975 (Kiyaga & Moores, 2003). Functioning as a teacher, evangelist, administrator, and public-relations specialist, Foster mentored and trained many deaf and hearing Africans to collaborate and continue the work of providing education and related services to deaf children in their own communities and beyond (Eleweke et al., 2015).

Eleweke et al. (2015) identified 'Dr Peter Mba (deceased), Dr Gabriel Adepoju (deceased), Dr Isaac Agboola, Ezekiel Sambo (deceased), Moses Ariobasa (deceased), Job Ayantola, Jonathan Erhiaganoma, Samuel Adesina, Timothy Owolabi (deceased), Adebayo Bella (deceased), Emmanuel Azodeh, Amos Akeju, Lucky Nepe, and Engineer Emmanual Ilabor' (p. 77) as among the people in Nigeria whom Foster inspired, trained, and mentored to be leaders in their own communities and beyond. Dr Tetteh-Ocloo can be named among many deaf people in Ghana whom Foster influenced to be leaders. Eleweke et al. (2015) further point out that Foster encouraged both deaf adults to pursue a college education at the Gallaudet University. Agboola (2014) remarks that upon completion, they became qualified deaf educators, leaders, and mentors. For example, 'Dr. Gabriel Adepoju founded the Kwara State School for the Deaf and Blind, Ilorin; Ezekiel Sambo established the Plateau School for the Deaf, Jos. Peter Mba not only worked as an educator of the deaf, founding schools in eastern Nigeria and elsewhere in the country, he was also a government consultant and advocated passionately for improved educational and related services for deaf people and other Nigerians with disabilities. He was instrumental in the establishment of the first Department of Special Education (at the University of Ibadan) in Nigeria and was its head for many years' (Eleweke et al., 2015, p. 77).

Outside the field of deaf education, Reverend Foster organized Bible meetings and Sunday schools for deaf individuals in many African countries. During these meetings, Foster taught deaf children and adults sign language. Kusters (2014) asserts that Reverend Foster was the first Christian deaf person to preach at Adamorobe, a village in Ghana where many deaf people are included in every facet of community life and where the whole community share a common sign language known as Adamorobe Sign Language (AdaSL). Kusters (2014) describes the interactions between Foster and the deaf people of Adamorobe as an exchange; they taught him AdaSL signs and he taught them American Sign Language signs. Reverend Foster also organized charitable donations: 'he regularly came to Adamorobe with a van with items such as rice, clothes, sandals, toothbrushes, oil, chocolate powder, soap, bread, sugar, milk, onions, peanuts, corn, towels, caps, and watches' (Kusters, 2014, p. 476). According to Kusters (2014), these donations continued even after Reverend Foster left Ghana in 1965 and it has resulted in the creation of a sense of neediness and dependency on the part of deaf people in Adamorobe. Kusters (2014) narrated that the deaf people in Adamorobe have equated church attendance to resources because the donations are given to those who come to church.

Deaf leadership in Africa and Ghana has not developed to the same level as in Western contexts, such as in the United States and Europe. Deaf leadership in Ghana occurs predominantly in the field of education, within faith-based organizations, and non-governmental organizations such as the Ghana National Association of the Deaf (GNAD), a major advocacy group and mouthpiece of deaf people in Ghana. Many deaf leaders and mentors are deaf teachers or deaf workers who carry out mentoring roles under the auspices of their schools or GNAD. Deaf leadership in Africa is a growing and important movement that seeks to empower and promote the rights of deaf individuals on the continent. Examples of deaf leadership initiatives and organizations in Africa include African Federation of the Deaf, Kenya Sign Language Research Project, Deaf Empowerment Society of Kenya, and Deaf Zimbabwe Trust. The African Federation of the Deaf is a regional organization that represents the interests of deaf people in Africa, by advocating for the rights and inclusion of deaf individuals, providing education and training programmes, and supporting the establishment of national deaf organizations. Kenya Sign Language Research Project is a research project that focuses on promoting the use and recognition of Kenyan Sign Language: it works with deaf individuals, teachers, and other stakeholders to develop and implement Kenyan Sign Language education and training programmes.

The Deaf Empowerment Society of Kenya is a non-profit organization that provides support services to deaf individuals in Kenya:it offers education and training programmes, supports the establishment of deaf businesses, and advocates for the rights and inclusion of deaf individuals. Deaf Zimbabwe Trust is a non-profit organization that works to promote the rights and inclusion of deaf individuals in Zimbabwe: it provides education and training programmes, supports the establishment of national deaf organizations, and advocates for the recognition of Zimbabwe Sign Language.

In Ghana, deaf adults rarely work with families and young deaf children in early care and education. In this situation, where there are few advocacy options for the deaf community as a whole (Cooper & Rashid, 2015), there are no formalized programmes that support partnerships between deaf individuals and families of deaf children. The majority of deaf children are not diagnosed until after their fifth birthdays, and they do not come into contact with deaf adults until they start formal education, which typically begins at 6 years of age (or later depending on when carers learned about the education of deaf children) in one of the schools for the deaf (Fobi & Oppong, 2019; Oppong & Fobi, 2019). Early possibilities to interact with deaf role models and be exposed to a deaf cultural identity are also lost during this key time for language and communication development. In Ghana's 16 administrative regions, there are currently 13 deaf schools that use Ghanaian Sign Language as their primary language of teaching. Three cohorts of teachers work at these schools with deaf students.

The three groups vary depending on the path taken by the teachers to become deaf educators. The first is deaf teachers who are also deaf received their training at a higher education facility in Ghana. They may or may not have received training in deaf education or studies, but because they are deaf, they are frequently assigned to deaf schools. The Ghana National Association of Teachers of the Deaf is made up of these teachers. The second group of educators consists of deaf teachers who have completed professional training programmes at the University of Education, Winneba's Department of Special Education. Following completion of their training, these teachers are frequently sent to deaf schools. Teachers who have gained training as normal teachers (not in deaf education or similar courses) from higher education institutions make up the final group of educators working in deaf schools. These teachers frequently have their first interactions with deaf students while also picking up sign language. The difficulty with the last category of teachers is that they must acquire the language they will use to instruct their students, and the majority of them are unaware of deafness or the pedagogies that are employed to teach deaf students. As a result, issues have arisen that are currently the focus of important parties involved in deaf education, and solutions are being sought.

Deaf leadership in Ghana has been steadily growing in recent years, with the establishment of various organizations and initiatives aimed at promoting the rights and inclusion of the deaf community in Ghana. GNAD was established in 1958 and is the oldest and largest organization representing the deaf community in Ghana (Fobi & Doku, 2022): it advocates for the rights and inclusion of deaf people in Ghana, provides education and training programmes, and offers support services to the deaf community. Other organizations for deaf people in Ghana include Ghana Deaf Football Association, Deaf Empowerment Ghana, and Ghana Deaf Youth Association.

The Ghana Deaf Football Association was established in 2003 and promotes football as a means of empowering and promoting the talents of deaf individuals in Ghana: it organizes tournaments and other events for deaf football players in Ghana, and has participated in international deaf football competitions. Deaf Empowerment Ghana on the other hand is a non-profit organization that focuses on empowering and promoting the rights of deaf women and girls in Ghana: it provides education and training programmes, offers support services to deaf women and girls, and advocates for their rights and inclusion. Ghana Deaf Youth Association is a youth-led organization that focuses on promoting the talents and skills of deaf youth in Ghana by offering education and training programmes, organizing events and competitions for deaf youth, and advocating for their rights and inclusion. Overall, deaf leadership in Ghana is making significant strides in promoting the rights and inclusion of the deaf community, and creating opportunities for deaf individuals to thrive and succeed. With the continued support and investment in deaf leadership initiatives and organizations, the deaf community in Ghana can continue to grow and make a positive impact in society.

Deaf Leadership as Revealed in Our Study

As part of our research activities 17 deaf leaders were interviewed to solicit their opinions on ECCE for young deaf children and their caregivers in Ghana. The aim of this part of our project was to examine the development of ECCE in Ghanaian sub-Saharan Africa focusing specifically on the perspectives of deaf adults on their roles in ECCE support and leadership. Our objectives were to provide context sensitive knowledge of the deaf adults that included their experiences, local expertise, and perspective in supporting ECCE for young deaf children and their caregivers in Ghana. Therefore, GNAD, we used Facebook Messenger and WhatsApp to ask regional and national executives as well as high-status deaf adults (mentors) who are respected by both deaf and hearing people to take part in the study. Seventeen of the 21 deaf leaders who agreed after going through the study's objectives participated in the study (for a list of participants, see Table 9.1). The participants were allowed to choose their response method, which could be either a video chat via Zoom, a video response, or written English, after the question items were discussed with them. The interviewer, was a skilled Ghanaian Sign Language user and interpreter with more than ten years of experience teaching and interpreting.

Our team, which primarily consists of Ghanaian deaf and hearing members, analysed and evaluated the data using our context linguistic and cultural backgrounds. To analyse and interpret the data from the interviews, we applied Braun and Clarke's (2019) thematic approach. We sought to create a shared understanding of the participants' comments during our weekly sessions by reading over these transcripts individually and bringing them. Five main discussion themes emerged from the data and have been discussed in the next sections.

Table 9.1 Overview of participants

SN	Participant	Designation	Gender	Preferred Response
1.	GDA1	GNAD Executive	M	Written response
2.	GDA2	GNAD Executive	M	Written response
3.	GDA3	GNAD-Executive	M	Video response
4.	GDA4	GNAD Executive	M	Video response
5.	GDA5	GNAD Executive	F	Video response
6.	GDA6	GNAD Executive	M	Written response
7.	DA7	Lecturer	M	Written response
8.	DA8	Teacher	M	Written response
9.	DA9	Teacher	M	Written response
10.	DA10	Teacher	M	Zoom Video chat
11.	DA11	Teacher	M	Written response
12.	DA12	Teacher	F	Written response
13.	DA13	Teacher	F	Written response
14.	DA14	Teacher	M	Written response
15.	DA15	Teacher	M	Written response
16.	DA16	Teacher/ Tertiary Student	M	Written response
17.	DA17	Teacher/ Tertiary student	M	Written response

Language and Communication

Providing multimodal language and communication support from deaf adults to deaf children was seen as a crucial language development and socialization tool for deaf children. Deaf adults can communicate with deaf children using sign language, such as American Sign Language, British Sign Language, Ghanaian Sign Language, or any other sign languages that they are fluent in. Sign language provides a visual and linguistic mode of communication that is accessible to deaf children. Participants shared how the GNAD supports the language and communication of deaf children and their families.

Recently GNAD started the production of sign language dictionary ... So, GNAD support by providing motivations to parents through the internet, books, and sign language apps so that the parents will decide on which one will help them best. (GDA3)

Parents of deaf children come to GNAD office sometimes and we teach them the basis of sign language for free. (GDA5)

I provide training for parents of children who are deaf and family with some basic Ghanaian sign language for them to be able to communicate at home. (GDA2)

Other forms of visual communications through visual aids, such as pictures, videos, and diagrams, can be used to support communication with deaf children. Visual aids can help deaf children understand complex concepts and language. Visual communication is an important mode of communication for deaf adults, as it allows them to communicate effectively with others without relying on spoken language.

In addition, deaf adults can provide contextual cues, such as pointing to objects or using facial expressions, to help deaf children understand the meaning of words and sentences. Again, deaf adults can encourage socialization between deaf children by facilitating opportunities for deaf children to interact with each other in sign language. Socialization helps deaf children develop language skills and a sense of identity within the deaf community. Overall, providing multimodal language and communication support from deaf adults to deaf children is essential for deaf children's language development and socialization. However, this approach needs to be adopted with sensitivity to culture-based norms in terms of the appropriate use of touch, gesture, and eye gaze in different communicative contexts (Lorié et al., 2017).

The deaf adults shared the roles they can play to facilitate ECCE for the young deaf children and their families. They stressed the importance of such roles in the lives of the children and their families.

> I think it's a good idea because it will help the children who are deaf to develop good language skills. (GDA4)

> Deaf adult mentors can offer visual communication to the young children in the form of storytelling. They can help socialize the children by introducing them to the deaf community and culture. Deaf Adults can introduce parents to the deaf community and CODA and PODC (parents of children who are deaf). (DA12)

Strategies and Programmes and Future Potential of Deaf Leadership

Again, it was evident that supporting deaf leadership is essential for ensuring that the deaf community has a strong voice and is represented in all aspects of society. This could be achieved through leadership training programmes for deaf individuals targeted at helping them develop the skills and confidence they need to become effective leaders. These programmes can include training in public speaking, advocacy, community organizing, and other leadership skills.

Mentorship programmes: Pairing deaf leaders with experienced mentors can provide valuable guidance and support as they navigate their leadership roles. Mentorship programmes can also help build connections between deaf leaders and the broader deaf community.

Funding and resources: Providing funding and resources to support deaf-led organizations and initiatives can help strengthen the capacity of deaf leaders to effect change in their communities. This can include funding for community events, advocacy campaigns, or professional development opportunities.

Collaboration and partnerships: Encouraging collaboration and partnerships between deaf leaders and other organizations can help amplify their voices and broaden their reach. For example, partnering with mainstream organizations or institutions can help deaf leaders advocate for greater access and inclusion for the deaf community.

Recognition and representation: Recognizing the achievements and contributions of deaf leaders can help increase their visibility and influence. This can include awards, public speaking opportunities, or representation on boards or committees.

Future Potential of Deaf Leadership

Furthermore, the study revealed that the future potential of deaf leadership is significant, and it is important to recognize the unique contributions that deaf leaders can make to society. As more deaf individuals enter leadership roles, they can advocate for greater representation and inclusion of the deaf community in all aspects of society. This includes in education, employment, healthcare, and other areas where deaf individuals have historically faced barriers. Deaf leaders can promote and celebrate deaf culture and identity, and help educate others about the rich history and diversity of the deaf community. This can help increase understanding and respect for deaf individuals and create a more inclusive society.

Deaf leaders bring unique perspectives and experiences to the table, which can lead to innovative solutions to problems. As more deaf individuals enter leadership roles, they can help drive innovation in fields such as technology, education, and healthcare. Deaf leaders can also serve as advocates for the deaf community, working to advance policies and initiatives that support the needs and interests of deaf individuals. This includes advocating for greater access to communication, education, and employment opportunities. Deaf leaders can serve as role models and mentors for the next generation of deaf leaders. By providing guidance, support, and inspiration, they can help develop a new generation of leaders who will continue to advance the interests of the deaf community. Sustaining the future potential of deaf leadership requires ongoing support, investment, and commitment.

While a goal of deaf leadership will be individuals with higher education degrees, some deaf mentors and role models in the early years programmes may not have had the opportunity for enrolling in higher education courses (Hamilton et al., 2020; Lynn et al., 2020). However, these mentors are often fluent in the use of sign language and are outstanding teachers of families and young deaf children in early years (Lynn et al., 2020). These mentors are often hired for these family-centred teaching positions and provided these services within the home (Hamilton et al., 2020). Similar positions could be available in spoken language for communication with families whose home language is not English and the available interpreter who is bilingually fluent does not have education at a post-secondary level, but has the pre-requisite skills to fulfil the needs of the position (Niklas et al., 2020). Furthermore, deaf leadership may also include parents of deaf children who are themselves deaf and who have been trained to provide support for other parents with deaf children or their children who are deaf (Marschark & Hauser, 2012).

ECCE Training Infrastructure

Early care and education training infrastructure was also revealed through the study as crucial for ensuring that young deaf children receive the support and services they need to thrive. Early care and education providers working with young deaf children should receive specialized training and education in deaf education, communication, and culture. This can include training on sign language, assistive technology, and other tools and strategies for supporting young deaf children.

Early care and education facilities should be designed to meet the needs of young deaf children, including appropriate lighting, acoustics, and assistive technology. Equipment such as hearing aids and cochlear implants should be readily available and properly maintained. Family involvement is critical in the early care and education of young deaf children. Parents and caregivers should be provided with information and resources to support their child's development, and should be included in decision-making regarding their child's education and care. Additionally, early care and education providers working with young deaf children should have access to ongoing professional development opportunities to stay up-to-date on the latest research, practices, and strategies for supporting young deaf children.

Finally, collaboration and partnerships between early care and education providers, deaf educators, and other professionals can help ensure that young deaf children receive the support and services they need. This can include partnerships with speech and language therapists, audiologists, and other healthcare professionals.

Collaboration with Other Practitioners

Collaboration between deaf leaders and other practitioners is essential in supporting deaf children. As evidenced in the study, by working together, deaf leaders and other practitioners can share their expertise, insights, and resources to provide the best possible support and services for deaf children. Here are some ways in which deaf leaders and other practitioners can collaborate to support deaf children:

Language development: Deaf leaders and practitioners can collaborate to support the language development of deaf children. Deaf leaders can provide insights into the use of sign language and visual communication, while practitioners can share their knowledge of language acquisition and development.

Advocacy: Deaf leaders and practitioners can collaborate to advocate for the rights of deaf children, including access to language, education, and employment. Together, they can work to remove barriers and create opportunities for deaf children to thrive.

Cultural awareness: Deaf leaders can help other practitioners develop cultural awareness and sensitivity when working with deaf children and their families. By understanding the unique needs and experiences of the deaf community, practitioners can provide more effective and respectful support.

Professional development: Deaf leaders can offer professional development opportunities for other practitioners to learn about deaf culture, language, and communication. This can help practitioners improve their skills and knowledge in working with deaf children and their families.

Collaboration on programmes and services: Deaf leaders and practitioners can collaborate on the development and implementation of programs and services for deaf children. By working together, they can ensure that these programmes and services are effective, culturally responsive, and meet the needs of the deaf community.

166   Care and Education of Deaf Children in Ghana

There are several professionals who can work with deaf adults to mentor young deaf children. Here are some examples:

Deaf mentors: Deaf mentors are deaf adults who have experience and expertise in working with deaf children. They can provide support and guidance to young deaf children and their families, and they can serve as positive role models for deaf children.

Teachers of the deaf: Teachers of the deaf are trained professionals who specialize in working with deaf children. They can provide educational support, language development guidance, and other resources to young deaf children and their families.

Speech and language therapists: Speech and language therapists can work with young deaf children to develop language skills and improve communication. They can also provide guidance to deaf adults on how to support language development in young deaf children.

Social workers: Social workers can provide support to young deaf children and their families in a variety of areas, such as accessing resources, navigating the healthcare system, and addressing mental health concerns.

Community leaders: Community leaders, such as members of the deaf community or leaders of deaf organizations, can work with deaf adults to mentor young deaf children. They can provide opportunities for young deaf children to connect with the deaf community, learn about deaf culture, and develop a sense of identity and pride.

Conclusion

In conclusion, deaf leadership has the potential to play a critical role in supporting the early care and education of young deaf children. Through their unique experiences and perspectives, deaf leaders are well-positioned to provide guidance, mentorship, and advocacy for deaf children and their families. To effectively support early care and education for young deaf children, deaf leaders can collaborate with other practitioners, promote culturally and linguistically responsive practices, and advocate for policies that prioritize the needs of the deaf community. By leveraging the strengths of deaf leadership, we can ensure that young deaf children have access to high-quality care and education that is responsive to their unique needs and experiences.

References

Agboola, I. O. (2014). Andrew Jackson Foster: The man, the vision, and the 30-year uphill climb. *Gallaudet University Deaf Studies Digital Journal*, 4. Retrieved from http://dsdj.gallau det.edu/assets/section/sec- tion2/entry177/DSDJ_entry177.pdf

Braun, V., & Clarke, V. (2019). Reflecting on reflexive thematic analysis. *Qualitative Research in Sport, Exercise and Health*, *11*(4), 589–597.

Breivik, J. K. (2005). Vulnerable but strong: Deaf people challenge established understandings of deafness. *Scandinavian Journal of Public Health*, *33*, 18–23.

Buchanan, R. M. (1999). *Illusions of equality: Deaf Americans in school and factory 1850–1950*. Gallaudet Press.

Carroll, C., & Marther, S. M. (1997). *Movers and shakers: Deaf people who have changed the world*. DawnSign Press.

Davis, L. J. (2007). Deafness and the riddle of identity. *The Chronicle Review*, *53*(19), B6.

Deaf Federation of South Africa (DeafSA). (2006). *Education position paper (draft)*. Retrieved from: www.deafsa.co.za.

Doe, T. (1999). Reconceptualizing deafness: Sex is to gender as deaf is to Deaf. *Conference proceedings of the deaf studies VI: Making the connection* (pp. 277–291). Gallaudet University Press.

Eleweke, C. J., Agboola, I. O., & Guteng, S. I. (2015). Reviewing the pioneering roles of Gallaudet University alumni in advancing deaf education and services in developing countries: Insights and challenges from Nigeria. *American Annals of the Deaf*, *160*(2), 75–83.

Fobi, D., & Oppong, A. M. (2019). Communication approaches for educating deaf and hard of hearing (DHH) children in Ghana: historical and contemporary issues. *Deafness & Education International*, *21*(4), 195–209. doi:10.1080/14643154.2018.1481594

Gale, E., Berke, M., Benedict, B., Olson, S., Putz, K., & Yoshinaga-Itano, C. (2021). Deaf adults in early intervention programs. *Deafness & Education International*, *23*(1), 3–24, DOI: 10.1080/14643154.2019.1664795

Hamilton, B., & Clark, M. D. M. (2020). The deaf mentor program: Benefits to families. *Psychology*, *11*(5), 713–736.

Hintermair, M. (2000). Hearing impairment, social networks, and coping: The need for families with hearing-impaired children to relate to other parents and to hearing-impaired adults. *American Annals of the Deaf*, *145*(1), 41–53. doi:10.1353/aad.2012.0244

Jackson, C. W. (2011). Family supports and resources for parents of children who are deaf or hard of hearing. *American Annals of the Deaf*, *156*(4), 343–362. doi:10.1353/aad.2011.0038

Joint Committee on Infant Hearing. (1995). Joint committee on infant hearing 1994 position statement. *Pediatrics*, *95*(1), 152–156.

Joint Committee on Infant Hearing. (2000). American Academy of Audiology, American Academy of Pediatrics, American speech-language-hearing association and directors of speech and hearing programs in state health and welfare agencies: Year 2000 position statement: Principles and guidelines for early hearing detection and intervention programs. *Pediatrics*, *106*, 798–817. doi:10.1542/peds.106.4.798

Joint Committee on Infant Hearing. (2007). Year 2007 position statement: Principles and guidelines for early hearing detection and Intervention programs. *Pediatrics*, *120*(4), 898–921.doi:10.1542/peds.2007-2333

Kamm-Larew, D., & Lamkin, M. (2008). Survey of leadership programs: Valued characteristics of leadership within the deaf community. *JADARA*, *42*(1). Retrieved from https://nsuworks. nova.edu/jadara/vol42/iss1/4

Kiyaga, N. B., & Moores, D. F. (2003). Deafness in sub-Saharan Africa. *American Annals of the Deaf*, *148*(1), 18–24.

Kusters, A. (2014). Deaf sociality and the deaf Lutheran church in Adamorobe, Ghana. *Sign Language Studies*, *14*(4), 466–487.

Lorié, Á., Reinero, D. A., Phillips, M., Zhang, L., & Riess, H. (2017). Culture and nonverbal expressions of empathy in clinical settings: A systematic review. *Patient Education and Counseling*, *100*(3), 411–424.

Lynn, M. A., Butcher, E., Cuculick, J. A., Barnett, S., Martina, C. A., Smith, S. R., Pollard, R. Q., & Simpson-Haidaris, P. J. (2020). A review of mentoring deaf and hard-of-hearing scholars. *Mentoring & Tutoring: Partnership in Learning*, *28*(2), 211–228.

Marschark, M. (1997). *Raising and educating a deaf child*. Oxford University Press.

Marschark, M., & Hauser, P. C. (2012). *How deaf children learn: What parents and teachers need to know*. OUP USA.

Moeller, M. P., Carr, G., Seaver, L., Stredler-Brown, A., & Holzinger, D. (2013). Best practices in family-centered early intervention for children who are deaf or hard of hearing: An international consensus statement. *Journal of Deaf Studies and Deaf Education*, *18*(4), 429–445. doi:10.1093/deafed/ent034

Moore, M. S., & Panera, R. F. (1996). *Great deaf Americans* (2nd ed.). Deaf Life Press.

Moores, D. F. (2007). Centripetal and centrifugal forces. *American Annals of the Deaf*, *152*(1), 3–4.

Muse, C., Harrison, J., Yoshinaga-Itano, C., Grimes, A., Brookhouser, P. E., Epstein, S., Buchman, C., Mehl, A., Vohr, B., Moeller, M. P., Martin, P., Benedict, B. S., Scoggins. B., Crace, J., King, M., Sette, A., Martin, B. (2013). Supplement to the JCIH 2007 position statement: Principles and guidelines for early intervention after confirmation that a child is deaf or hard of hearing. *Pediatrics*, *131*(4), e1324–e1349. doi:10.1542/peds.2013-0008

Napier, J., & Leeson, L. (2016). *Sign language in action*. London: Palgrave Macmillan UK.

National Deaf Children's Society (no date). *Communicating with your deaf child*. http//.www.ndcs.or.uk

Niklas, F., Tayler, C., & Cohrssen, C. (2020). Bilingual children's language learning in Australian early childhood education and care settings. In W. Smidt, & S. Lehrl (Eds.), *Teacher–child interactions in early childhood education and care classrooms* (pp. 134–150). Routledge.

Oppong, A. M., & Fobi, D. (2019). Deaf Education in Ghana. In H. Knoors, M. Brons, & M. Marschark (Eds.), *Deaf Education beyond the Western World – Context, Challenges and Prospects for Agenda 2030* (pp. 53–72). New York: Oxford University Press. doi:10.1093/oso/9780190880514.003.0004

Rogers, K. D., & Young, A. M. (2011). Being a deaf role model: Deaf people's experiences of working with families and deaf young people. *Deafness & Education International*, *13*(1), 2–16. doi:10.1179/1557069X10Y.0000000004

Ross, E., Storbeck, C., & Wemmer, K. (2004). Psychosocial issues in prelingual deafness. In E. Ross, & A. Deverell (Eds.), *Psychosocial approaches to health, illness and disability: a reader for health care professionals* (pp. 255–292). Van Schaik.

Vijaylaxmi, J. (2009). *An ecosystemic perspective on the raising of deaf children by hearing parents in South Africa: A mixed method study*. Faculty of Education, University of KwaZulu-Natal, Durban.

Watkins, S., Pittman, P., & Walden, B. (1998). The deaf mentor experimental project for young children who are deaf and their families. *American Annals of the Deaf*, *143*(1), 29–34. doi:10.1353/aad.2012.0098

Wax, T. M. (2019). Deaf community leaders as liaisons between mental health and deaf cultures. *JADARA*, *24*(2). Retrieved from https://repository.wcsu.edu/jadara/vol24/iss2/5

10

Early Childhood Care and Education of Deaf Children

The Development of Knowledge, Theory, and Practice

Ruth Swanwick and Daniel Fobi

Introduction: Early Education for All

The 2007 United Nations Education for All initiative set out to realize Article 26 of the 1948 Universal Declaration of Human Rights that 'Everyone has the right to education' and aims to address barriers to universal education through targets that are disability inclusive. This is articulated in Sustainable Development Goal 4.2 that states that all children should have access to quality early childhood development, care, and pre-primary education. In pursuit of this goal the International Commission on Financing Global Education Opportunity, the 2018 World Bank Development Report, and the Global Education Monitoring Reports 3, 4, and 5 have all endorsed the need to invest in and develop effective pre-primary education that enables children reach their fullest potential. Our work on the early care and education of deaf children in Ghana sits within this broad context and the specific focus on investment in the development of infants and young children in Africa, as identified in the United Nations Global Monitoring report of 2007 (UNESCO, 2007). This report emphasized the need for improving early years provision for the most disadvantaged children in the world. Of the 130 million children under 6 years old in sub-Saharan Africa (SSA) more than half are shelter deprived and 40% are water deprived. The report calls on African countries to improve their early childhood care and education (ECCE) and invest in their young children.

Ruth Swanwick and Daniel Fobi, *Early Childhood Care and Education of Deaf Children* In: *The Early Care and Education of Deaf Children in Ghana*. Edited by: Ruth Swanwick, Daniel Fobi, Yaw Offei, and Alexander Oppong, Oxford University Press. © Ruth Swanwick and Daniel Fobi 2024. DOI: 10.1093/oso/9780192872272.003.0010

The 2019 UNICEF global report, 'A World Ready to Learn', analyses progress towards SDG goal 4.2 and recognizes the multiple systemic and individual barriers to early childhood education in low- and middle-income countries (LMICs) and specifically for the most disadvantaged and vulnerable children. The strategies and measures undertaken to challenge these inequities that are outlined in this report all begin with an analysis of why certain marginalized communities are not receiving services. The identified barriers centre on policy development and enactment, the logistics and costs of access to services, and social awareness and stigma. Steps taken to mitigate these barriers to reaching all children emphasize the need for multi-professional cooperation in order to achieve holistic, accessible, and effective ECCE services.

Deaf Children: Left Behind from the Start

A legacy of the call to action has been a growth in ECCE research and development work including intervention and evaluation studies (Garcia et al., 2008; Penn & Lloyd, 2007) along with the development of critical perspectives on the provenance and assumptions underlying ECCE research, reporting and evaluation, and efforts to globalize provision (Nsamenang, 2008; Singal & Muthukrishna, 2014). However, deaf children are barely visible in this research, development, and action planning in Africa and other LMICs, even though an estimated 180,000 children are born with permanent hearing loss in SSA annually. The high prevalence of hearing impairment in children and adolescents in SSA that is estimated to be at least 1.9% (vs 0.4% in high income contexts) highlights the severity of the burden for this context where most children with hearing loss are living (Desalew et al., 2020).

This state of affairs is perplexing given that international policy has been developed to protect deaf children's entitlement to early care and education, and specifically their rights to grow up with access to language and communication. Specific goals focusing on disability are set out in the United Nations Convention on the Rights of the Child (UNCRC) that was adopted by the UN General Assembly in 1989.

Article 23(1) CRC 1989 reads that 'States Parties recognize that a mentally or physically disabled child should enjoy a full and decent life, in conditions which ensure dignity, promote self-reliance, and facilitate the child's active participation in the community.'

The Convention on the Rights of Persons with Disabilities (CRPD, 2006) further obligates governments to respect the rights of children with disabilities as soon as they born and afford them the same freedoms and rights as other children. Articles in the CRPD specify sensory impairment and respect for individual identities. This is explicit in Article 21 in relation to 'Freedom of expression and opinion, and access to information' that calls on States Parties to provide access through 'all forms of communication' (21b) and the recognition and promotion of sign languages (21e). Article 24 is further specific in relation to recognizing the right of persons with disabilities to education, without discrimination and based on equal opportunity. It calls on all State Parties to facilitate the learning of sign language and the promotion of the linguistic identity of the deaf community (24.3b), access to education through the most appropriate means of communication (24.3c) and the provision of appropriate training in sign language for educators (24.4).

What this means in the context of the education of deaf children is spelled out in further detail in a position paper produced by the World Federation of the Deaf. This paper does not specify early education but emphasizes the implications of the CRPD statements in terms of 'early exposure to sign language and multilingualism, combined with strong family support for sign languages' as well as the importance of visual language and access to a quality education in children's native sign language(s), regardless of any technological devices they may use (World Federation of the Deaf, 2016).

Alongside these international conventions the aligned objectives of the African Charter on the Rights and Welfare of the Child (1990) and the African Charter on the Rights of Persons with Disabilities (2018) emphasize the universal human rights for Africans with disabilities. Specifically, the 2018 protocol seeks to adopt accountable measures to improve the lives of African people with disabilities and to address urgent issues of poverty, systemic discrimination, and harmful practices that have the most disproportionate impact on people with disabilities.

Despite international policy and legalisation, deaf children and those with other disabilities are still missing out on quality inclusive ECCE particularly in the poorest countries where the intersecting factors of poverty and discrimination further marginalize the children who would benefit from quality ECCE most (Rose & Zubairi, 2017). Ghana, as an example, is one of the African nations that has made a strong response to the call for ECCE at a national, district, and community level and has a national Early Child Development (ECD) coordinating committee and secretariat. However, the needs of young deaf children are not served within this remit. Consequently, as shown through the case study work in Chapters 5–9, the experience of exclusion from early childhood education and subsequent access to language, communication, and eventual participation in society starts at birth. It is important to try to understand why that is.

Inclusive ECCE Research, Development, and Practice

The Knowledge Base

One of the constraints on the development of an ECCE agenda that is inclusive of deaf children in southern contexts such as Africa is the dominant knowledge base that drives the development and evaluation of ECCE provision. Knowledge that is derived from largely Western research and understandings of childhood and caregiving lead the international ECCE dialogue despite efforts in the Global Monitoring Report to provide a pluralistic account using case studies (Pence & Marfo, 2008). Specifically, Nsamenang (2007) makes the point that the ideological and theoretical positioning of ECCE narratives and debates are not inclusive of African knowledge systems and values or indeed of the majority world. This means many early childhood programmes and interventions embody rather narrow and ethnocentric development theories that neglect a more diverse understanding of child development and parenting and the different ways in which community, family shape childhood experience (LeVine, 2004, Super & Harkness, 2008).

Countries of the South and LMICs are further excluded by the 'investment narrative' underpinning ECCE recommendations, programmes, and interventions, that links early childhood, neuro-science, and economics (Doyle et al., 2007). Such models fail to acknowledge the deep inequalities and fundamental hardships experienced by so many children in the low-income contexts and neglect the local realities and cultural context for early development and care (Nsamenang, 2008).

These issues are reflected in specific context of early childhood deaf education where models of intervention are driven by Western research that is infused with assumptions about nuclear families, constructs of a child-oriented talk, the play environment, and the pedagogic role of parents (Curtin et al., 2021). These models are not a fit for most of the worlds' deaf children: They do not include attention to different cultural values around the role of children in society and diverse approaches to child rearing (Pence & Marfo, 2008) or consider the intersection between poverty and disability (Grech, 2009). An additional lacuna is that the wider issues of stigma and marginalization around deafness and other disabilities are not acknowledged (Opoku et al., 2020). For these reasons deaf children from LMICs of the South are not served by current ECCE guidelines, protocols, and policy development.

The Research Context

Young deaf children and their caregivers are also missing from the ECCE research literature. The research dialogue around the early support of deaf children and their caregivers includes very little reference to the experiences of children and families in contexts that lack a robust ECCE infrastructure and resource and where a missed or very late confirmation of deafness is compounded by the absence of maintained hearing technologies and impoverished opportunities develop early language and communication skills. Research that examines the early childhood care and education of deaf children focuses largely on communication and language development and subsequent impacts of childhood deafness on cognitive and social development, participation, and inclusion. These issues are typically examined from a Western perspective. Topics in deaf ECCE identified as pertinent (see, e.g., Taylor et al., 2023) including literacy and language development, phonology, autonomy, self-advocacy, curriculum, and assessment are often discussed from a particular view of childhood experience where 'watching television, helping a family member bake a cake, singing songs or playing a video game' (p.6) are considered to be typical. Constructs of language deprivation that are often rehearsed in this literature are largely contextualized within Western cultures (Hall et al., 2019; Rowley et al., 2022). More understanding is needed of what being 'language deprived' looks like in a context where there are intersecting issues of poverty, health, and stigma in order for the research to include and impact on caregivers in such contexts.

A further significant lacuna concerns the attention to the multilingual realities of the lives of young deaf children and the families in contexts where there are multiple spoken languages in use in the home and designated local languages valorized in the early education context, alongside the use of an official languages associated with later primary and secondary education, and where the only access to sign language is in the school for the deaf where English is the taught spoken/written language. Research into multilingualism in deaf children and their families is growing but tends to focus on nations of the global North and populations and this has led to the development of a knowledge base that neglects underrepresented socio-cultural contexts and minorities.

Much can be learned from countries of the South about different multilingual repertoires, language practices, and language users not represented in current research and who present a unique perspective on multilingual language development and use. Whilst the potential of early exposure bilingual/

174   Care and Education of Deaf Children in Ghana

bimodal language use is increasingly examined in the deaf ECCE literature, this research assumes an early identification window, and access to protocol and services that align with the early hearing detection and intervention (EHDI) guidelines, and a universal relevance of social models of disability and understandings of deaf and cultural identity (Clarke et al., 2020). Research, for example, that identifies the use of sign language as an 'efficacious choice' for families (Clark et al., 2020, p. 1341), constructs of caregiver choice, and advocacy around language and communication need to be problematized.

Without research that is inclusive of these contexts and experiences, the research field of deaf ECCE, that then drives policy and international guidelines, represents and applies only to a minority of deaf children and families. A more inclusive research agenda would diversify the flow of information and knowledge (usually from North to South) to include southern livelihoods, voices, and theoretical perspectives and more emphatically bring the needs of most deaf children in the world to the attention of governments, international organizations, development agencies, and charities.

Developing Practice

Insights from the case study work that we undertook in Ghana contribute to the development of the deaf ECCE knowledge base and the theoretical frameworks that can inform policy and practice development. There are pointers from this work towards ways in which the early support of deaf children and their caregivers can be responsive to the needs of caregivers and their children in cultural settings beyond the Western world where the child development context, daily routines, parenting practices, and surrounding societal attitudes and expectations diverge from Western paradigms. We have used the bioecological framework that we adopted for the project work to reflect on what has been learned in terms of the proximal and distal influences on early development, caregiving, and support.

In thinking about the day-to-day contexts of children's lives (home, school, community), and the relationships and interactions within that context that involve the child (the microsystem), ECCE programmes need to take account of who is the social and physical setting for caregiving, who is involved, and what this looks like. As we observed in the Ghana study, caregiving in many African contexts is shared among available adults in the community space, grandparents, and older siblings in physical settings that are often shared and communal Nsamenang (2010),). Early intervention and specifically communication support including access to sign language tuition or links with the school for the deaf that is normally targeted towards main caregivers needs to encompass the full range of caregiving encounters at home and in school so that the skills and confidence develop across the actors involved with young deaf children on a daily basis. Caregivers of deaf children may not consistently be the biological parents but are sometimes the carers in residential schools for the deaf or other members of the community around the family, especially where accommodation is in shared compound houses. Nsamenang (2010, p. 20) uses the term 'first educator' to refer to ways in which family life, caregiving responsibilities, and routines depart from Western practices.

The nature of the support around communication also needs to be contextually appropriate. We learned from our observations and interviews with caregivers that children's learning and development takes place through taking part in family and community life. There is little emphasis on one-to-one dialogic parent–child interactions around toys and books but rather an expectation that young children spend their time being alongside adults in the home and community as they go about their daily routines and chores of the family and the community. Caregivers in our study talked about involving their deaf children in sweeping the house, the cooking and shopping, and general fetching and carrying. Through these routines it is expected that young children graduate to contributing to family and community life. Development and learning thus comes about through participation rather than scaffolded instruction from parents. ECCE intervention for deaf children in such a context needs to be tailored around these practices. The communication support offered also needs to account for the complexities of the multilingual environment around the child so that local languages are valorized but at the same time the links for caregivers to the languages used (GhSL and English) in the schools for the deaf ECCE are facilitated. The scaffolding of communication around the child's needs, that is construed in the Western models of support as taking place between parent and child dyads thus needs to be understood and supported by professionals in ways that are relevant.

Most of the caregivers that we spoke to were concerned about the financial burden of the educational and technology needs of their deaf child and did not have the means to seek independent support, training facilities, or equipment. Their financial situations and working commitments also impeded their involvement with their child's school life (in regional schools for the deaf) due to the costs of travel and impacted on opportunities for their young children to spend time at home during the school term time. ECCE programmes in such a context need to be developed with an awareness of the intersecting disadvantages of poverty and deprivation that impact the lives of deaf children and their caregivers with a strong focus on the local and community-based support alongside work with the school-based 'house parents' who have a substantial caregiving and intermediary role in young deaf children's lives.

An ECCE programme in this context whilst being child-centred would also ideally undertake the training of the parents and the wider caregiving community with a focus on embedding expertise, resources, and practices within the local community. Along with a focus on the development of resources and capacity, close work with caregivers would be usefully focused on developing the understanding and confidence that they need to advocate for the needs of their children and encourage this agency among other caregivers (Storbeck and Moodley, 2011). ECCE intervention in this context could usefully be conceptualized as support across the different environments and microsystems of home, community, and school that surround the child, that is support for the mesosystem that facilitates the optimal conditions for child development and assured caregiving.

Increasing the Workforce

Increasing the professional work force in ECCE for deaf children is critical if an equitable and quality service is to exist throughout countries such as Ghana, that is one that is inclusive of rural areas. Insights from our research highlight the importance of identifying a range of providers with the motivation and pre-requisite skills to be trained to provide early intervention specific to children who are deaf. This includes deaf individuals, educators, clinicians, and highly respected community members. The ECCE workforce can also be effectively increased through the proactive development of parent professionals. Although we were not able to talk to any deaf caregivers in this research, it is well documented that some of the most effective mentors/teachers of other families are deaf parents who have experience in how to parent a new deaf baby and extensive communication strategies (Hamilton & Clark, 2020). Family-to-family support and the role of parents and families in collaboration with deaf community are critical components discussed in both the Joint Committee on Infant Hearing and the Family Centred Early Intervention documents that could be effectively developed in different global contexts (Moeller, 2000). Working with local communities to provide such services, support, and training is key to the effectiveness of such initiatives.

Whilst we saw limited use of remote technologies in our study other than the reported use of tele-interpreting during the pandemic, there is great potential for building tele-intervention services particularly around sign language tuition for families, early language, and learning, as well as tele-health and tele-therapy for audiological services and medical services. This technology also provides a mechanism to train educators within communities and to thus build the provision and workforce beyond the more populated and economically advantaged urban areas (Nelson et al., 2022; Yaribakht & Movallali, 2020).

A Blended Approach

To take this work forward in practical ways we might usefully adopt a blended approach as described by Nsamenang (2010) that recognizes the inevitable co-existence of Western models of deaf ECCE with approaches that recognize and build on indigenous childrearing practices and traditions. A blended approach to the early support of deaf children and their caregivers would imply recognition of the intersecting disadvantages of health and poverty often associated with deafness in low-income contexts that impact on the support systems, societal attitudes, and caregiver experience. However, through focused work with community leaders such an approach could challenge the negative connotations and stigma associated with deafness and sign language in Southern contexts, improve local and national deaf awareness, and mitigate polarized views around the use of spoken and/or sign language by promoting bilingual educational provision. A blended approach to capacity building is a powerful argument for using the available funds of knowledge among academics, practitioners, and families and communities but at the same time building confidence and skills to extend and share this knowledge.

An Epistemic Journey

Alongside these implications for practice, this text contributes to theory development in ECCE by disrupting northern epistemologies of early childhood, caregiving, and intervention, and looking to incorporate southern perspectives into the growing science of ECE.

Whilst concepts of inclusive education are curated in the global North (Kamenopoulou, 2020) so too are constructs of early child development, education, and care on which best practice models for deaf children and their caregivers are based (Moeller et al., 2013). The project work described in this text demonstrates the extent to which these models need renovation to make them relevant to southern contexts. ECCE policy—that according to Nsamenang (p.22) suffers from 'poverty of knowledge'—also needs to be developed with a greater understanding of where and how the majority of the worlds' deaf children live. Our examination of the deaf ECCE context in Ghana and exposition of the realities of childhood deafness and caregiving highlight the need for a critical approach to the literature, caution around the transfer of constructs across cultures and geographies, and reveal the potential for new knowledge. This epistemic challenge pushes at assumptions about parenting practices, communication and interactional styles, the multilingual language context, and social understandings of deafness and demands a re-framing of the caregiving context. We see this as a process, or a journey towards, more inclusive ECCE for deaf children globally.

More widely this work touches the politics of disability and impairment and challenges dominant discourses of disability rights and inclusion that are embedded within international policy (such as the Convention on the Rights of Persons with Disabilities) and the Sustainable Development Goals. The construct of 'rights', as Grech points out (2011) is a Western invention and as such needs to be re-examined as an framework for research and development work in disability education in southern contexts. This need for reflexivity is echoed by other disability scholars who work beyond the global North. Meekosah (2011), for example, urges critical awareness around the use of constructs such as discrimination, marginalization, and emancipation arguing that these are socially constructed concepts and ideologies that potentially neglect examination of the wider intersecting categories of experience. In the field of deaf studies and education, the need for criticality is especially pertinent where ideological binaries have led to an inauthentic division between social and medical perspectives on deafness and polarized discourse around the educational approach and communication choices (Kusters et al., 2017).

We extend this debate to the early education and care of deaf children, and the support of families in southern contexts where the support and empowerment of caregivers needs to be enacted with an understanding of the social worlds and livelihoods of families, their caregiving and languaging practices as well as wider societal structures, attitudes, and beliefs surrounding deafness and the use of sign language. Our encounters with families of deaf children, the communities around families, and deaf and hearing practitioners required us to reframe our position on rights and embrace a southern emphasis on collective rather than individual needs and behaviours and emphasis on moral conduct rather than entitlement (Singal, 2010). We signal this ambition and the tension around it from the start in our introductory positioning around the social model of disability, acknowledging that this model has been constructed in the global North (mainly by scholars in the UK) and focuses largely on social systems not relevant to many other world cultures (Connell, 2011).

Developing Research Methods and Tools

To continue this epistemic journey, we must increase the visibility of young deaf children and their families from different global contexts in the ECCE research. This requires a shift in the way in which research projects are conceptualized, framed, and designed. Because of the predominant structure and provenance of international research funding there is always a risk that the way in which the research premise, questions, and methods are determined fail to reflect the priorities and concerns of all the contexts involved. The aims and questions for an international project should ideally be co-constructed through preliminary work with stakeholders and co-investigators so that the conceptual approach from the start is shared and contextually appropriate. At the point of the Ghana funding application, we found it useful to talk to local and regional educational and health practitioners about their deaf ECCE experiences and concerns. In preparation we also worked together to develop a conceptual bioecological framework for the work planned that we felt would enable us to look deeply, focus on the resources in context, and avoid being led by preconceived expectations of what ECCE should look like for deaf children.

In terms of methodological approach, there is a strong case for more ethnographic work with nationally and culturally diverse research teams that provide thick description and reflexive interpretation that challenge research assumptions and facilitate the global dissemination of ECCE practices and ideas. Tobin (2022) talks about the 'productive tensions' (p. 300) that can arise from ethnographic research that looks across diverse setting and challenges core assumptions. Comparisons across cultures and contexts can be useful but only if we allow them to 'complicate and deepen' (p. 302) our understanding of practices and approaches. This kind of approach relies on a diverse research team who have the linguistic and cultural knowledge of the context as well as the intercultural understandings needed to ensure successful communication and working practices across the team. The work undertaken in Ghana would not have succeeded without the co-ordination of a mixed hearing and deaf multilingual Ghana team with understanding of the early years' context for families of deaf children, and a project coordinator with awareness of the research contexts in Ghana and the UK.

To really see inside the ECCE contexts, we would also advocate for the use of more participatory and visual methods with children and families to gain insights in caregiving practices and experience, language use, and communication strategies (Adair & Kurban 2019; Valente 2019). Participatory methods need to be tailored to the context of people's lives and their experience of research. Methods such as 'go-alongs' or walking interviews that blend interview and their observation techniques are an example of an accessible way of learning about people's lived experience (Evans & Jones, 2011; Kusenbach, 2003). Researchers walk with participants to elicit responses that relate to their environment and their connections with, attitudes towards, and behaviours in different spaces. This approach enables the researcher to capture a richer understanding of place and how languages are used in the different locations of participants' lives.

Visual methods are also suited to work with families who may have limited experiences of interview formats, who may be uncertain about voicing opinions and reflections, and prefer a visual approach to telling and sharing. Strategies might include the use of pre-made images, such as photos, drawings, postcards, videos, and text messages, that can be used as prompts during interviews with children and caregivers to bridge communication gaps and ensure that the participants have some control over the interview process. As well, created images by participants, ecomaps (Rogers, 2017) and other artefacts can provide useful springboards for discussion. Creating opportunities for expression through the visual artefact is a useful way to ensure that interviews are hospitable to and reflect participants' values and cultures (O'Brien, 2021).

A central part of early intervention work with deaf children and their families is the support of language development and shared communication. For the most part this support centres on hearing caregivers of deaf children who are likely to have limited experience of childhood deafness and the use of sign language. To analyse and learn about language development and communication among young deaf children and their caregivers across different cultural contexts, we argue that a multimodal rather than a language-based approach provides the opportunity to understand the different ways in which caregivers deploy and coordinate different embodied multimodal resources (touch, gesture, and eye-gaze) in their interactions with their deaf infants. Detailed multimodal analysis of child and parent interaction can show how the use of these resources facilitates mutual understanding in the presence of sensorial asymmetries (Adami & Swanwick 2019). This knowledge provides an important basis for supporting the development of caregivers' visual communication in culturally sensitive ways that build on their established repertoire of strategies.

South–North Research Partnerships

Undertaking research in to ECCE as a mixed deaf -hearing cross-cultural team offered creative research possibilities as well as challenges. We spent much of the early cross-context discussion time unravelling our different expectations of quality ECCE for deaf children. A significant challenge for us was to avoid the importation of ideas, methods, and practices from North to South from the very start. This involved reversing the typical direction of the flow of knowledge and research 'know how' from North to South and developing strategies to 'privilege the insights of insiders' (Tobin, 2022, p.297). This was, and continues to be, difficult to achieve. Even for culturally diverse and multilingual research teams challenges of inequity exist with project documentation, reporting, and publication where English is the lingua franca of the funder and thus the project. The expectations of the academy, research funders, and journal editors inexorably drive the focus of research activities, outcomes, and a focus on metrics. In this situation, often the norm for international projects, it becomes easier and convenient for the first language English speaking team members to take on the role of lead author across project written project outcomes. There is then a danger that one perspective comes though the reports and papers and of the project outputs leading with Western philosophies, theories, and methods (Hayashi, 2021).

In the Ghana project we have tried to counter this in various ways. One of our tasks was to ensure that the cultural heritage of the Ghanaian team members was valued by the Ghanaian team members themselves who at the start tended to underestimate the potential of their own insider perspectives, defer to UK values and academic practices, and default to importing ideas and solutions from well-resourced contexts. We also invested time in the development of a critical reading and writing skills across the project team from the start, and for the preparation of papers and chapters we have worked consistently in mentoring pairs. Since Ghanaian Sign Language is one of our team languages, we have also invited video contributions to project outputs from deaf team members that they have themselves translated into English for text-based materials. Whilst this is still not fully equitable, such solutions go some way to addressing issues of power, culture, and language as discussed by Valente (2017), and also ensures that the insider knowledge of deaf researchers from within the indigenous deaf communities influences the project structure and approaches taken (Graham & Horejes 2017).

A further challenge that we experienced was how to negotiate a universally acceptable research code of ethics across the North and South universities and enact this in culturally sensitive ways. We found, as suggested by McMahon and Milligan (2023), that over and above an ethical agreement there was a need for an on-going dialogue across the project team about the most ethical way of approaching each new encounter and that this involved returning to the ecological values and principles underpinning the project questions. Our approach to start with the resources and practices around the thus provided an anchor for the context-sensitive design of data collection and analysis methods and tools.

As we continue to work together to develop the impact of the research our focus is increasingly on the development of professional and academic skills and confidence of the deaf and hearing actors involved in the support of young deaf children and their caregivers *in situ*. This comprises work with the deaf community to develop a strong deaf-informed input into intervention planning and cross-sectoral partnerships with parents and communities to grow parent education projects that are not only attached to the schools for the deaf. In this way we are building capacity to provide deaf-led and community-based mentoring of caregivers that supports visual communication strategies among children and families that enhance but do not replace cultural ways of being and doing (Nsamenang 2008).

We are also 'training the trainers' and special educators in total communication approaches and have established of mentoring writing and research partnerships across the UK and Ghana settings. This work that draws on established funds of knowledge encourages more writing about deaf ECCE through the lens of southern theory and facilitates new knowledge production. Across these developments it is our priority that the expertise and know-how being developed is deployed with an understanding of family and community resources and practices, and local understandings of childhood.

Conclusion

In both mainstream and deaf education ECCE is a growing area for international research and development. However, young deaf children and their caregivers in Africa and other southern, low-income contexts have slipped through a gap in the research debates and are also missing in international and local policy development. Whilst statistics on childhood deafness globally are readily available, policies and service planning that addresses the combined impacts of the medical and social impacts of childhood deafness are mainly oriented to Western contexts (for one notable exception see Storbeck & Moodley, 2011). To minimize the disruption to development caused by childhood deafness in the context of the language deprivation, the social lives of deaf children and their caregivers need to be an integral part of the measures of support following detection in African countries (Olusanya et al., 2006). It is therefore important that deaf ECCE researchers and practitioners join the critical debates in this arena that problematize theoretical and ideological drivers and review the task of embedding ECCE practices within local understandings of childhood (Marfo et al., 2011). Throughout this project we have sought to examine ECCE thinking and propose actions that are relevant to African childhood and parenting paradigms and to bring the experience of parenting a deaf child in the global South to the fore in research and policy development. We have also proposed an engagement with southern perspective and methodologies in an effort to extend epistemologies surrounding childhood deafness and caregiving beyond the global North (Nguyen, 2018).This is the start of a longer-term decolonization project in this field that we hope will fuel deaf ECCE policy development that is cross-sector, holistic, and that integrates health, education, and well-being and that is supported by multiprofessional partnerships that includes parents, communities, and international organizations.

References

(2019). Year 2019 Position Statement: Principles and Guidelines for Early Hearing Detection and Intervention Programs. *Journal of Early Hearing Detection and Intervention, 4*(2), 1–44. DOI: https://doi.org/10.15142/fptk-b748 Retrieved from

Adair, J. K., & Kurban, F. (2019). Video-cued ethnographic data collection as a tool toward participant voice. *Anthropology & Education Quarterly, 50*(3), 313–332.

Adami, E., & Swanwick, R. (2019). Signs of understanding and turns-as-actions: a multimodal analysis of deaf–hearing interaction. *Visual Communication*, 147035721985477. DOI: 10.1177/1470357219854776

Clark, M. D., Cue, K. R., Delgado, N. J., Greene-Woods, A. N., & Wolsey, J.-L. A. (2020). Early intervention protocols: Proposing a default bimodal bilingual approach for deaf children. *Maternal and Child Health Journal, 24*, 1339–1344.

Connell, R. (2011). Southern bodies and disability: Re-thinking concepts. *Third World Quarterly, 32*(8), 1369–1381.

Curtin, M., Dirks, E., Cruice, M., Herman, R., Newman, L., Rodgers, L., Morgan, G. (2021). Assessing parent behaviours in parent–child interactions with deaf and hard of hearing infants aged 0–3 years: a systematic review. *Journal of Clinical Medicine, 10*(15), 1–30.

Desalew, A., Feto Gelano, T., Semahegn, A., Geda, B., & Ali, T. (2020). *Childhood hearing impairment and its associated factors in sub-Saharan Africa in the 21st century: A systematic review and meta-analysis. SAGE Open Medicine, 8*, 2050312120919240.

Doyle, O., Tremblay, R. E., Harmon, C., & Heckman, J. J. (2007). Early childhood intervention: rationale, timing, and efficacy. *Working Paper University College Dublin, Geary Institute Series.*

Evans, J., & Jones, P. (2011). The walking interview: Methodology, mobility and place. *Applied Geography, 31*(2), 849–858. DOI: 10.1016/j.apgeog.2010.09.005

Garcia, M. H., Pence, A., & Evans, J. (2008). *Africa's future, Africa's challenge: early childhood care and development in Sub-Saharan* Africa. World Bank Publications.

Graham, P. J., & Horejes, T. P. (2017). Why positionality matters in deaf education research: An insider ethnographic perspective. In S. Cawthon & C. L. Garberoglio (Eds.), *Research in deaf education: Contexts, challenges, and considerations* (pp. 55–74). Oxford University Press.

Grech, S. (2011). Recolonising debates or perpetuated coloniality? Decentring the spaces of disability, development and community in the global South. *International Journal of Inclusive Education, 15*(1), 87–100.

Grech, S., 2009. Disability, poverty and development: critical reflections on the majority world debate. *Disability in Society 24*(6), 771–784.

Hall, M. L., Hall, W. C., & Caselli, N. K. (2019). Deaf children need language, not (just) speech. *First Language, 39*(4), 367–395.

Hamilton, B., & Clark, M. D. M. (2020). The deaf mentor program: Benefits to families. *Psychology, 11*(5), 713–736.

Hayashi, A. (2021). Some Japanese ways of conducting comparative educational research. *Comparative Education, 57*(2), 147–158.

International Commission on Financing Global Education Opportunity (2016), *The Learning Generation: Investing in education for a changing world, Education Commission*, New York, <https://bit.ly/2T1DA4T>, accessed 10 March 2023.

Kamenopoulou, L. (2020). Decolonising inclusive education: an example from a research in Colombia. *Disability and the Global South, 7*(1), 1792–1812.

Kusenbach, M. (2003). Street phenomenology: The go-along as ethnographic research tool. *Ethnography, 4*(3), 455–485. DOI: 10.1177/146613810343007

Kusters, A., De Meulder, M., & O'Brien, D. (2017). Innovations in deaf studies: Critically mapping the field. In A. Kusters, M. De Meulder, & D. O'Brien (Eds.), *Innovations in deaf studies: The role of deaf scholars* (pp. 1–53). Oxford University Press.

LeVine, R. A. (2004). Challenging expert knowledge: Findings from an African study of infant care and development. In U. P. Gielen, & J. Roopnarine (Eds.), *Childhood and adolescence: cross-cultural perspectives and applications* (pp. 149–165). Praeger.

Marfo, K., Pence, A., LeVine, R. A., & LeVine, S. (2011). Strengthening Africa's contributions to child development research: Introduction. *Child Development Perspectives, 5*(2), 104–111.

McMahon, E., & Milligan, L. O. (2023). A framework for ethical research in international and comparative education. *Compare: A Journal of Comparative and International Education, 53*(1), 72–78.

Meekosha, H. (2011). Decolonising disability: thinking and acting globally. *Disability & Society, 26*(6), 667–682.

Moeller, M. P. (2000). Early intervention and language development in children who are deaf and hard of hearing. *Pediatrics, 106*(3), E43. doi: 10.1542/peds.106.3.e43

Moeller, M. P., G. Carr, L. Seaver, A. Stredler-Brown, & Holzinger, D. (2013). Best practices in family-centered early intervention for children who are deaf or hard of hearing: An International Consensus Statement. *Journal of Deaf Studies and Deaf Education 18*(4), 429–445. doi:10.1093/deafed/ent034

Nelson, L. H., Rudge, A. M., Dawson, P., Culianos, D., Broekelmann, C., & Stredler-Brown, A. (2022). Parents' perspectives about tele-intervention services for their children who are deaf or hard of hearing. *Journal of Early Hearing Detection and Intervention, 7*(2), 9–21.

Nguyen, X. T. (2018). Critical disability studies at the edge of global development: Why do we need to engage with southern theory? *Canadian Journal of Disability Studies, 7*(1), 1–25.

Nsamenang, A. B. (2007). A critical peek at early childhood care and education in Africa. *Child Health and Education, 1*(1), 14–26.

Nsamenang, A. B. (2008). (Mis)understanding ECD in Africa: The force of local and global motive. In J. E. Garcia-Albea, A. Pence, & A. D. Evans (Eds.), *Africa's future, Africa's challenge: Early childhood care and development in sub-Saharan Africa* (pp. 135–149). Washington World Bank.

Nsamenang, A. B. (2010). Issues in and challenges to professionalism in Africa's cultural settings. *Contemporary Issues in Early Childhood*, *11*(1), 20–28.

O'Brien, D. (2021). Theorising the deaf body: Using Lefebvre and Bourdieu to understand deaf spatial experience. *Cultural Geographies*, *28*(4), 645–660. DOI: 10.1177/14744740211003632

Olusanya, B., Luxon, L., & Wirz, S. (2006). Maternal views on infant hearing loss in a developing country. *International Journal of Pediatric Otorhinolaryngology*, *70*(4), 619–623.

Opoku, M. P., Nketsia, W., Benefo, E. B., & Mprah, W. K. (2020). Understanding the parental experiences of raising deaf children in Ghana. *Journal of Family Studies*, *28*(4), 1235–1254. doi:10.1080/13229400.2020.1815557

Pence, A. R., & Marfo, K. (2008). Early childhood development in Africa: Interrogating constraints of prevailing knowledge bases. *International Journal Psychology*, *43*(2), 78–87.

Penn, H., & Lloyd, E. (2007). Richness or rigour? A discussion of systematic reviews and evidence-based policy in early childhood. *Contemporary Issues in Early Childhood*, *8*(1), 3–18.

Rogers, J. (2017). Eco-maps and photo elicitation: reflections on the use of visual methods in social work research with children and young people in the UK. *Journal of Applied Youth Studies*, *1*(4), 45–60.

Rose, P., & Zubairi, A. (2017). *Bright and Early: How financing pre-primary education gives every child a fair start in life*. Theirworld. UK

Rowley, K., Snoddon, K., & O'Neill, R. (2022). Supporting families and young deaf children with a bimodal bilingual approach. *International Journal of Birth & Parent Education*, *9*(3), 15–20.

Singal, N. (2010). Doing disability research in a Southern context: challenges and possibilities. *Disability & Society*, *25*(4), 415–426. doi:10.1080/09687591003755807

Singal, N., & Muthukrishna, N. (2014). Education, childhood and disability in countries of the South–Re-positioning the debates. *Childhood*, *21*(3), 293–307.

Storbeck, C., & Moodley, S. (2011). ECD policies in South Africa–What about children with disabilities? *Journal of African Studies and Development*, *3*(1), 1–8.

Super, C. M., & Harkness, S. (2008). Globalization and its discontents: Challenges to developmental theory and practice in Africa. *International Journal of Psychology*, *43*(2), 107–113.

Taylor, K., Neild, R., & Fitzpatrick, M. (2023). Universal design for learning: Promoting access in early childhood education for deaf and hard of hearing children. *Perspectives on Early Childhood Psychology and Education*, *5*(2), 4.

Tobin, J. (2022). Learning from comparative ethnographic studies of early childhood education and care. *Comparative Education*, *58*(3), 297–314.

UN General Assembly, *Convention on the Rights of the Child*, 20 November 1989, United Nations, Treaty Series, vol. *1577*, p. 3. Retrieved 26 June 2023 from https://www.refworld.org/docid/3ae6b38f0.html

United Nations Educational Scientific and Cultural Organization (UNESCO), (2007), *Education for All Global Monitoring Report: Strong foundations – Early childhood care and education*, UNESCO, Paris, <https://unesdoc.unesco.org/ark:/48223/pf0000147794>;

Valente, J. M. (2017). Anxiety as a tool for Critical Disability Studies fieldwork. *Review of Disability Studies: An International Journal*, *13*(2), 1–14.

Valente, J. M. (2019). A deaf lens: Adapting video-cued multivocal ethnography for the 'Kindergartens for the Deaf in Three Countries' project. *Anthropology & Education Quarterly*, *50*(3), 340–347.

World Bank. (2018). *World Development Report 2018: Learning to realize education's promise*, World Bank, Washington, D.C., <www. worldbank.org/en/publication/wdr2018>, accessed 10 March 2023.

World Federation of the Deaf. (2016, September). WFD position paper on the sign language rights of deaf children. https://wfdeaf.org/news/resources-category/statements/

Yaribakht, M., & Movallali, G. (2020). The effectiveness of an early family-centered tele-intervention program on pre-verbal and listening skills of deaf children under 2 years old. *Iranian Rehabilitation Journal, 18*(2), 117–124.

Index

For the benefit of digital users, indexed terms that span two pages (e.g., 52–53) may, on occasion, appear on only one of those pages.

Adamorobe Sign Language 111–12, 114
Adaptive Auditory Screening Test
    (AAST) 13
African Charter on the Rights of Persons
    with Disabilities (2018) 171
African Charter on the Rights and Welfare of
    the Child (1990) 171
African knowledge systems and values 172
Agona Duakwa, Salvation Army
    Rehabilitation Centre 133, 135,
    141–42
Akan language 93, 111, 112, 113, 115, 118,
    122, 127–28
ambulances 139
Appau, Obed 9–10
Ashanti School for the Deaf 135
Asomaning, Derrick 5–7, 128
audiological services, Ghana 65, 66–68,
    176–77
    outdated and non-functional basic
        equipment 138
    outreach, mobile ambulances 139
Automated Auditory Brainstem Response
    (AABR) test 23–24, 66

bioecological theory of parenting 45, 82–87
    caregiving experiences and practices 85
    development of methodology 83–86
    ethical challenges 45, 86–87
    position and agency of caregivers 45, 85
    shortcomings 45, 84
    summary 88
    see also ecological systems theory (1977)
book layout 1–19
    collective vision 14–15
    contributor stories 3–14
    core writing team 15
    geographical definitions 1–2

introduction 1–3
research *see* Ghana: ECCE research/
    intervention project
structure 15–19
Bourdieusian constructs, power and
    agency 84

caregivers
    case studies 114–24
        Boateng family 120–22
        Dazie family 118–20
        Opuku family 122–24
        Owusu family 115–18
        reflections on family
            experience 124–26
    counselling and emotional support 138
    funding 94
    influences on communication practices
        and choices 84
    methodology of research/intervention
        project 92–95
        Bronfenbrenner bioecological
            framework 92–95
    parent–professional partnerships 139–40
    participative research and 87
    resources (liabilities and assets) 84
    summary/conclusion 106–7
Centre for Hearing and Speech Services
    (CHSS), Winneba 13, 66, 133, 139
    history 135–37
child development, influences *see also*
        bioecological theory of parenting
childbearing
    religious beliefs 41–42
    rural and urban settings 42
CHSS *see* Centre for Hearing and Speech
    Services (CHSS), Winneba
clinic system 140–43

188 Index

clinicians *see* professionals
cochlear implant 14, 25–26, 127–28, 145,
    164–65
collectives, role in early education/care,
    Ghana and other African societies 81
communication 99–101, 104–6, 109–10,
    161–62
  multilingualism 109–10
Community Based Rehabilitation Centre,
    Agona Duakwa 133, 135, 141–42
contributor stories 3–14
Conventions *see* United Nations
Covid restrictions 86, 92, 135–36
culturally competent practice 30–31
culture, Western context, constructs of child-
    oriented talk, play environment,
    pedagogic role of parents 172

Deaf Leadership International Alliance
    (DLIA) *vi*
deafness *see* ECCE for deaf children (deaf
    ECCE); hearing loss in SSA
Demonstration School for the Deaf,
    Mampong Akuapem 10, 135
disability
  exclusion from education 52–53
  leading causes worldwide 21
  parenting issues 51–52
  traditional indigenous beliefs in SSA 52
  Ubuntu model 16
distortion product evoked otoacoustic
    emissions (DPOAE) tests 23–24
Doku, Richard 10–11, 127

Early Child Development (ECD)
    platform 83
early childhood care and education *see*
    ECCE
Early Hearing Detection and Intervention
    (EHDI) guidelines 81
ECCE
  deaf adult participation and
    leadership 149–56
  defined 58–59, 62
  exclusion, 'investment narrative' 181–82
  models of intervention driven by Western
    research 172
  research and development 170
  research project (this book) *see* ECCE
    research/intervention project

South–North epistemologies 177–82
  see also Ghana, ECCE delivery in Ghana
ECCE for deaf children (deaf ECCE) 169–71
  developing practice 174–77
  inclusive research, development and
    practice 172–74
  increasing professional workforce 176–77
  multilingual societies 109, 113
  policy development 182–83
  research context deficiencies 173–74
  sign language 99–101, 103, 161–62
  UN Education for All initiative 169–70
  Western culture assumptions 173–74
  blended approach 177
ECCE delivery in Ghana
  age at which deafness is detected 64–65
  audiological services 65, 66–68, 176–77
  constitution and ECCE policy 59–61
  Disability Act 2006 Act 715 70
  formal early education 61–63
    kindergarten (KG) unit 61
  government policy 69–71
  increasing professional
    workforce 176–77
  language policy and use 112–14
  (late) identification of hearing loss 59
  (no) early provision for deaf
    children 63–64
  (no) newborn hearing screening 64–65,
    134
  (no) rights of deaf people 114
  preschool support 67–68, 73
  schools 101–2
    support services and challenges 101–2
    teacher posting practices 86
    teacher training 69–73
    training infrastructure 164–65
ECCE research/intervention project 1, 4–5,
    59–63, 79–82
  aims/goals 79–80, 88, 91–92
  bioecological approach 82–87, 137
  blended approach 177
  caregiver experiences 97–104
  communication 99–101, 104–6, 161–62
  counselling and emotional support 138
  Covid safety protocols 135–37
  cultural heritage of Ghanaian team
    members 181
  data analysis 137
    main discussion themes 160

Index **189**

documentary videos 11
ethical challenges 80–82, 86–87
ethical practice 78–79
Ghanaian Sign Languages (GhSL) 181
identification and confirmation of
  deafness 59, 97–99
inclusivity, knowledge base 172
longer-term decolonization
  project 182–83
methodology 92–95
  Bronfenbrenner bioecological
    framework 92–95
  participants 95–96, 96t, 135–37
    professional/clinician
      participants 135–37
personal responses by parents 103–4
practice 174–77
project findings 80–82, 137–45
relevance to Southern contexts 177–82
research context 173–74
research methods and tools 172–74,
  179–80
research team 91–92
schools and 67–70
South–North research
  partnerships 181–82
summary and conclusion 182–83
team member reflections 104–6
ecological systems theory (1977) 45, 82
  macrosystem 83
  microsystem/mesosystem/
    exosystem 82–83, 85–86
  see also bioecological theory of parenting
education
  deaf adult participation and
    leadership 150–56
  models of intervention driven by Western
    research 172
  policies/funding in LMICs 34–36,
    172–74
  research context 173–74
Effutu language 118–20

faith see religion
family life
  parenting constructs 42–44
  structure and caretaking role 50–51
Fante language 5, 93
Fobi, Daniel 4–5
Fobi, Joyce 7

Ga language 5, 120
Ghana
  health and wellbeing services 29–31
  indigenous spoken and written
    languages 110, 111
  multilingualism 110–12
  national service 8
  non-governmental organizations
    (NGOs) 61, 68, 141–42, 146
  see also education
Ghana National Association of the Deaf
  (GNAD) 6, 10–11, 31, 106, 114, 134,
  158–61
Ghanaian Sign Languages (GhSL) 3, 6, 9–11,
  111–12
  advocacy 9–10
  curriculum development 10–11
  documentation 111–12
Gibbah, Linda Amanvida 8–9, 126, 143–45
Global Education Monitoring Reports 169–70

hearing aids, cost 101–2
Hearing Assessment and Research Klinic
  (HARK) 139
hearing loss in SSA
  age at diagnosis 25
  bilateral 22–23
  burden on caregivers 64–65
  causes and prevalence 21
  early identification and intervention 22–
    23, 139–40
  exclusion from education 171
  gender and 95–96
  identity, Western context 12
  inequality of resources 25
  late diagnosis 134
  numbers 22–23, 63, 170
hearing screening in SSA 12, 22–26
  hospital-based vs
    community-based 23–24
    inequality of resources 25
  newborns in Ghana 64–65, 134
  procedures 23–25
  staffing 24–25
  training by principal investigator
    (PI) 24–25
hearing screening in West 81
HI HOPES early intervention partnership,
  Ghana 66–67
hospitals, neonatal hearing screening 23–24, 25

190   Index

inclusive education 34–36
Instituut voor Doven (IVD) 142
International Commission on
     Financing Global Education
     Opportunity 169–70
'investment narrative' 181–82

kindergarten (KG)/nursery units, Ghana 61, 62
  curriculum 62–63
  implementation/advocacy 62
Komfo-Anokye Teaching Hospital,
    Kumasi 139
Korle Bu Teaching Hospital, Accra 66, 68, 139

language
  indigenous spoken and written in
    Ghana 111
  lingua franca 181
  multilingual societies 109–10
  see also sign languages
Liliane Foundation (LF), Winneba 142
LittlEARS (MED-EL) Auditory
    Questionnaire (LEAQ) 13, 66
LMICs *see* low-and-middle-income countries
low-and-middle-income countries
    (LMICs) 1–2
  education policies/funding 34–36
  exclusion, 'investment narrative' 181–82
  models of intervention driven by Western
    research 172

Mampong Akuapem, Demonstration School
    for the Deaf 10, 135
missionaries, Jackson Foster 156–57
mobile audiology ambulance (HARK) 139
multilingual societies
  adult reflections on growing up 126–29
    Derrick 128
    Linda 8–9, 126, 143–45
    Richard 127
    summary 129–30

Nanabin Sign Language 111–12, 114
Netherlands
  Instituut voor Doven (IVD) 142
  Liliane Foundation (LF) 142
Nigeria
  missionaries' foundation work 156–57
  neonatal hearing screening 23–25
non-governmental organizations (NGOs) in
    Ghana 61, 68, 141–42, 146
  see also Salvation Army

Offei, Yaw Nyadu 13–14
Oppong, Alexander Mills 3–4
outreach services 139, 141, 146

parenting
  collective responsibility theory of
    parenting 42
  see also bioecological theory of
    parenting
parenting constructs, SSA context 42–44
  children with disability 51–52
  socio-economic background 48
  theories of childrearing 44–45
  traditional practices vs urbanization 45–49
professionals
  collaboration among 140–43, 145–47, 165–66
  development opportunities 165–66
  parent–professional partnerships 139–40
  research context 134
  research definition 133

Rehabilitation Centre, Agona Duakwa 133,
    135, 141–42
religion
  access to 24–25
  beliefs 11, 29, 41, 51, 98, 113
  commitment to deaf people 120
reproductive health education 49
research partnerships, global
    South–North 181–82
research project *see* ECCE research/
    intervention project
rural and remote settings 22, 27, 42, 44, 47,
    50–51, 62, 81, 105–6, 134
  inclusivity 176
  migration to cities 48–49
  need for outreach services 139
  wealth insecurity 77–78

Salvation Army Rehabilitation Centre, Agona
    Duakwa 133, 135, 141–42
Samuel Wellington Botwey Foundation,
    Accra 141–42
Savelugu School for the Deaf 135
schools
  ECCE delivery in Ghana 101–2
  ECCE research/intervention
    project 67–70
  house parents *see* caregivers
  late enrolment 103–4
  marginalization/stigma 105–6
  see also education

sign languages 99–101, 103, 111–12, 137, 161–62
  dictionary 161
  Ghana constitutional commitment 103, 113–14
  knowledge of 104–5
  see also Ghanaian Sign Languages (GhSL)
'snake' children 52
social exclusion and marginalization 26–36, 105–6, 171
  access to health and wellbeing services 29–31
  hearing loss, exclusion from education 171
  material deprivation 27
socio-cultural norms (of adult control), theory of parenting 44
'South'
  countries of see South–North research; sub-Saharan Africa (SSA)
  global South, defined 1–2
South Africa
  deafness, late identification and intervention 25
  health care 25
  neonatal hearing screening 23, 25
South–North research
  epistemologies 177–82
  partnerships 181–82
spatial exclusions 28–29
special needs education 35–36
speech and language therapist 138
Starkey Group of Companies 142
sub-Saharan Africa (SSA) 1–2
  disadvantaged children, numbers 169, 170
  early childhood deafness 21–26
    prevalence 170–71
  education, deaf adult participation and leadership 156–66
  exclusion, 'investment narrative' 181–82
  indigenous languages 93, 111
  negative cultural beliefs and practices 22
  neonatal hearing screening 12, 22
  see also hearing loss in SSA; hearing screening in SSA
Swanwick, Ruth 12–13

tele-intervention (TI) 30
  need for outreach services 139
  rural and remote settings 27, 30, 139

Transient Evoked Otoacoustic Emissions (TEOAE) testing 23–25
Twi language 93, 111

UK–Ghana, early childhood care and education (ECCE) joint project 1, 58
UNESCO
  direct involvement in pre-primary education 62
  ECCE defined 58–59
  Global Monitoring report of 2007 169
UNICEF global education monitoring reports, A World Ready to Learn 170
United Nations
  Convention on the Rights of the Child (UNCRC) 170–71
  Convention on the Rights of Persons with Disabilities (UNCRPD) 113–14, 170–71
  Education for All initiative 169–70
  Universal Declaration of Human Rights (1948) 169–70
  Sustainable Development Goals 4.2 169–70
University of Education Winneba see Centre for Hearing and Speech Services (CHSS), Winneba

Video Relay Services (VRS) 30

Western context
  construct of 'rights' 178
  constructs of child-oriented talk, play environment, pedagogic role of parents 172
  constructs of identity, hearing loss in SSA 12
  dominant knowledge base 79, 155–56, 172, 174, 182–83
    critical stance towards 85–86
  early hearing screening 81
  nuclear families 50–51, 109–10, 172
  understandings of attachment 78
Winneba
  Liliane Foundation 142
  see also Centre for Hearing and Speech Services (CHSS), Winneba
World Bank Development Report (2018) 169–70
World Federation of the Deaf 171
World Health Organization (WHO) 21
  deafness causes and prevalence 21